Contents

About this book

Starting out

This book is full of information, exercises and advice designed to help you achieve the best results from your GCSE English course. It will also help you with English Literature. There is advice on how to improve your coursework and on how to practise and revise effectively for examinations, in order to achieve higher grades in both subjects.

To help you practise and improve, there are also exercises for you to do, and the chance to check your progress as you go along. Finally, there is up-to-date information on the examinations you will be sitting and the kinds of question you will have to face. Of course, some of the advice given here will echo what your teacher tells you already, though it has the great advantage of being written down, which might increase your chances of remembering it! Remember, too, that while reading this book may be useful, only constant practice – putting the advice to use when, and wherever, you are actually doing your work – will be the test of whether you have understood what you have read.

Who this book is for

This book is designed for three groups of students. The first group is all the fifteen- and sixteen-year-olds who are working through Key Stage 4 of the National Curriculum in years 10 and 11 of secondary school. If you are in this group, you have to take a GCSE English examination at the end of your course.

The second group is made up of older students in schools and colleges who want to improve on their GCSE grades, perhaps by moving from a Grade D to a C to enable them to start a college course at a higher level. The third group includes students at college, or individuals working on their own, who may, or may not, have already taken a GCSE, GCE or CSE examination. If you are in this group, your aim will probably be to achieve a better qualification but you could be taking the examination simply to improve your mind and keep your brain ticking over! Whoever you are, and whatever your starting point, if you want to sit an English examination and do well, this book is for you.

English in the National Curriculum

The National Curriculum is the starting point for all the GCSE examination syllabuses in English and what it says about study in English has to be reflected in all of them. That explains why the syllabuses are broadly similar – although they do have some differences, as you will discover. The National Curriculum breaks the study of English up into three main areas. These are Speaking and Listening (also known as En1), Reading (En2) and Writing (En3). Because the curriculum sets targets for students in each area, they are known as **attainment targets**. The targets are set out as a mixture of skills and knowledge so, in English, they include such varied requirements as discussing in groups, reading Shakespeare's plays and spelling more accurately. At the end of Key Stages 1, 2 and 3, for five- to fourteen-year-olds, there are assessments and tests which give a numbered level for each child's performance in English (1, 2, 3) but, at GCSE level, letter grades (A*, A, B to G) are used instead.

GCSE syllabuses in English

A GCSE syllabus is a document that explains how the requirements of the.National Curriculum at Key Stage 4 will be assessed. It tells teachers what to teach and explains what kind of work the students have to produce for assessment. It explains about the examinations as well. GCSE syllabuses are run by examining boards or groups. These organisations assess coursework, set the examination papers and mark them and report the results to schools and colleges. There are four of them in England, one in Wales and one in Northern Ireland. Scotland has a different examining system which is based on a different curriculum. Each examining board offers one syllabus for English although if you are at college you may encounter a variety of it that has been modified for older students.

GCSE syllabuses in English Literature

All the examining boards also offer GCSE examinations in English Literature. These syllabuses require more reading than in English and, in schools, students often work on both subjects together. To make this easier, the coursework for the two examinations overlaps, although the subjects are given grades quite separately. If you are up to it, and enjoy reading, working on both subjects at the same time gives you an extra GCSE for less than twice the work. This book, especially the sections on reading, will help you if you are studying English Literature.

About GCSE English

In some ways, English is very different from your other GCSE subjects. For many of you it is the first language you learnt. You were listening to and speaking English for years before you learnt to read and write it. There can be very few of you who could say that everything you know about English has been taught to you in school. Your language abilities will have grown and developed in many ways because of the experiences you have had outside school, the way you talk to your family and friends and the way you read all sorts of written English, from signs in shop windows to newspapers and novels.

In other words, you are already a competent user of language. Imagine how odd life would be otherwise. You could be out with your friends and ask a question and they would all look at you strangely and ask you to say it again, or more slowly. Or, they might ask you to correct what you were saying and rephrase it! Luckily, people do communicate what they mean without any difficulty most of the time. But there are occasions when you have to write or say something which you find difficult or unfamiliar. Giving a talk to an audience, writing a letter to a boyfriend or girlfriend saying that you no longer want to see them, phoning up someone you don't know to ask for a job, making a complaint in a shop, summarising something you've read in school or following a difficult set of instructions when loading a new computer game are all occasions when your use of language can be stretched to the limits.

These are the kinds of situations where practice can help. You know that is true because the second time you do something it is always a little bit easier. It is also true that someone who practises a particular language skill outside school will be more competent at that use of English than other people of the same age, regardless of what school has taught him or her. For example, students whose parents are in the catering business are often skilled at making polite conversation with unfamiliar adults. So your command of English is a skill which will be improved by all your experiences throughout your life, not something which is confined to the years you spend at school.

English and the literary heritage

This book will also help you with English Literature examinations and coursework. Like English, English Literature builds on what you already know about reading and the reading you already do. So it isn't surprising that students who belong to libraries and read lots of fiction are often good story writers as well as skilled readers.

The study of literature is not expected to make you a faster reader or anything like that, but it does give you the chance to think more about the books you read and to write down and discuss your views of them. There are two good reasons for this. First, when you discuss the kind of music you like or talk about why you liked a particular film, you use the sorts of language skills that a literature course develops. But you may also use the same kind of vocabulary to discuss motorbikes, sport, food or politicians whenever you want to evaluate, make comparisons or judge what something is worth.

The second reason is more complicated. A GCSE course in English or English Literature will certainly require you to read books, poetry and plays which you would not otherwise read. Sometimes that can be off-putting but it can also introduce you to some of the novelists, poets and dramatists who make up our shared culture. If that sounds rather self-important and irrelevant, try thinking about it in this kind of way. Take a very well-known play of the kind you might be asked to study – like Shakespeare's *Romeo and Juliet.* First of all it has a story which you may well enjoy. The idea of two young lovers kept apart by the feuding between their families is a timeless one and you may well have come across the same plot in television soap operas, comics, other films and books. You may also have read real-life accounts of people trapped in this sort of situation or be able to relate it to events in the lives of people you know, or even to yourself. Shakespeare's play is part of all this – people faced the same problems when he wrote it, and that is how the play can come alive for a modern audience.

Over the course of hundreds of years, the play itself has become part of our culture so that when we think of young lovers who are forced apart by circumstance, most people think of the story of *Romeo and Juliet.* Because of this, the story keeps cropping up in different ways, so that there are modern versions of the play like the musical *West Side Story* and rock songs like *Romeo and Juliet* by Dire Straits, while newspaper editors often talk about 'Fearless Romeos' or 'Modern-day Romeos and Juliets' in their headlines.

That is what it means to say that a play, a book or a poem is part of our culture. If you know about what Noah did in his spare time, what the Ancient Mariner shot, where Alice ended up after following a rabbit and who asked for more soup, then you are part of that culture. But, you are also part of it if you can name Bart Simpson's family, list most of the

xaminer's tip

the main aims of
glish course is to
ce you to the writers
ve most influenced
ure.

current top ten records or remember what is on television this evening. In other words, you can't help being part of the culture within which you live. One reason for the choice of the books, plays and poetry you have to read for GCSE is to introduce you to some of the best-known and most influential writers in our culture.

If you are at school, it is likely that you will be taking English and English Literature together. You will probably have one folder for your coursework and you will be studying the same books for each subject. In fact, sometimes it will be hard for you to tell whether a piece of coursework is for English or English Literature and, sometimes, it can count towards both subjects.

Something about you

Not all of the readers of this book will be between the ages of fourteen and sixteen. It will be clear that those of you who are undertaking GCSE at college or as mature students are likely to have certain advantages over the conventional GCSE age group, simply by having wider experience of language in the 'real' world.

It is also likely that those of you who speak another language as well as English will have the advantage of insight you may gain by comparing the way the two languages work. You may have grandparents who speak a different dialect of English from your own. You may have learnt French or German in school and begun to see how the grammar of languages differs. When you were little, you may have been told stories, in another language or in a dialect which is different from the standard English used in books.

Improving your English is not a matter of trying to learn another language for when you have to write. Being aware of and interested in all sorts of language in your own life: adverts, films, TV plays, poems, and so on, will also enrich your English. Reading a newspaper each day, or the occasional novel, will underline the fact that the more you bring to reading this book, the more you get out of it. This book does not set out to teach you English: it will help you to use the English you have acquired to the best advantage when tackling your GCSE work.

How to use this book

The sections in this book relate to the different skills you have to practise in English and the variety of written work you have to complete. Each section gives you an opportunity to practise what you have learned and offers you tips for success. That means you can go directly to a particular section to find immediate help in an area where you know your work is weak. There is advice to cover both the final examination and the coursework you have to do leading up to it.

Throughout the book you will also find:

aminer's tip

Examiner's tips Some of these cover the little things which can help you get your work right, from remembering to check it for specific mistakes to including a title. Others give you more insight into the GCSE course and help you prepare for – and pass – your examinations.

Putting this into practice For the main sections of the book, these go over exactly what you should have learned from the section. If you are unsure about them, you know you need to work through that section again.

The study of English

What is English?

The forms of the English language you have to study and the skills you must master are set out in your syllabus. Put at its simplest, what is required for any GCSE English course are linked opportunities for speaking and listening, reading and writing. For example, you could read a story, discuss it with your group and then write one of your own. Or you could watch a play, discuss it with your teacher and write about a character in it. In these examples you would be doing some reading, some writing, some talking and some listening.

On another occasion you might just do some writing, maybe after watching a film or perhaps after being given the title of a story. If you think about it for a moment, you will see that it is really only possible to tell how well you read by what you say or write afterwards. Reading aloud does not help you understand what you read. Only writing or talking about it will show that you have understood what you have read, and only writing is permanent enough to be looked at much later and to show how much you understand.

So you could think of the relationship between reading, writing and speaking and listening like this. The diagram shows how important your written work is:

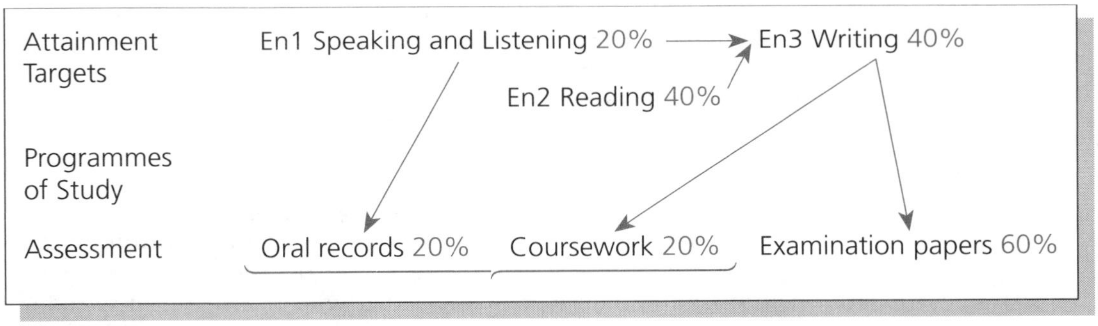

It is important not to forget how these aspects of English overlap, especially because syllabuses often talk about Speaking and Listening, Reading and Writing separately. Bearing this in mind, we can go on to look at the different GCSE requirements for each of these areas. Remember that, whatever syllabus you choose, it must cover these three areas.

Speaking and Listening (En1)

Each examination board has to give teachers and examiners guidelines about how to grade your coursework and examination answers. The exact words vary a little from syllabus to syllabus, though the skills you have to demonstrate and the standards expected for each grade are similar because, whichever GCSE you are taking, you are still following Key Stage 4 of the National Curriculum.

The 'marking criteria' on p.6 for grades A, C and E are as they appear in one syllabus. Studying them will give you a clear idea of what you have to show you can do to gain a particular GCSE grade in English whichever syllabus you are following.

MARKING CRITERIA FOR SPEAKING AND LISTENING

	General Criteria	Specific Criteria		
		Explain, Describe, Narrate	Explore, Analyse, Imagine	Discuss, Argue, Persuade
A	Candidated initiate speech and take a leading role in discussion, responding in detail to the ideas of others. They understand and discuss aspects of challenging content. They show an assured use of standard English vocabulary and grammar in a range of situations and for a variety of purposes. They listen and respond to a range of complex speech.	• show cogency and explicit depth of detail when required • use a range of highly developed vocabulary to suit a range of purposes and processes • skilfully involve listeners	• articulate and analyse complex ideas and information • identify priorities • synthesise essential points, resolving outcomes	• initiate and sustain discussion through a variety of sensitive contributions • respond persuasively and engagingly
C	Candidates speak with fluency and make significant contributions to talk in a variety of different contexts. They show a competent use of standard English vocabulary and grammar in situations which demand it. They adapt their talk to a range of different audiences, showing judgement in their choice of style and delivery to interest listeners. They listen closely and sympathetically, responding as appropriate.	• use varied and appropriate vocabulary and expression • sustain the interest of the listener • show a consistent style of delivery	• show order and precise use of vocabulary to communicate ideas and issues • respond with understanding to ideas of varying complexity	• make a significant contribution to discussion • engage with others' ideas, recognising obvious assumptions and biases • are able to promote a point of view
E	Candidates speak confidently in different contexts, showing sensitivity to situation and audience. They generally use standard English vocabulary and grammar where appropriate. They listen with concentration to a range of talk.	• use straightforward and appropriate language to fit audience and purpose • give structured, and on occasions, developed accounts, responding to requests for clarification when asked	• respond to familiar and less familiar subject matter • show some ability to develop a line of enquiry	• listen with concentration and respond with some order • express an opinion and make a useful contribution • occasionally make decisive points to good effect

MEG English Syllabus

At first sight, what you have to do and the ways in which you have to perform may seem very challenging and difficult. It is important to remember that these criteria were written for teachers to use rather than pupils. They give more detail than you would usually require. In fact, they describe the skills you need to develop in three main areas of activity:

- explaining, describing, narrating;
- exploring, analysing, imagining;
- discussing, arguing, persuading.

Whatever syllabus you follow, there must be plenty of opportunities for speaking and listening. You will be assessed on the best three occasions when you demonstrate these skills. And it is important to remember that your assessment in speaking and listening contributes one-fifth of your final grade for the subject as a whole. There is more detail on exactly what you have to do for this part of your course in Section Two.

Standard English

Languages vary all over the world and each single language also varies according to the particular area where it is spoken. A dialect is a version of a language which changes the words in the language, or their order. An accent is a version of the language which is pronounced slightly differently. In fact, the language of any area always features variations in both dialect and accent. It is not really correct, for example, to say that cockneys or Americans speak a different version of the English language, because there is no single language to which they can be compared. However, in practice, people compare other dialects of English to what people agree is the correct form for writing – the dialect called standard English.

Standard English differs from most regional dialects because it is used by, and can be understood by, English speakers all over the world. People from other countries who want to learn English are taught standard English. Standard English can be spoken with any accent and should not be confused with 'talking posh'. The mix-up arises because some standard English speakers also have a Received Pronunciation (RP) accent. This is the kind of accent you hear on old newsreels and, occasionally, from television and radio newsreaders. It is, in fact, perfectly possible to speak standard English with any regional accent.

Examiner's tip

Using standard English in speaking depends on who you are talking to (your audience) and why (your purpose). It is not required on every occasion.

In some parts of England, the local dialect is very similar to standard English but, for most people, standard English is a dialect they learn at school. If you live in an area where many people speak a dialect, you will need to learn about the differences between your local way of speaking and standard English so that you can adapt your speech when it seems necessary to do so.

If you speak with a very pronounced or strong regional accent, there may be some situations where you have to adapt that, too, in order to to make yourself understood. If you are talking to people who live a long way from where you live, for example, they may not be familiar with your way of speaking.

Your written English will be almost entirely standard English. Of course, it is easier to write than to speak, because you have more time to think and to make changes when you are writing. Speech is immediate and you can't really alter it once you've opened your mouth, so you may need to practise standard English until it becomes a habit and feels natural.

Reading (En2)

In the same way as for Speaking and Listening, it is possible to pick out the main areas you must study and the skills you must demonstrate for assessment in Reading:

- reading a range of texts, including media, non-fiction and texts from other cultures;
- responding to literature, including Shakespeare and other well-known writers;
- using reading skills to find information;
- analysing and evaluating how ideas are presented in texts.

MARKING CRITERIA FOR READING

General Criteria		Specific Criteria		
		Response to Shakespeare	Response to Poetry	Response to Prose
A	Candidates appreciate and analyse alternative interpretations, making cross-references where appropriate. They develop their ideas and refer in detail to aspects of language, structure and presentation, making apt and careful comparison within and between texts.	Candidates show analytical and interpretative skill when evaluating		
		• the play's moral and philosophical context • significant achievements within the dramatic genre • Shakespeare's exploitation of language for dramatic, poetic and figurative effect	• moral and philosophical context of poems • significant achievements within the poetic genre • the poet's exploitation of language for emotive, aural and figurative effect	• moral and philosophi context of text • significant achievements withi the prose genre • the writer's exploitation of language for emoti and figurative effec
C	Candidates give personal and critical responses to literary texts, which show understanding of the ways in which meaning is conveyed. They refer to aspects of language, structure and themes to support their views.	Candidates show insight when discussing		
		• the nature of the play, its implication and relevance • characters, structure and stagecraft • Shakespeare's use of language	• the nature of poetry, its implications and relevance • verse style, structure and tone • the poet's characteristic use of language	• the nature of the te its implications and relevance • style, structure and characters • the writer's characteristic use of language
E	Candidates make personal responses to texts commenting on key ideas, themes, events and characters. They make inferences and deductions and identify some features of language and structure. They refer to aspects of the text when explaining their views.	They show familiarity when describing		
		• the nature of the play, its meanings and ideas • sequence of events and variety of characters • the impact on an audience	• the nature of the poem's meaning and ideas • the range and variety of language • the impact on the reader	• the nature of the text's subject matter • the variety of character, situation, narration • the impact on the reader

The syllabuses also want you to look at as wide a range of literary and non-fiction texts as possible. Literary texts are books, short stories, plays, poems which someone has written – the words to a song could be a literary text. Non-fiction texts are magazine or newspaper articles, sets of instructions or advertisements. There is more detail on exactly what you have to do for this part of your English course in Section Three.

Writing (En3)

The main areas where you have to show what you can achieve in writing are similar to those for Speaking and Listening. You have to write for a range of audiences and purposes. These are:

- exploring, imagining, entertaining;
- informing, explaining, describing;
- arguing, persuading, instructing;
- analysing, reviewing, commenting.

The marking criteria below cover three of these areas for Grades A, C and E.

You also have to spell correctly, use legible handwriting and present your work neatly. Section Four gives more details of exactly what you have to do for the writing element of English.

MARKING CRITERIA FOR WRITING

	General Criteria	Specific Criteria		
		Inform, Explain, Describe	Explore, Imagine, Entertain	Analyse, Review, Comment
		Candidates		
A	Candidates' writing has shape and assured control of a range of styles. A wide range of grammatical constructions is used accurately; paragraphs are well-constructed and linked to clarify the organisation of the writing as a whole. Vocabulary and punctuation are often ambitious and usually accurate.	• communicate effectively and accurately, making responses to difficult tasks quite clear to the reader • use language which is consistently clear, accurate, helpful to the reader, and confident	• writing is enjoyable for its originality • for its fluency of style • and in its security and control of structure	• control the entire writing securely and balance analysis of main ideas with the use of detail; show a strong grasp of appropriate language
C	Candidates' writing engages and sustains readers' interest. It shows adaptation of style and register to different forms. Candidates use a range of sentence structures and varied vocabulary to create effects. Spelling is accurate; paragraphing and punctuation are correct. Handwriting is neat and legible, and work is presented clearly.	• communicate clearly and fully in different forms • control and order explanations and begin to handle detail in processes and reports • adapt style and register to audience and form	• write well-balanced stories with some explanation of interesting events, characters and backgrounds • use language and structure for effect	• write intelligently and at some length, extend some of their ideas and justify them in appropriate, secure language
E	Candidates' writing attempts to match style and form to purpose and audience, developing ideas within appropriate structures and showing some grasp of organising sentences into paragraphs. Candidates make some use of complex sentences. Common and some irregular words are spelt correctly and a range of punctuation is employed.	• communicate clearly in a range of forms including those that require explanation of processes • give full and orderly descriptions • make some conscious choice of vocabulary to improve clarity	• begin to develop stories and add detail for the reader's benefit • begin to write other types of imaginative writing • occasionally use language to make writing attractive to the reader	• begin to comment effectively on reading material and give more extended impressions of everyday experience

MEG English Syllabus

The English syllabuses

When you are entered for a GCSE examination in English, you follow the syllabus set down by one of the examining groups. This syllabus must include everything required by the National Curriculum Programmes of Study. The GCSE National Criteria for English sets down exactly for the examining groups how their syllabuses must relate to the National Curriculum.

That is why all the English syllabuses are so similar. Often, they take their exact wording from the criteria document so that they read in exactly the same way. There are some differences, however, in they way that the syllabuses organise the work which has to be done and in the way that teachers must record and assess it. There can be differences in the amount or type of coursework required or the topics covered by the examination papers.

Reading the English syllabuses

At school, you are unlikely to have any choice over the English syllabus you follow. Your teachers will already have made that decision and the similarities between syllabuses are so extensive that it would be a waste of your time to try and change or to follow a syllabus that is not taught by your school. However, if you are taking English GCSE as a mature or an external candidate, it might be worth your while to shop around the different syllabuses and to make a choice. In every syllabus you will find the same kinds of main headings.

Examiner's tip

If you have a choice, shop around. Look at sample examination papers to help you decide.

❶ A statement about weightings

For English, the attainment targets are weighted. This means that some attainment targets make a greater contribution than others to your final grade. These weightings are laid down by the National Criteria for English. They are the same for all GCSE English syllabuses.

En1	Speaking and Listening	20%
En2	Reading	40%
En3	Writing	40%

The same National Criteria also state that En1 must be assessed through coursework and that coursework as a whole can only add up to 40% of the assessment in total. The syllabus therefore shows the combination of terminal examination and coursework which is used.

	Terminal examination	Coursework
Speaking and Listening		20%
Reading	30%	10%
Writing	30%	10%
Totals	60%	40%

xaminer's tip

'cross-over' require-
s are complicated. Ask
eacher to explain them
ı look at a particular
us or work out what
nean with a friend.

2 A statement about syllabus overlap

To make it easier for teachers, and to reduce the burden of coursework, all GCSE English syllabuses overlap with similar syllabuses in English Literature. Schools are encouraged to teach both subjects in the same lesson and to keep just one coursework folder. Then the same coursework may be used for both subjects and English coursework for Reading can be based on books studied for English Literature. The completed folder containing work for both subjects will then be checked by only one marker (the teacher) and one moderator (an examining group assessor).

3 Aims and objectives

The aims and objectives of each syllabus are closely related to the National Curriculum requirements for English as set out below.

En1 Successful candidates should be able to:
- use the vocabulary and grammar of standard English;
- formulate, clarify and express their ideas;
- adapt their speech to a widening range of circumstances and demands;
- listen, understand and respond appropriately to others.

En2 They should:
- read accurately, fluently and with understanding;
- understand and respond to the texts they read;
- read, analyse and evaluate a wide range of texts, including literature from the English literary heritage and from other cultures and traditions.

En3 They should be taught to use:
- compositional skills – developing ideas and communicating meaning to a reader, using a wide-ranging vocabulary and an effective style;
- presentational skills – accurate punctuation, correct spelling and legible handwriting;
- a variety of writing types for different purposes.

The broad aims are turned into specific assessment objectives.

En1 Successful candidates should show that they can:
- communicate clearly, structuring and organising their talk and adapting it to different situations;
- use standard English;
- listen to and understand varied speech;
- participate in discussion, judging the nature and purposes of contributions and the roles of participants.

En2 That they can:
- read, with insight and engagement, making appropriate references to texts and developing and sustaining interpretations of them;
- distinguish between fact and opinion and evaluate how information is presented;
- follow an argument, identifying implications and recognising inconsistencies;
- select material appropriate to their purpose, collate material from different sources, and make cross-references;
- understand and evaluate how writers use linguistic, structural and presentational devices to achieve their effects, and comment on ways language varies and changes.

En3 That they can:
- communicate clearly, adapting their writing for a wide range of purposes and audiences;
- use and adapt forms and genres for specific purposes and effects;
- organise ideas into sentences, paragraphs and whole texts;
- use accurate spelling and punctuation, and present work neatly and clearly;
- use the grammatical structures of standard English and a wide vocabulary to express meaning with clarity and precision.

And a list of activities is provided.

En1 The range must include talk to:
- explain, describe, narrate;
- explore, analyse, imagine;
- discuss, argue, persuade.

En2 The range must include:
- prose, poetry and drama;
- a play by Shakespeare;
- work published before 1900 by one of the authors of fiction or poetry listed in the National Curriculum Order;
- work by an author published after 1900;
- texts from other cultures and traditions;
- non-fiction texts (e.g. autobiographies, biographies, journals, diaries, letters, travel writing, leaflets);
- media texts (e.g. magazines, newspapers, radio, television and film).

En3 The range must include, in a variety of forms and genres, writing to:
- explore, imagine, entertain;
- inform, explain, describe;
- argue, persuade, instruct;
- analyse, review, comment.

adapted from English in the National Curriculum

English (GCSE)
En1 Assessment Form

Year of Examination ☐

Name of Centre .... Centre No. ☐☐☐☐☐

Candidate's Surname .... Candidate No. ☐☐☐☐

Other Names ....

Teacher's summative comments	Overall mark for En1 ☐ (out of 54)		explain describe narrate A	explore analyse imagine B	discuss argue persuade C
Unit 1	❑ Formal ❑ Individual ❑ Pair	❑ Informal ❑ Group	❑	❑	❑
Unit 1	❑ Formal ❑ Individual ❑ Pair	❑ Informal ❑ Group	❑	❑	❑
Unit 1	❑ Formal ❑ Individual ❑ Pair	❑ Informal ❑ Group	❑	❑	❑
Use boxes to give brief details of activities within each Unit, including texts or other stimulus materials used.	Tick appropriate categories above to indicate context of each unit.		Tick boxes above to indicate group(s) of skills (A, B, C) assessed in each Unit (1, 2, 3).		

4 A scheme of assessment

In English, the final assessment is made up from a number of components. Marks from the separate components are added together to give mark totals for each Attainment Target and a grade for the subject. These components include:

- **An oral record** giving evidence for En1 about your performance in speaking and listening, and for En2 where you have commented on your reading by talking about what you have read.
- **Written coursework** showing how well you can write for En3 and your response to reading for En2.

  Every examining group requires you to include a piece of coursework to show you have studied a play by Shakespeare and a piece to show that you have read other literary texts written before and after 1900. In addition, you will have to include at least one piece of your best writing, for example a story you have written, or a collection of your own poems.

  There should also be at least four pieces of written coursework in your folder. Your teacher will give you guidance about exactly what your syllabus requires as you work through your course. At least one assignment must be handwritten, so that your handwriting can be assessed.
- **Examination papers 1 and 2** showing how well you can write for En3 and respond to reading for En2. Both papers test both attainment targets. One paper will test your response to literary texts, the other your reading of non-fiction or media texts.

You can see from this that, for En2 and En3, up to three components contribute to your final grade. The advantage of this is that if you do badly in the examination, your coursework can then help to give you a higher grade. The disadvantage is that to do really well, you have to achieve high marks for each component.

One other complication is that the examination papers are **tiered**. In a tiered system, different examination papers are set for (or target) a limited range of grades. The idea behind this is that candidates who expect to do very well at English can be set a paper with difficult reading material or questions which might be too hard for the average candidate. Because the examination is designed to show how well you can do against a scale of grades of difficulty from G–A*, it is important that the questions target grades quite closely. To understand this better, imagine taking a test in a foreign language which you knew enough of to chat to people, to shop and to order food in restaurants. If a test asked you to do these things, then you would probably score quite highly. But suppose your test asked you to translate a highly technical article or a complicated novel and left you completely confused. Then you would do worse than you deserved to and your grade would not be a fair one.

In some GCSE subjects there are three tiers but for English and English Literature there are only **two**. There is a lower tier, **Foundation**, which covers **grades G–C** and an upper tier, **Higher**, covering **grades D–A***. On either tier, if you score lower than the lowest allowed grade, you will be unclassified (**grade U**.) This means that if you enter for the Higher Tier papers, you must be quite confident of gaining a C grade under examination conditions, or you may be running the risk of ending up with no GCSE pass at all. The tasks on the Foundation Tier papers are slightly more straightforward, so it may be easier for you to show a good level of achievement than on the Higher Tier paper. However, no matter how well you do on a Foundation Tier paper, you cannot be given a B or an A grade, so the decision about which paper will give you the better chance of a good grade is not an easy one. If you are at school, your teacher will be able to give you advice and guidance about this.

To answer an obvious question, you are not allowed to enter for both tiers! The examinations take place at the same time and the regulations forbid it. Remember also that only the examination is tiered – the coursework and other records are always the same.

5 The examination papers

As indicated above, the examination papers vary in how they test attainment targets. They also vary slightly in length and in the kinds of things they ask you to do. For one syllabus you could be asked to write a report, for another an imaginative story. Some papers set more questions than others. Some papers are set with a common theme for all of the questions. In assessment terms, the form of the examination paper will probably not make any difference to your overall result but, if you have a choice, this is one section of the syllabuses you should definitely look at.

For each paper in the syllabus you should find the following information:

Title	Tier code	Target grades	Allowed grades	Duration	Weighting	
e.g.					En2	En3
Paper 5: Media (Unseen)	Higher	C–A*	D–A*	2 hours	10%	20%

The syllabus will also contain a more detailed description of each examination paper. For example:

Media (Unseen)

Paper 5 (Higher Tier)

Terminal Examination: 2 hours

These papers will assess 30% of the total English mark (50% of the Terminal Examination) and will assess Reading (10%) and Writing (20%).

These papers will assess candidates' responses to one or more unseen media texts.

Candidates will be given three questions consisting of:
- one question, which will be assessed for Reading, selecting material appropriate for purpose and evaluating presentation of material;
- two questions on the material, which will be assessed for Writing, requiring candidates to
  (a) argue, persuade and instruct
  (b) analyse, review and comment

London Examinations English Syllabus

6 Coursework

xaminer's tip

submit an incomplete
work folder – your
s will suffer!

All English syllabuses give detailed guidance on the coursework which you must submit at the end of the course. These regulations are very important. Submitting an incomplete folder will severely reduce your marks. The folder is supposed to give evidence of your highest attainment in the subject and for each attainment target. That means it will be assessed as if it is your best work. Most syllabuses ask that some of the coursework has been supervised by a teacher. This is done so that the teacher can guarantee that the work is your own and that you are not getting an unacceptable level of help from other people.

The precise contents of the coursework vary from syllabus to syllabus, although between them the coursework and the examination papers must cover all aspects of the attainment targets. For En1, Speaking and Listening, where coursework is the only evidence of performance, the record must show that each group of skills has been assessed. For En2, Reading, and En3, Writing, coursework must cover those skills for which it is most suited, especially those which are not assessed in the examination paper. Skills such as re-drafting written work or attempting a range of types of writing might come into this group.

There are slight differences between the coursework requirements for different English syllabuses, but in general the completed folder must contain records and enough written work to provide evidence of:

- achievements in speaking and listening;
- the study of at least two whole works of literature (one written before 1900 and one after);
- a response to a play by Shakespeare;
- your best original writing;
- your handwriting and spelling skills;
- work done under teacher supervision.

While this may seem a lot to do, the pieces of work can overlap so that a single one covers more than one of the requirements. For example, a comparison of two short stories, produced under supervision, could cover at least three of these requirements.

In practice there is a lot of discussion about how much work has to be included. The sensible principle to work on is that you do not need to show the moderator that you can do something more than once, but you do need to include your best work. As a rough guide, expect to have to include:

- around five pieces of written work covering the area above, some of which must be handwritten;
- a written record of three speaking and listening activities; which have been formally assessed;
- a written record or cover sheet showing the texts you have studied.

The five pieces of written work could include a piece on a Shakespeare play, a piece on another work of literature – poetry or fiction written before and after 1900 – and a piece based on some non-fiction material like a newspaper report, advertising materials or a television programme. Then the other pieces could be imaginative or creative writing, letters and reports, persuasive speeches or other forms of writing. However, it is important to check this against the fine print of your chosen syllabus, as there are clear differences between them.

The syllabus will also give advice on the presentation of the coursework folder. It should normally:

- be A4 in size with a flat cover – not a ring binder;
- be clearly labelled with your name and examination codes and numbers;
- include a form – supplied by the examining group – which lists its contents. For an example, see p.16.

In addition, each piece of writing should:

- be clearly headed with your name and the date;
- include a title and, where relevant, the source or text upon which your work is based;
- have been marked by your teacher;
- not have been altered by you after marking.

There will be a statement for you to sign which states that the work in the folder is your own and that you have completed it without an unreasonable amount of help. There is more advice on coursework in Section Five.

WELSH JOINT EDUCATION COMMITTEE
CYD-BWYLLGOR ADDYSG CYMRU

E2

GCSE ENGLISH

Coursework sample

Centre .... Candidate's Name ....

Centre No. .... Candidate's No. ....

Title/Brief Description of Stimulus/Background to Assignment	Mark /20
1. Shakespeare Play	
2. Pre-1900 (N.C.)	
3. Other Cultures	
4. Writing	
TOTAL /80	

	Assignment No.
Teacher supervised	
Poetry	

Further details of oral assignments must be given overleaf.

N.B. At least one assignment must be handwritten.

This folder is my own work. I have not copied any part of it from anyone else.

Candidate's signature .... Date ....

Supporting Comments

Teacher's signature .... Date ....

Syllabus analysis

Choosing the right syllabus

Some of the information in this section is quite complicated as it unravels differences between syllabuses. If you are uncertain about exactly what a syllabus is asking from you, ask a teacher to help to clarify exactly what it says.

Most advice suggests that it makes sense to follow the same examining group's syllabuses for English and English Literature, but you should also study the coursework requirements and the set books you will have to study before making up your mind.

Special syllabuses for older students

There are some syllabuses intended for mature candidates in full-time or part-time education and for external candidates, who do not attend a college. The content of these courses is different, since they are meant to appeal to older students who have probably already taken a GCSE syllabus and want to do something different at college. However, their structure is identical to other syllabuses and the work load involved is exactly the same. They all have coursework. This may mean that if you are not in full-time education and would like to take an examination in English you will have to become part of a class at a college of further education or take school evening classes, unless the examining group allows you to send your coursework directly to a moderator. The syllabus will tell you this.

Your own syllabus

Complete a copy of this chart to make sure that you know all the details of the syllabus you are following. Ask your English teacher to lend you the syllabus. He or she should be able to give you some help. It is possible to buy syllabuses direct from the examining groups. You will find their addresses and an analysis of each syllabus on pp.19–25.

Syllabus title: English

Examining group:

Syllabus code or number: Tier: Foundation/Higher

Component no.	Title	Weighting	How assessed?	No. of pieces/ length of examination
Speaking and Listening (i.e. oral coursework)				
Written coursework	1 2 3 4 5			
Examination Paper 1	Section A: Section B:			
Examination Paper 2	Section A: Section B:			

Northern Examinations and Assessment Board (NEAB)

Devas Street, Manchester M15 6EX Tel: 0161 953 1180

Essential support materials

A poetry anthology focusing on the works of three poets plus a selection drawn from other cultures and traditions.

Coursework

40% of total marks

- **Speaking and Listening:** *20% of total marks*
  Three assessed units - explaining, exploring and discussing - for defined purposes.
- **Reading:** *10% of total marks*
  1 Shakespeare
  2 Wide reading
- **Reading/Writing:** 3 Media
- **Writing:** *10% of total marks*
  4 Original writing

Written Paper 1

2 hours
30% of total marks

- **Section A: Reading** *15% of total marks*
  One task, or tasks, set in response to unprepared non-fiction.
- **Section B: Writing** *15% of total marks*
  One task that calls for argument, persuasion or instruction linked to topic in Section A.

Written Paper 2

2 hours
30% of total marks

- **Section A: Reading** *15% of total marks*
  Two tasks, set in response to poetry from anthology: one on a specific poet; the other on poems from other cultures and traditions. Alternative tasks are set.
- **Section B: Writing** *15% of total marks*
  One task to inform, explain or describe that may be linked to Section A.

Southern Examining Group (SEG)

Stag Hill House, Guildford, Surrey GU2 5XJ Tel: 01483 506506

Essential support materials

Pre-release booklet made up of: Section A Media texts; Section B Non-fiction; and Section C Texts from other cultures and traditions.

Coursework

40% of total marks

- **Speaking and Listening:** *20% of total marks*
  Three assessed units - explaining, exploring and discussing - for defined purposes.
- **Reading:** *10% of total marks*
  1 Personal writing – fiction
  2 Personal writing – non-fiction
- **Writing:** *10% of total marks*
  3 Shakespeare
  4 Pre-1900 author
  5 Post-1900 author
  (*Note: In Units 4 and 5, prose and poetry must both be included.*)

Written Paper 1

2 hours
30% of total marks

- **Reading:** *20% of total marks*
  Section A: Response to media texts
  Section B: Response to non-fiction texts
- **Writing:** *10% of total marks*
  Section C: Writing an argument

Written Paper 2

2 hours
30% of total marks

- **Reading:** *10% of total marks*
  Section A: Response to texts from other cultures and traditions
- **Writing:** *20% of total marks*
  Section B: Analytical writing
  Section C: Persuasive writing

Midland Examining Group (MEG)

Syndicate Buildings, 1 Hills Road, Cambridge CB1 2EU Tel: 01223 553311

Essential support materials

For Papers One and Three, a pre-released text will indicate the general theme of the paper, while a pre-released prose text will be used as the basis for Papers Two and Four. An anthology, required for English Literature, is recommended as the basis for Unit 3 of the coursework on poetry post-1900.

Coursework

40% of total marks

- **Speaking and Listening:** *20% of total marks*
  Three assessed units – explaining, exploring and discussing – for defined purposes.
- **Reading:** *10% of total marks*
  Unit 3: Reading in the literary heritage (analysing, reviewing and commenting on drama, prose and poetry from the heritage, Shakespeare, pre-1900 writer, post-1900 writer).
- **Writing:** *10% of total marks*
  Unit 1: Non-fiction
  Unit 2: Imaginative and creative

Written Paper 1

2 hours + 10 mins. reading time
30% of total marks

- **Section A: Reading** *20% of total marks*
  Two responses – selecting, evaluating, commenting – to unprepared non-fiction and media texts.
- **Section B: Writing** *10% of total marks*
  One task in response to Section A materials including argument, persuasion and instruction – in forms such as letters, reports and interviews.

(*Note: Higher Tier paper is known as Paper Three*)

Written Paper 2

2 hours + 10 mins. reading time
30% of total marks

- **Section A: Reading** *10% of total marks*
  One response – character, setting , theme, language – based on pre-released short story or chapter from a book from another culture or tradition.
- **Section B: Writing** *20% of total marks*
  Two tasks linked to pre-released passage: one to inform, explain and describe; the other to explore, imagine, entertain.

(*Note: Higher Tier paper is known as Paper Four*)

London Examinations (part of EdExcel)

Stewart House, 32 Russell Square, London WC1B 5DN Tel: 0171 331 4000

Essential support materials
A pre-released booklet of 20th-century poetry and non-fiction.

Coursework
40% of total marks

- **Speaking and Listening:** *20% of total marks*
  Three assessed units – explaining, exploring and discussing – for defined purposes.
- **Reading:** *10% of total marks*
  Unit 3: Shakespeare
  Unit 4: Pre-1900 prose author
- **Reading/Writing:** Unit 2: Other cultures and traditions (must include analyses, reviews and comment)
- **Writing:** *10% of total marks*
  Unit 1: Personal and imaginative writing

Written Paper 1
2 hours
30% of total marks

- **Reading:** *20% of total marks*
  Two questions based on close reading of pre-released booklet.
- **Writing:** *10% of total marks*
  One task to inform, explain or describe.

(Note: Foundation Tier paper is known as Paper Two, Higher Tier paper is known as Paper Four)

Written Paper 2
2 hours
30% of total marks

- **Reading:** *10% of total marks*
  One question selecting and evaluating from unseen media material.
- **Writing:** *20% of total marks*
  Two tasks: one to argue, persuade and instruct; the other to analyse, review and comment.

(Note: Foundation Tier paper is known as Paper Three, Higher Tier paper is known as Paper Five)

Welsh Joint Education Committee (WJEC)

245 Western Avenue, Llandaff, Cardiff CF5 2YX Tel: 01222 265000

Coursework

40% of total marks

- **Speaking and Listening:** *20% of total marks*
  Three assessed units – explaining, exploring and discussing – for defined purposes.
- **Reading:** *15% of total marks*
  Assignment 1: Shakespeare
  Assignment 2: Poetry
  Assignment 3: Further reading – prose , poetry or drama
  (*Note: Either Assignment 2 or 3 must include an author taken from English Order pre-1900*)
- **Writing:** *5% of total marks*
  Assignment 4: Best writing

Written Paper 1

2 hours
30% of total marks

- **Section A: Reading** *10% of total marks*
  Response in structured questions to prose passage post-1900.
- **Section B: Writing** *20% of total marks*
  Two tasks: one to describe; the other to explore, imagine, entertain.

Written Paper 2

2 hours
30% of total marks

- **Section A: Reading** *15% of total marks*
  Response in structured questions to non-fiction and media texts, with visual material included.
- **Section B: Writing** *15% of total marks*
  Two tasks covering some of inform, argue, explain, analyse, review and comment; one linked to Section A.

Northern Ireland Council for Curriculum, Examinations and Assessment (NICCEA)

Clarendon Dock, 29 Clarendon Road, Belfast BT1 3BG Tel: 01232 261200

Coursework
40% of total marks

- **Speaking and Listening:** *20% of total marks*
  Three assessed units – explaining, exploring and discussing – for defined purposes.
- **Reading:** *10% of total marks*
  Assignment A: Poetry (pre- and post-1900)
  Assignment B: Shakespeare and Media (appreciation of a play in performance)
- **Writing:** *10% of total marks*
  Assignment C: Writing to argue, persuade
  Assignment D: Writing to explore, imagine, entertain

Written Paper 1
2 hours
30% of total marks

- **Section A: Reading** *15% of total marks*
  Response to prose fiction passage post-1900.
- **Section B: Writing** *15% of total marks*
  One task – analyse, review, comment – based on visual stimulus material.

Written Paper 2
2 hours
30% of total marks

- **Section A: Writing** *15% of total marks*
  One task – inform, explain, describe – based on information sheet.
- **Section B: Reading** *15% of total marks*
  Response to non-literary reading.

Scottish Qualifications Authority (SQA, formerly SEB)

Ironmills Road, Dalkeith, Midlothian, EH22 1LE Tel: 0131 6636601

The Scottish examination system is quite different from that in the rest of the United Kingdom although, in English, the areas that have to be covered are similar. In the Standard Grade examination, the closest equivalent to GCSE English, Speaking and Listening is broken down into Listening and Talking when it is taught, and known simply as Talking when it is assessed. This is carried out by teachers. Reading and Writing are assessed separately as in GCSE English, using a mixture of coursework (known as folio) and examinations set at three levels – Foundation, General and Credit. The result is a numbered grade from 1–6 with 1 being the highest. The reading test lasts for 50 minutes and the writing test for 75 minutes and the coursework and the examination contribute equally to the final result.

If you are using this book in Scotland you will find that all of the main sections help you with Talking, Reading and Writing but you should obtain sample test papers to practise from for reading.

Chapter 1
Your own language

1.1 Building on what you know

You certainly are not starting from scratch as a speaker and listener. You have been doing these things since before you can even remember: at home, at school, with your friends, in shops, maybe even at work. So, what more is there to learn? If you want to gain a high grade in your GCSE, the answer is, quite a lot. This section aims to show you what you have to do and how to do it better.

It also goes into the detail of what your assessment of speaking and listening should consist of and the way in which your work in this area will be assessed. Of course, exactly how this is done will depend on where you are studying. A college of further education or an evening class may have to provide more structured opportunities for this kind of work than a school does.

This section shows you the skills and knowledge you need to reach the higher grades of speaking and listening assessment. It also gives you some ideas for activities you can undertake to practise the skills you will need to use in school.

1.2 Dialects and standard English

In your area there is probably a local dialect and a local accent. If you have lived there a long time then you may not notice it – probably because you speak it to some extent! Listening to old people talking can often give you a chance to hear good examples of local accents and dialects. The reason why this is so gives you an insight into dialects and standard English.

Only a hundred years ago, people rarely travelled far out of their own local area. Books were very expensive compared to their cost today, there were few national newspapers and no radio or television. In fact, most people spent their time talking and listening. Only a limited amount of reading and writing went on and many people were illiterate (unable to read or write). In these circumstances local dialects flourished and people spoke the way their ancestors had spoken for generations. A woman from Cornwall would only have to travel as far as London to find herself in a place where people spoke what was almost a different language.

Sometimes it is hard to take in just how much things have changed. You are used to owning books and having them around, to reading magazines and newspapers and to a choice of national television and radio. You watch video tapes and know about satellite broadcasting and cable television and you, and everyone around you, is used to travelling not just in the British Isles but all over the world. Distances have shrunk. It might have taken that Cornishwoman three days to travel to London. Now it takes about an hour by air, less than four hours by train and less than six by road.

The result of this is that the language we use is becoming more national and the old regional accents and dialects are dying out. Writing, printing and broadcasting have speeded up this process as one dialect has come to be used by more and more people. This is the dialect called standard English which was first used outside London in the south and east Midlands. From there it became the standard form for writing and printing and, later still, the standard form for speaking in formal situations.

Putting this into practice

Why is talk important?

Find four people, two male and two female; two between the ages of 30 and 50 and two over the age of 50. Ask them if they would answer these questions for you. If you can, tape their answers.

- What do you remember about talking in school?
- What do you remember about listening?
- What do you think children need to be taught about speaking and listening in school nowadays?
- How important is it to be good at talking? Do you need to be a good speaker and listener to do your job?
- Do you think it is as important to be a good speaker and listener as it is to be a good reader and writer?
- In what ways are speaking and listening important to you in your home life?

- What does talking properly mean to you? What is the right way to talk?
- Do you think that you speak with any accent or dialect? Have you noticed that accents and dialects are now heard less often than they used to be?

If you can, carry out this investigation with a friend. Discuss your findings. Ask yourself what you have learned about:

the nature of spoken language;
how spoken language changes;
social attitudes towards spoken language.

Even if you don't follow up your initial investigations, you will have found out that the English language is something everyone knows about and has opinions about. You may even have heard opinions that you disagreed with. One thing you will almost certainly have discovered is that we take our ability to talk very much for granted. Only people who for some reason have found it difficult to learn to speak, such as people with hearing or speech impairments, appreciate how difficult it would make our everyday lives to be without it.

You may have discovered from your interviews that, for many older people, talking at school was often considered 'bad behaviour', even though it is important to be able to talk well when work and social situations demand it. But times change and the National Curriculum in English recognises changing attitudes to the importance of talk by putting it first on the list of things you must learn to use in English.

Chapter 2
GCSE coursework in Speaking and Listening

As you know from Section One, your skills as a speaker and listener will account for 20% of your final assessment. Unlike reading or writing, all of your talk will be assessed by your teacher, as there is no final examination, so this is one area where you will need to improve your skills and demonstrate them in school or college right the way through your English course. You will find the advice in this section useful in other subjects where talk plays a part in your work.

There are three clusters of skills that are assessed. In classroom activities, these will often overlap. They will sometimes be connected with your reading and writing activities. You will find plenty more opportunities to practise your talk in later sections as well.

2.1 What do I need to know how to do?

The speaking and listening achievements which the GCSE assesses are grouped together in this way:

- explaining, describing and narrating;
- exploring, analysing, imagining;
- discussing, arguing, persuading.

Or, in more detail:

❶ **Explaining, describing and narrating** – your ability to talk about your own experiences, your ideas, your knowledge and your feelings.

This could involve anything, from telling your friends about what you did at the weekend, to giving a talk to the class about a book you have read, or giving instructions and explanations. At the simplest level, this could be a matter of seeing if you do what you are told. At the most complex level, it could involve you in demonstrating to a group of total strangers how to undertake a fairly complicated task, for example, explaining how you use tape and video recorders to help you with oral work on a school Open Evening.

❷ **Exploring, analysing and imagining** – this cluster of purposes of talk is all about your ability to use language to explain your creative thought processes.

You could be in a group at school trying to make sense of the ideas in a poem you have just read, or working on a role play where you have to cope with a problem you are not likely to have faced in real life - like how to survive in the alien environment of Mars when your space station malfunctions and you end up stranded there.

❸ **Discussing, arguing and persuading** – these are all functions of talk which allow you to express and explain your own opinions with the intention of getting listeners to agree that you are correct.

You could be talking informally with a group of friends about which type of music is the best, or you could be doing something much more formal, like taking part in a debate, or making a speech to your class.

To gain some idea of how your teacher will judge if you are doing these tasks well, you need to take a look at the assessment objectives listed on pp.10–11 and the assessment criteria listed on p.6.

xaminer's tip

xaminer wants to see ou can adjust how you according to who you lking to and what you o say.

You will see that you need to show that you can:

- participate co-operatively in pairs and groups;
- listen effectively and respond to what others say;
- adapt your way of talking to suit the situation - which means being able to speak standard English confidently when more formal situations demand it.

Different syllabuses set the speaking and listening skills out in slightly different ways, but these are the ones your English teacher will assess. Over the next few pages, you will be reading about how you can improve in each of these three areas.

❶ Explaining, describing and narrating

Well, you take the first, no, the second left. No, it's not, it's right. Then you walk down the High Street until you get to Boots, or is it W.H. Smith's? Well, if you get there you've gone past it, but this is the easiest way....

Explaining

By the time you start your GCSE English course, you will have had plenty of practice at following instructions and acting on information, both at home and at school. At the highest assessment levels, it is more or less taken for granted that you are able to listen carefully and to carry out accurately the task you have been given. In real life, of course, we all know that some simple instructions, like: 'Tidy that bedroom, NOW!' and 'Give your homework in tomorrow morning', are very difficult for a highly-intelligent GCSE student to follow.

Explaining clearly and accurately is something you will need to do outside school and in many other lessons apart from English, so it is worth practising. Most of us have had the experience of asking someone in a strange town how to find the railway station, for example, and been given information like this:

'Well, you take the first, no, the second left. No, it's not, it's right. Then you walk down the High Street until you get to Boots, or is it W.H. Smith's? Well, if you get there you've gone past it, but this is the easiest way...' and so on, and so on!

Putting this into practice

Could you do better? Practise, with a friend, giving as wide a variety of explanations as you can. The less familiar the listener is with what he or she is being told, the better. As far as possible, use words only; use diagrams and demonstrations as a last resort.

Try out these ideas. Tell each other how to:

- get from one place to another;
- programme your video recorder;
- dub a tape on your stereo;
- play a card game;
- cast off a row of knitting;
- get to the next level or 'world' in a computer game.

It doesn't really matter *what* the task is, though if you intend to follow each other's instructions as they are given, avoid tasks which could result in danger or damage if things go wrong! Finally, each of you should compile a list of between five and ten instructions about how to give clear, precise explanations. Compare your lists.

Describing

Being able to talk about emotions and responses, both your own and those of others, is a little different from many of the other sorts of talk you will read about in this section. Most talking skills will be useful to you in many of your school subjects. Talking about feelings is something you are more likely to do in your English classroom than anywhere else. You will find yourself discussing your feelings about your own experiences, the books you read, and the feelings of the characters in the books you read.

Empathy (the ability to identify with the feelings of other people) is a skill you cannot be without to succeed in English. The starting point is being able to talk about how you feel about things yourself.

This is not easy for some people: British culture seems to encourage an attitude that feelings are private, and only for sharing with a circle of intimate friends. Talking about feelings in groups can be quite awkward for a lot of people. Don't worry if you find it difficult at first, and remember that talking about the difficulties faced by characters in books or on television and film may be much easier than talking about similar problems in your own life.

Narrating

A Cream Cracker Under the Settee by Alan Bennett

(Doris is in her seventies and the play is set in the living room and hallway of her semi-detached house. She is sitting awkwardly on a low chair and rubbing her leg. It is morning.)
It's such a silly thing to have done.
Pause.
I should never have tried to dust. Zulema says to me every time she comes, "Doris. Do not attempt to dust. That's what the council pay me for. You are now a lady of leisure." Which would be all right providing she did dust. But Zulema doesn't dust. She half-dusts.
When she's going she says, "Doris. I don't want to hear you've been touching the sweeper. You're on trial here." I said, "What for?" She said, "For being on you own. For not behaving like a woman of seventy-five who has a pacemaker and dizzy spells and doesn't have the sense she was born with." I said, "Yes, Zulema."
She says, "What you don't understand, Doris, is that I'm the only person that stands between you and Stafford House. I have to report on you. They bend over backwards to keep you in your own home. But, Doris, you've got to meet them half way. Pull your horns in. Let the dirt wait. I'm here every week."
I was glad she'd gone, dictating. I sat for a bit looking up at me and Wilfred on the wedding photo. And I thought, "Well, Zulema, I bet you haven't dusted on top of that." So I got the stool and climbed up. And she hadn't. Thick with dust. Home help! Home hindrance. You're better off doing it yourself. And I was just wiping it over when, oh hell, the flaming stool went over.
Pause.
I think I'm all right. My leg's a bit numb. I'm just going to sit and come round a bit.
Pause.
Shan't let on I was dusting.
She looks down at the wedding photo on the floor.
Cracked the photo. We're cracked, Wilfred.
Pause.
The gate's open again. Dogs coming in, all sorts. You see Zulema should have closed that, only she didn't.
Pause.
The sneck's loose, that's the root cause of it. I kept saying to Wilfred, "When are you going to get round to that gate?" But oh no. It was always the same refrain. "Don't worry, Mother. I've got it on my list." I never saw no list. He'd no system at all, Wilfred. "When I get a minute, Doris." Well, he's got a minute now, bless him.
Pause.
Feels funny this leg. Not there.
Pause.
Some leaves coming down now. Zulema won't touch them. Says if I want leaves swept it's Parks Department. They're next door's leaves. We've only got one bush and it's an evergreen, so I'm certain they're not my leaves. Only other folks won't know that. I ought to put a note on the gate. 'Not my leaves!'; Not my leg either, the way it feels. Gone to sleep.
Pause.
I didn't even want the bush. I said, "Dad, is it a bush that'll make a mess?" He said, "Doris. Rest assured," and fetches out the catalogue. "'This labour-saving variety is much favoured by retired people.' Anyway," he says, "the garden is my department." I said, "Given a choice, Wilfred, I'd have concrete." He said, "Doris, concrete has no character." Well, he's got his little garden now. Only I bet it's covered in leaves. Graves, gardens, everything's to follow.
I'll make a move in a minute. Put the kettle on. Come on leg. Wake up.
Black out.

Come up on Doris sitting on the floor with her back to the wall.
Fancy, there's a cream cracker under the settee. She's not half done this place, Zulema. I'm going to save that cream cracker and show it her. I'll say, "Don't Stafford House me, lady. I've only got to send this cream cracker to the Social

" Services Department and you'll be on the carpet. Same as the cream cracker. I'll be in Stafford House, Zulema, but you'll be in the Unemployment Exchange."
I'm en route for the window only I'm not making much headway. I'll bang on it. Alert somebody. Don't know who. Don't know anybody round here now. Folks opposite, I don't know them. Used to be the Marsdens. There for years. Then he died, and she died and the daughter went away somewhere and folks started to come and go. You lose track. I don't think they're married half of them. You see all sorts.
Ought to have had a dog. Then it could have been barking for someone. Wilfred was always hankering after a dog. I wasn't keen. Hairs all up and down, then having to take it outside every five minutes. Wilfred said that would be his province. I said, "Yes, and whose province would all the little hairs be?" We never got one either. It was the growing mushrooms saga all over again. He never got round to it. Like the fretwork, making toys and forts and whatnot. No end of money he was going to make. Then there was this phantom allotment. "We can be self-sufficient in the vegetable department, Doris." Never materialised. I was glad. It'd've meant muck somehow.

She looks in the place where the pram was.
I wanted to call him John. The midwife said he wasn't fit to be called anything and had we any newspaper? Wilfred said, "Oh yes, she saves newspapers. Shoeboxes as well." I must have fallen asleep because when I woke up she'd gone. I wanted to see him. Wrapping him in newspaper as if he was dirty. He wasn't dirty, little thing. I don't think Wilfred minded. A kiddy. Same as the allotment and the fretwork. Just a craze. He said, "We're better off, Doris. Just the two of us." Then he started talking about a dog.
If it had lived I might have had grandchildren now. Wouldn't have been in this fix. Daughters are the best. They don't migrate.
Pause.

We were always on our own, me and Wilfred. We weren't gregarious. He thought he was, but he wasn't. Mix. I don't want to mix. Comes to the finish and they suddenly think you want to mix. I don't want to be stuck with a lot of old lasses. You go daft there. Wearing somebody else's frock. They even mix up your teeth. I am H.A.P.P.Y. I am not H.A.P.P.Y. I am un H.A.P.P.Y. Or I would be.
And Zulema says, "You don't understand, Doris. You're not up to date. They have lockers now. Flowerbeds. They go on trips to Wharfedale." I said, "Yes, smelling of pee." She said, "You're prejudiced, you." I said, "I am where hygiene is concerned."
When people were clean and the streets were clean and it was all clean and you could walk down the street and folks smiled and passed the time of day, I'd leave the door on the latch and go on to the end for some toffee, and when I came back Dad was home and the cloth was on and we'd have our tea. And I'd wash up while he read the paper and we'd eat the toffees and listen to the wireless all them years ago when we were first married and I was having the baby.
Doris and Wilfred. They don't get called Doris now. Or Wilfred. Museum, names like that. That's what they're all called in Stafford House. Alice, Mabel, Doris. Antiques. Keep them under lock and key. "What's your name? Doris? Right. Pack your case."
A home. Not me. No fear.

Long pause.
You've done it now, Doris. Done it now, Wilfred.
Pause.
I wish I was ready for bed. All washed and in a clean nightie and the bottle in, all sweet and crisp and clean like when I was little on Baking Night, sat in front of the fire with my long hair still.
Her eyes close and she sings a little to herself.
Pause.
Never mind. It's done now, anyway.
Light fades. "

We all tell stories about our experiences. We tell them in conversations to entertain our friends; we tell them to explain our feelings and to illustrate points we are making. Some stories are mainly intended to teach the listener something. Consider how often your teachers in school use anecdotes to help you understand and remember something they are explaining to you.

Storytelling is something you have been doing all your life, both in and out of school, quite spontaneously. You will be well aware that some people are better at this than others: they hold their listeners spellbound while they talk about their experiences. How do they do it?

Putting this into practice

Spend a day listening to the way people use anecdotes: on the bus, at school, at home, on the television and radio. Make brief notes about as many of the stories as you can. Use these headings to help you:

- Who was telling it?
- Who to?
- For what reason?
- How? As a monologue or as part of a conversation? Was it rehearsed or spontaneous?
- What skills did the teller have (or not have) that made it a good (or bad) story?

At the end of the day, consider all the information you have collected and decide which were the best three stories you heard. Use the notes you have made to put together a list of rules for good storytelling.

Now have a go yourself. Think about something interesting that you did recently, or a vivid memory. Find two people to tell it to, such as a younger sister or brother, an older member of the family or a neighbour, or one of your friends.

- Tape yourself so you can listen to the two different versions afterwards.
- Think in advance about the interesting details you want to keep in and the boring bits you want to leave out.
- Think how you would begin and end your story.
- Think about where you might need to include descriptive details of people and places, and where you might want to comment on how you felt about the events that happened. Make some brief notes if you are not sure you can trust your memory.
- Think about the importance of eye-contact: how can you tell your listener is understanding you, or is interested in what you are saying? What do you do if they are not?
- Think about ways in which the speed, the intonation and gestures you use might help to make your storytelling better.

Afterwards, listen to your tape. As you listen, think about how the story was changed to suit the different audiences. For example, you would probably use simpler vocabulary when talking to a child, and tell the story more slowly, perhaps with more explanation of unfamiliar experiences, than you would if you were talking to a close friend. Talking to someone older, who is less familiar to you, you might find that you avoided slang and chose to highlight slightly different events in the story.

Remember that suiting the way you talk to a particular audience, and being able to explain the choices you make, is a skill you need to develop to become a 'high-grade' talker.

2 Exploring, analysing and imagining

Putting this into practice

Read the script that follows. A group of four GCSE students, James, Gemma, Carl and Nasreen, are discussing the ideas in a poem they have read. Your task is to spot the occasions when these four show skills in using talk to think aloud about abstract ideas and problems.

Complete the chart on p.37 by filling in the words spoken which show each of the four students using language to analyse and explore the poem *Song of the Battery Hen*.

What grade would you award to each student for this group discussion?

James: OK then, this poem. Nasreen can read it and Gemma can make notes.
Nasreen: James, Gemma was secretary last time. Don't you think she should have a go at chairing?
Carl: Yeah, and James can report. I hate doing that.
Gemma: Nas, I'm no good, why did you...
James: Go on then Nas. Gemma chairs, Carl reports.
Carl and Gemma: Oh no!
Nasreen: Go on Gem, you can.
Gemma: All right. Nas, read the poem. Then we've got to, er...
James: Discuss whether...
Nasreen: Go on, Gem.
Gemma: Yeah, we have to say whether factory farming is cruel. We have to say why it's, er... unhuman...
Carl: Inhumane.
Gemma: Oh, yeah, inhumane for the hens. And we have to decide whether... er... there are advantages for people that, like... er...
Nasreen: Justify it?
Gemma: Yeah. Justify it.
Carl: 'Course it's worth it, because free range eggs cost a fortune, don't they? And besides, they're only a load of hens...
Gemma: Carl, let's read the poem first. OK, Nasreen?
(Nasreen reads.)

Song of the Battery Hen

We can't grumble about the accommodation:
we have a new concrete floor that's
always dry, four walls that are
painted white, and a sheet-iron roof
the rain drums on. A fan blows warm air
beneath our feet to disperse the smell
of chicken-shit and, on dull days,
fluorescent lighting sees us.

You can tell me: if you come by
the North door, I am in the twelfth pen
on the left-hand side of the third row
from the floor; and in that pen
I am usually the middle one of three.
But, even without directions, you'd
discover me. I have the same orange-
red comb, yellow beak and auburn
feathers, but as the door opens and you
hear above the electric fan a kind of
one-word wail, I am the one
who sounds loudest in my head.

Listen. Outside this house there's an
orchard with small moss-green apple
trees; beyond that, two fields of
cabbages; then, on the far side of
the road, a broiler house. Listen:
one cockerel grows out of there, as
tall and proud as the first hour of the sun.
Sometimes I stop calling with the others
to listen, and wonder if he hears me.

The next time you come here, look for me.
Notice the way I sound inside my head.
God made us all quite differently,
and blessed us with this expensive home.

Edwin Brock

James: Well, that's all about inhumanity isn't it? I mean, look at what it says about it never seeing daylight. That's really...
Gemma: Good point, James. Hey... no one's taking notes. James, would you? Write it down before you forget. Carl, do you still think it doesn't matter because they're only hens?
Carl: Well... er... this bit here is a bit tight...
Nasreen: Which? Read it to us.
Carl: Where it says...
James: I think...
Gemma: Can Carl explain why, first? Sorry, James. Are you writing it down, then?...
Carl: It says about the smell of chicken...
Nasreen: Trust you to choose that bit!
Carl: No, seriously, it says about a fan blowing the air, and electic lights, and a roof that keeps the rain off. It's kind of all about how it's not natural for an animal - a bird - it should be out in the open.
Nasreen: That's right - and it says about the cockerel outside 'tall and proud' - and - like she's never seen it or anything, but she imagines what it's like and where it is.
Gemma: That's really sad - she'll never have little chicks and do what hens naturally do.

Carl:	Yeah, but like I said, though, it's only a bird isn't it? Birds can't really think or anything! If you live on a farm, well, that's what you do, isn't it? You have to sell things at a price people can afford.
James:	Like that other poem, in our anthology, 'The Early Purges', remember?
Gemma:	Yeah - really tight - about drowning poor little kittens.
James:	It's what Carl's talking about - how sentimental we are about animals - but on a farm you can't be because it's a business isn't it? It's not so inhumane to keep chickens like this as it would be to ....
Nasreen:	Have them loose in a farmyard full of millions of starving cats pouncing on all their little chicks.
James:	Now that really is nature isn't it? Red in tooth and claw - literally!
Carl:	What are you two on about? All I'm saying is not many people would pay for them free-range eggs. I never said anything about cats.
Nasreen:	No, you're right, in a way, Carl. We do tend to think animals have feelings like humans, and farmers don't think about it like that.
Gemma:	But I still think it's dead cruel to keep animals in cages like that. You can still get cheap eggs without them being in a cage. They sell them in our supermarket. They're ... the chickens ... they're inside, but not trapped.
James:	True. And that's a good compromise, I think we'd all agree.
Gemma:	What have you written, James? We need some ideas to report. Read it and we'll check ....

Skill	**Carl**	**Gemma**	**James**	**Nasreen**
Understands the main ideas **(Grade F)**				
Shows ability to develop a line of enquiry **(Grade E)**				
Interprets the central issues **(Grade D)**				
Responds to complex ideas **(Grade C)**				
Communicates using precise vocabulary **(Grade C)**				
Interprets information and develops significant points **(Grade B)**				
Draws ideas together to reach a shared conclusion **(Grade A)**				
Shows original thinking in bringing in ideas from other sources **(Grade A*)**				

Develop your skills as a pair or group worker

You will spend a great deal of time working and talking together with other members of your class. Your skills as a **collaborative** talker will be assessed by many of your teachers: nearly all GCSE subjects have some assessment relating to oral communication.

Examiner's tip

Being a better listener

There is a lot more to good listening than simply sitting in silence. It is possible to do that and be thinking of something completely different from what you are hearing. Two reasons why people are poor listeners are either that they find it hard to sustain concentration listening to others, or that they are very confident talkers and prefer that to listening.

If you recognise these faults, practise the following skills:

- Show that you are listening. Making eye contact with the person speaking is one way of doing this. So is appropriate body language: face the speaker; lean towards them; nod or shake your head; smile; look interested; look puzzled. Your facial expressions show whether you are listening and understanding what you are hearing.
- Verbal encouragement is useful too. Say 'mm' and 'yes' if you agree. Ask for more details or for clarification if they are trying to make a point that you cannot understand.
- Don't be in a tearing hurry to make your contribution. Ask others in the group if they agree or disagree, and listen to what they have to say.
- Rephrase or summarise what has been said so far, if it seems useful. You do not always have to make a new point.

- Give quieter members of the group time to talk. Encourage good listening skills in the others.
- Try not to interrupt or change the subject until you are sure the speaker has finished.
- Being able to explain what you think and your reasons for holding an opinion are skills you need to work hard at during your English course. Forming and explaining well-thought-out points of view will be influenced by:
  how well you listen to the opinions of others;
  how carefully you read materials that help you form opinions;
  how you use all these other sources of information to make sense of what you think yourself.

Who listens best?

Did you know that girls are generally better listeners than boys and that, contrary to popular belief, boys tend to talk more than girls in group discussions? You could test this out by observing different people talking in groups and, in your own groups, you could encourage the boys to listen and give the girls space to talk.

An American linguist called Deborah Tannen has suggested that there are two different ways of interrupting. One way is to talk over the top of what someone else is saying, changing the subject and showing that you were not listening to or did not care about what they were saying.

The other sort of interruption, she suggests, is when someone is so interested in what another person is saying that they join in and start relating it to their own experience and feelings. She suggests that men usually interrupt the first way (maybe because they are not such good listeners), whilst women usually interrupt in the second way. Try observing people working in groups at school and see if you think she is correct!

❸ Discussing, arguing, persuading

This is the kind of talk which will give you the opportunity to put forward your opinions about things - so listeners can understand why you hold your beliefs and, sometimes, be so convinced by what you say, that they agree that you are right.

But first, you need to have some opinions and views which will give you the chance to talk impressively. Reading newspapers and taking an interest in current affairs programmes on radio and television is a good way of building up information, so that the views you express are based on evidence rather than prejudice. Reading a broadsheet quality paper, like the *Independent*, *Telegraph* or *Guardian* is a good idea. All newspapers have some sort of bias, but you will find more reasons and explanations backing up the points of view in the quality papers, whereas the tabloid papers like the *Sun* and the *Star* tend to present their readers with opinions which appeal to emotions rather than logical thought.

Editorial and opinion columns from any newspaper are a good starting point for discussing points of view. The less reasoned they are, the more you will find to say to put an opposing point of view and, therefore, to make your point in an argument.

Putting this into practice

Read this newspaper article. It is taken from a Sunday newspaper – *The News of the World*. You should be able to detect four separate opinions being presented here:

❶ that football hooliganism is a disgrace;
❷ that German football hooligans are as bad as English ones;
❸ that English teams should only be banned from European football if German ones are;
❹ that the cause of football hooliganism could be violence on television.

> **THE VOICE OF REASON**
>
> Woodrow Wyatt
>
> English football hooligans disgraced us in Sweden. German football hooligans disgraced Germany after they were beaten by Denmark.
>
> They were just as violent as the English. It'd be monstrous if English teams were prevented from competing on the Continent unless German teams were too.
>
> Perhaps TV provokes the terrifying behaviour. Flicking from channel to channel, scenes of brutality are an all day, every day matter.
>
> That's whether it's the news or what passes for entertainment. As the young everywhere see people beat each other about the head they've begun to think this is normal life.

This article presents one person's opinion. There is very little justification given for any of the opinions presented, and anyone might disagree with some or all of them.

What are your views on the last argument – that television encourages football violence? You might think that the causes of football hooliganism are a lot more complicated than the programmes people watch on television. After all:

- millions of people watch television and do not become football hooligans;
- some psychologists even say that watching violence makes people less likely to want to participate in it;
- there are many more theories to explain football hooliganism: poor home backgrounds, mob pressure, etc. Recently, a government politician suggested that if children were taught more English grammar in school, it would reduce hooliganism!

Now add two more reasons of your own to explain why you either agree or disagree with the theory that there is a link between violence on television and hooliganism. Ask friends or relatives to discuss the topic. If possible, audiotape your discussion so you can listen to it afterwards.

Examiner's tip

- State your points of view clearly and back them up with well-thought-out reasons for what you say.
- Listen to the points of view of the person you are talking to.
- Be ready to ask them to explain in more detail if you do not see the logic in what they are saying.
- Be prepared to explain why you think some of the points they make are unsound. Use evidence to do this.
- Be willing to modify your opinion if they make a good point which you had not thought of.
- Be careful not to resort to prejudice, or to rely on comments like, 'It's obvious', or 'everyone knows that'.

Remember that you do not have to 'win' an argument to have a good discussion. You *may* persuade someone to agree with you, but even if you still hold different points of view, you should have better understanding of your reasons for holding them.

As you listen to your tape, check off which of these skills you used. Ask the other person or people you talked to for their assessment as well.

Working in larger groups: roles

Working in pairs is easy enough, so long as you are both prepared to listen and both take part in talking. Once groups get larger than two, they take more organising and more understanding about how language works in groups. It can help if different members of the group take on different jobs and all members know what their job is.

Groups usually function best if they have:

A chairperson, who
- should make sure the group is clear about the task;
- should make sure the task gets done;
- should make sure everyone in the group is involved in the task.

A secretary, who
- should make sure that any conclusions the group reaches are written down, especially if information is to be passed on or shared with other groups during or after the activity.

A reporter, who
- is the group's messenger or spokesperson and should be able to pass on information or conclusions from the group to other groups.

In a way, everything you have read in this section has involved knowledge about spoken language.

Revise what you have learned by looking at who does what in a good group meeting or discussion.

Putting this into practice

List four of the speaking and listening skills mentioned in this chapter which you think a good chairperson would need.

1 ______________________________

2 ______________________________

3 ______________________________

4 ______________________________

Which four speaking and listening skills do you think a good secretary would need?

1 ______________________________

2 ______________________________

3 ______________________________

4 ______________________________

Which four speaking and listening skills do you think a good reporter would need?

1 ______________________________

2 ______________________________

3 ______________________________

4 ______________________________

Which four speaking and listening skills would be the most important to group members?

1 ______________________________

2 ______________________________

3 ______________________________

4 ______________________________

Finally, take a second look at the group discussion (pp.35–7) and see how well the four students fulfil these roles.

Examiner's tip

The bigger the group, the more skilful you need to be. Once a group gets bigger than four people, you need all your skills to make it work: confident talkers tend to take over and quieter members get left out. Make sure you do not take on the same role every time you work in a group. It is easy for quieter members to find they are always secretary, while the more confident members of the group do the chairing and reporting. Make sure roles are swapped: you will not learn how to do a job if you never try it out. Also, the roles of Chair and Secretary are highly skilled jobs. If you show you can do these well, you will be on your way to achieving a high mark for your collaborative skills.

Making a speech

Once you feel confident about arguing your case in conversation, you will be ready to practise something more difficult: presenting a well-thought-out, extended statement of your opinion on a difficult subject is one of the skills that will help you to gain the highest possible grade for your speaking and listening assessment. Many people, including very articulate adults, find this a nerve-racking experience. If the thought of making a speech to your own class at school, let alone to a larger group of complete strangers, fills you with trepidation, you can be sure you are not alone in feeling like that.

2.2 Case study

Jessica has been asked to give a talk to her class on a topic she feels strongly about. She is a vegetarian, so it seemed natural to talk about that. That topic seemed too broad for a short talk so her teacher suggested that she focus on one idea – the way that animals are raised with factory farming methods.

The first thing Jessica did was to think hard about the opinions people hold on the subject.

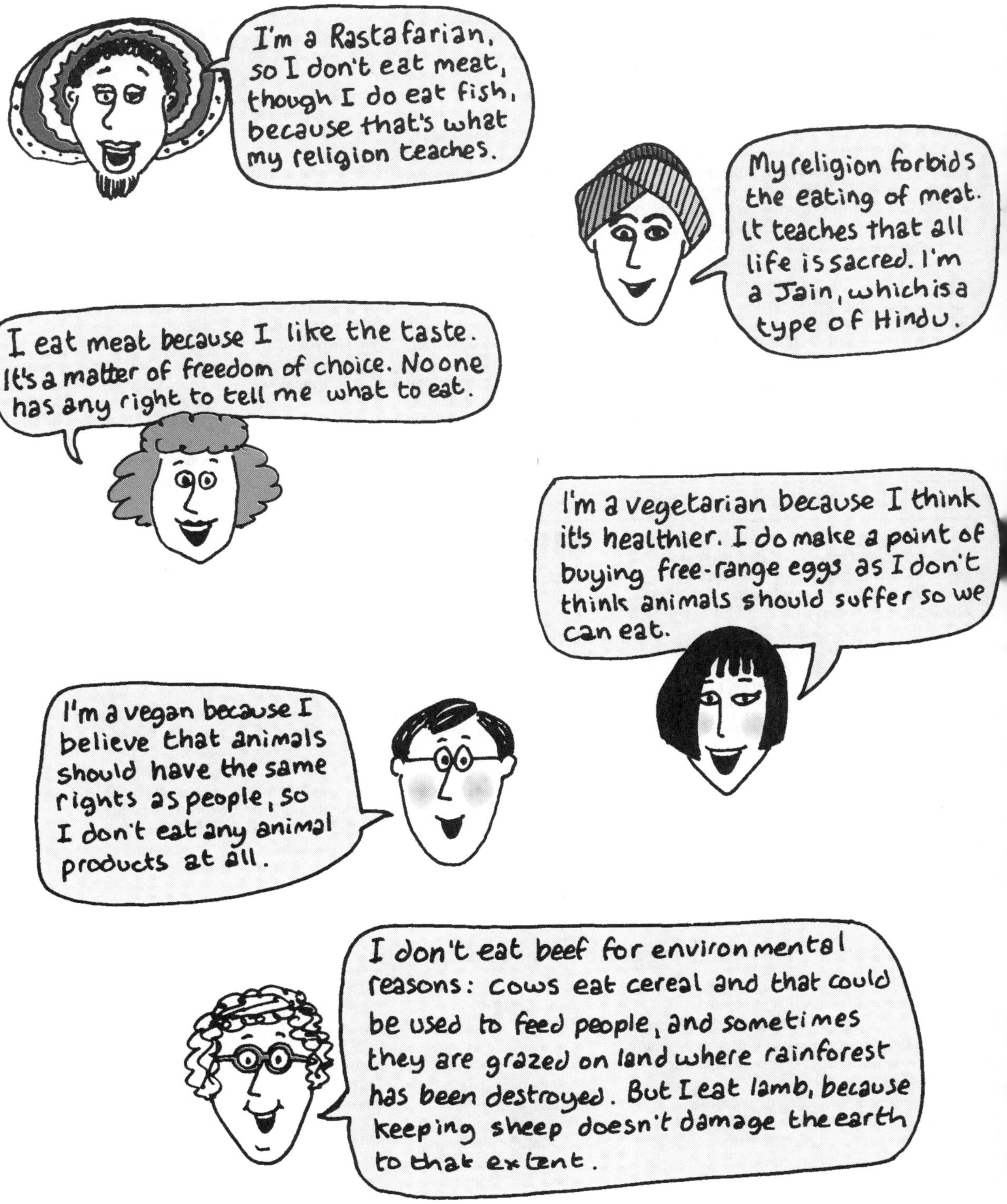
I'm a Rastafarian, so I don't eat meat, though I do eat fish, because that's what my religion teaches.
My religion forbids the eating of meat. It teaches that all life is sacred. I'm a Jain, which is a type of Hindu.
I eat meat because I like the taste. It's a matter of freedom of choice. No one has any right to tell me what to eat.
I'm a vegetarian because I think it's healthier. I do make a point of buying free-range eggs as I don't think animals should suffer so we can eat.
I'm a vegan because I believe that animals should have the same rights as people, so I don't eat any animal products at all.
I don't eat beef for environmental reasons: cows eat cereal and that could be used to feed people, and sometimes they are grazed on land where rainforest has been destroyed. But I eat lamb, because keeping sheep doesn't damage the earth to that extent.

Then she did some reading in the library.

The *Indy* guide to life without meat

Vegetarians are growing in number and are no longer considered freaks. **Anne Churchward** and **Louise Hurst** explain how to take the meat out of your diet. They reveal the life in a factory farm and name some famous veggies along the way.

BECOMING A vegetarian doesn't just mean giving up the odd beef doorstep sandwich from your school lunch, and existing on a diet of soggy lettuce and nut roast.

Here are a few tips which might make life a little easier if you decide you want to be a veggie and don't warm to the prospect of boiled cabbage and Brussels sprouts for dinner every night.

1 You don't have to subject yourself to eating mounds of Brussels sprouts for dinner and sticks of celery for lunch! There are loads of good vegetarian cookbooks around, so pop down to your nearest bookshop to investigate.

2 Quorn is a form of soya protein which can take the place of meat as the protein content of your diet. When cooked, e.g. in a vegetable stew, it takes the flavour of what it is cooked in.

3 If you decide to become a vegetarian because you are opposed to the cruelty inflicted upon factory-farmed animals, then you may also choose to eat free-range eggs, laid by chickens who live happily out in a farmyard, instead of battery-farmed eggs.

4 The invisible ingredients warning: many everyday foods and sweets contain ingredients derived from animals. You may think that by not eating meat or fish you are excluding animal foods from your diet, and are a fully-fledged vegetarian.

But if you are serious about becoming a vegetarian you should try to *avoid* the following.

- **a** Gelatine – this is glue-like and derived from a protein called collagen which is found in animal tissues. Gelatine often crops up in chewy sweets and similar confectionery.
- **b** Animal fat – this is used in a wide variety of foods, ranging from margarine, suet, cooking fats, biscuits and cakes to sweets; look carefully if you want to avoid it.
- **c** Rennet – rennet is obtained from calf's stomachs and is used to curdle milk. This means it turns up in hard cheeses, such as cheddar. If you want to avoid rennet it is best to steer well clear of pizzas, cauliflower cheese, cheese sandwiches or any other foods which contain non-vegetarian cheese.

5 Many people who want to become vegetarians are put off by their mum or dad. If your parents moan and say, 'No you can't become vegetarian… I'm not cooking two separate dinners… don't be such a pain!', try sitting down and reasoning with them.

Explain why you want to become a vegetarian, and suggest that your mum or dad tries cooking some vegetarian meals for the whole family. You could even volunteer to help with the cooking, but make sure they are sitting down when you tell them, so they don't collapse from shock!

6 You are now ready to become a successful vegetarian. Remember, when you go into fast-food restaurant, beefburgers are out of the question. However, Wimpy do sell beanburgers as an alternative.

Why be a vegetarian?

Being a vegetarian does not make you an anaemic, pale-faced freak!

* The vegetarian diet is very similar to the recommendations issued by the government on medical aspects of food policy.
* The average fibre content of a vegetarian diet is almost twice that of a meat-eater.
* The total daily calorie intake of fat per person could be reduced by 10 per cent by cutting out meat.
* British milk is among Europe's worst, as most of our cows are pumped full of antibiotics.
* Diseases such as diabetes, gout and kidney stones are more common among meat-eaters.
* Millions of children in Third-World countries go blind because they do not get enough of vitamin A, which is abundant in a vegetarian diet.

Eating without meat is healthy and kind says **Joe Newman**, age 15 of Simonstock School, Maidstone

Why I am a vegetarian

I TURNED vegetarian three years ago, when I was twelve, and have not eaten meat since. At first it was difficult and there were many problems. One of these was eating at someone else's house. Gradually I and other people got used to it. Half of my family were already vegetarian.

The change of diet was difficult though. Now I check the ingredients of every type of food before I eat it. For example, Polos have gelatine in which is made from animals.

I turned vegetarian when I found out what was going on within the meat industry and, more importantly, on the factory farms. The most disturbing was the animal cruelty going on there.

I do not eat eggs either because battery hens are put into cages measuring four inches wide. In such a small space there is no room to walk, make dustbaths, spread their wings, lay their eggs in nests, scratch or peck.

Pigs are also kept in appalling conditions, where they are kept in crates on cold concrete floors. These crates are only two feet wide, where there is no room to even turn around.

The same kind of treatment is given to cows, chickens, turkeys and sheep. None of these animals take exercise, feel fresh air, experience freedom of movement or natural companionship with their own species. They face a sentence of life imprisonment.

Another reason I turned vegetarian was because it is more healthy than a meat eating diet. Meat has a high fat content. A vegetarian diet has a high fibre content. It also provides carbohydrates, some fat, vitamins and minerals, which all add up to a healthy, balanced diet.

Such a diet can reduce the risks of heart disease, cancer of the colon (in your stomach), obesity and hernias (internal ruptures). A reduction in fatty foods can reduce the risk of cardiovascular disease (in the heart's blood vessels) which is the UK's biggest killer, with 180,000 deaths each year.

The meat industry is also responsible for environment damage, such as water pollution and loss of wildlife. Tropical rainforests the size of Wales are cut down every month to make way for cattle ranching.

One hectare of land will feed enough animals to produce meat to make just 1,000 hamburgers, each costing half a tonne of rainforest.

Next time you are eating your dinner, think about it.

The shocking facts for you meat eaters

Many people are now choosing not to eat meat because they object to the cruel process of factory farming

* Almost half-a-billion animals every year are killed for food in Britain alone.
* Battery hens are kept in rows of wire cages about the size of a piece of typing paper (they cannot spread their wings for the whole of their lives).
* The cramped space makes them susceptible to illness and disease.
* The hens become aggressive in small spaces, so the farmers cut their beaks off to stop them pecking their neighbours to death. This causes severe pain, yet more than 1,000 hens per farm per day are still mutilated.
* Pigs are stunned with electric shocks before being killed. However, this does not always make them unconscious to pain.
* Many pigs are still fully awake when they are hung upside down to have their throats slit!
* Most hens are killed on a conveyor belt system, by an automatic throat slitter. If the birds are too large or too small then the knife will miss their throats and cut their heads or lower neck.
* In some abattoirs (slaughter-houses) sheep are stunned through the eyeball.
* In a lifetime one British person eats on average 8 cows, 346 pigs, 36 sheep, 750 poultry.
* There are 2 million vegetarians in Britain alone, and the number is constantly increasing.
* 1 in 9 students are vegetarians.
* 2 million battery hens die in their cages every year.
* 6 million livestock die each year before they reach the abattoir.
* Vegetarian have a 20 per cent lower blood cholesterol level on average than meat eaters.
* 100 acres of tropical rainforest is destroyed every minute. A lot of the land is used to rear

Types of vegetarians

14 per cent of under-16s in Britain are one of three types of vegetarian.

1) Ovovegetarians eat a diet of vegetables, milk, cheese and eggs.
2) Lactovegetarians eat a diet of all vegetables, milk, cheese but no eggs.
3) Pure vegetarians, vegans, eat a diet of all vegetables, and will not eat any product of animal origin, (i.e. milk or eggs).

She made some notes:

Many methods of raising animals for meat are inhumane.

There are laws which should prevent real cruelty.

Raising animals for meat is wasteful and damages the environment.

Some people have moral and religious reasons for not eating meat.

People should be allowed to choose for themselves.

A meatless diet is healthier than one containing meat.

Jessica now had the beginnings of her speech.

Jessica's notes	What she said
Burgers *Rainforest*	Remember tucking into your last Big Burger? The fresh warm bun; the tasty ozone-layer relish; the succulent burger? But did you think about where that burger came from? A lump of minced-up cow, grazed on land that ought to be rainforest. Did you ever think that you were doing your bit for the destruction of the ozone layer?

Technical tips: Notice *three* things Jessica does to make what she says strike home. She *asks a series of questions* which set a trap for the listeners and makes them question their behaviour. She *uses emotive words* ('minced-up cow', 'destruction') which help sway the audience to adopt her point of view. She also *lists things in groups of three.* This is sometimes called the 'rule of three'. It is a way of reinforcing your point by making it three times in slightly different ways.

Once Jessica had the attention of her audience, she could use any number of persuasive techniques. She could:

- shock them with facts about factory farming;
- scare them by emphasising health risks;
- appeal to their sympathy by describing the suffering of animals;
- appeal to their common sense.

The end of a speech is as important as the beginning. Jessica needed to leave her audience in no doubt about the main point she was trying to make.

Jessica's notes	What she said
No meat *Health* *Suffering of animals* *Damage to environment*	So, I think you'll agree that it's best not to eat meat. For the sake of your own health; to avoid causing unnecessary suffering to animals; to protect our planet. Next time you pick up a juicy Big Burger, just think about all that!

2.3 Talking standard English

In this kind of public performance you have to think about your use of standard English. Look back at Section One for an outline of what standard English is. If you have already carried out the assignment on telling stories (p.34), you will have begun to consider the way you adapt how you speak to suit different listeners: a child, a friend your own age or an elderly relative, for example.

Skilful talkers are also aware of how we need to adapt our use of English to suit different occasions. Suppose you turned up at a party dressed very casually and then realised you were the only one there not wearing a formal suit or a long dress. You would feel quite out of place, because your clothes were not appropriate for the occasion.

There are some occasions which call for the language equivalent of 'best clothes'. This is one of the skills you will need to develop during your English course. To achieve a high grade, you will need to show that you recognise where it is appropriate to use standard English and to demonstrate that you adapt your everyday speech to do this when appropriate.

Formal situations, where you are attempting to make a good impression, are the most likely to require standard English. These might include:

- job interviews;
- speeches to a large audience;
- showing an important visitor around your school;
- phoning to make an appointment or a complaint, etc.

xaminer's tip

't make your use of
dard English sound false
ilted. Let it develop
ly.

Which dialect features might I need to alter?

Vocabulary is the simplest part of language to change. If you know you sometimes use words which are local dialect words, you need to 'translate' these into words which any English speaker might also understand. In formal situations, you will also need to avoid slang and colloquial expressions. Even though these might be understood by anyone, they will not be appropriate in formal speech.

Grammar is more difficult to adapt. You will need to know how your local grammar differs from standard English.

- **This might include the way you form verb tenses.**
  In the North of England you might hear a local dialect speaker say, 'I were stood at the bus stop for more than an hour,' where a standard English speaker would say 'I was standing…'.

- **It might include the way you use adverbs.**
  In Yorkshire you might hear someone say, 'I waited while the rain stopped,' where the standard English speaker would say 'I waited until…'.

- **You might find there are different pronouns in your dialect.**
  In some Irish dialects there is a plural form of 'you': 'Which one of youse did this?', where standard English uses the same word for singular and plural.

- **You may notice different use of prepositions.**
  Some Scottish speakers say, 'We went by my house,' where a standard English speaker would say, 'We went to my house.'

Being a local dialect speaker is not a disadvantage. You will learn a great deal about English grammar by taking an interest in dialect and by talking about it to other people, and you will also improve your skills in writing and speaking standard English.

Putting this into practice

Making a formal speech

Now, prepare a short speech giving **your** views on the causes of football hooliganism. First, note down your opinions and then try to back up each one with evidence or examples. Keep the points you want to make as clear and simple as you can. Make a conscious attempt to use standard English.

If you are able to, videotape your performance. If that is not possible, try giving your speech as you look in a mirror. You will find it very hard to give a speech to just one or two friends. Speeches are 'public' and sound odd in personal situations or small groups.

Examiner's tip

- Making speeches really does get easier with practice: the more times you do it, the more confident you will become.
- Advance preparation is essential. Know your facts and prepare notes in advance. Trying it out either on a friend, or on tape or in front of a mirror, will make you feel much more confident when you finally face a larger audience.
- Take a few deep breaths before you start. Having a table in front of you on which to steady yourself will make you feel less like a quivering jelly.
- Work from notes – not a written speech. Make your notes on a bundle of cards (about postcard size), one point to each card. If your hands shake with nerves, it is a lot less obvious to those watching you if you are holding small cards, rather than a large, quivering sheet of paper! Grip your cards in one hand, and hang onto the table with the other.
- Use visual aids (posters, pictures, facts on an overhead projector) to emphasise your points, but make sure your audience can see them properly.
- Make each point clearly. Use 'tricks of the trade' to involve your audience. Vary tone, volume and pace of voice. Use pauses to give your audience time to think. Try to use eye contact and gestures.
- Start with something to make your audience to sit up and take notice. Shock them, surprise them. Make sure you have a strong beginning and end to your speech.

Using role-play

Examiner's tip

Use role-play to explore the characters you encounter in books and remember that this work can be assessed.

You will probably already have had experience of taking part in a variety of larger group performances during your English course. You might be taking on roles of people with different opinions to argue out differing points of view about various topical issues, improvising scenes, sometimes of your own invention, sometimes based on your reading, and acting out scripted plays, written by members of your class, or plays you were studying.

- Working in a group on a drama or role-play allows you to develop your collaborative skills.
- Role-playing allows you to demonstrate your ability to argue a case or to give information.
- Group performances based on the books you are reading may allow your teacher to assess your understanding of what you have read as an alternative to written essays.
- Role-playing may be used to help you gather information in preparation for writing essays about varying points of view on a topic.
- Improvisation can help you to refine ideas for writing a script or a story.

All of these are skills which you can develop to reach the highest grades in Reading and Writing, in addition to Speaking and Listening.

2.4 Recording your achievements

At the end of the course, your teacher has to send a detailed written summary of your speaking and listening skills to the examination board. All examining groups have a form for teachers to complete (see p.12). If a talk assignment is used as evidence of your reading skills, then your teacher may have to note this on your coursework cover sheet.

Self-assessment

Sometimes your teacher may ask you to fill in ready-prepared forms to record and assess what you have done in lessons where most of the work is speaking and listening.

English/English Literature (GCSE)

En2/Literature
Oral Assessment Form

Year of Examination [ ]

Name of Centre .... Centre No. [ ][ ][ ][ ][ ]

Candidate's Surname .... Candidate No. [ ][ ][ ][ ][ ]

Other Names ....

Notice

This form must be included in the candidate's folder if an oral response to any of the categories below is included in the coursework submission. Please tick appropriate box(es) to indicate subject(s) and category applicable. **A brief written evaluation of the activity by the candidate must be attched to this form.**

Please tick appropriate box(es) to indicate subject(s)and category applicable.

Subjects

☐ *English* ☐ *English Literature*

Coursework category

☐ Shakespeare ☐ Wide Reading ☐ 20th Century Drama

Teacher's account of activity e.g. content, stimulus, etc.

Teacher's assessment of candidate's performance

Teacher's signature ....

NEAB English Syllabus

Sometimes you may be asked to observe another pupil and to record what they have done. All of this is useful in helping you to develop your own speaking skills, as well as providing your teacher with much more information than it would be possible to record when watching twenty or thirty pupils at the same time.

All the way through this section, you have been building up your own knowledge about speaking and listening skills. If you put these into practice, you will be a better speaker and listener. Reflecting on your own performance as a speaker is useful, because:

- if you know what your strengths and weaknesses are, then you will be able to make efforts to improve specific skills;
- most of the talking you do in school goes on in a busy classroom, and a great deal of it vanishes into thin air: it would not be possible to tape or video every single thing you said for the two years of your GCSE course. Written records of self-assessment will be a great help to your teacher when it comes to recording your overall achievement and are a requirement in some English Literature syllabuses. You may even need to make a transcript of what was said.

Keeping a talk log

The most thorough way of recording your speaking and listening is to keep a diary in which you can record all your significant achievements. This is most useful because it allows you to write about talk in other lessons, not just English, as well as any achievements out of school, like taking part in a play or a debating competition.

If you have not done this before, it might be difficult to decide what is worth writing about, so here are some ideas to start you off:

- **You can write about work you have done in pairs**
  What was the work you did? Who did you work with? Did you work well together? Did you help each other get the work done well? Did you solve any problems together? Could you make any improvements if you worked with that person again?
- **You can write about group work**
  Who was in your group? What was the work you did? Did you have a particular job (chair, secretary)? Did your group work well? What did you (or other people) do that helped to get the work done? What did you (or other people) do that made it difficult to work? Could you make any improvements if you worked with that group again?
- **You can write about drama work – role-play, improvisation, working with a script, etc**
  Who did you work with? What was the work you did? What part did you play? Did you do well? What about the others in the group?
  Were there any problems with the work? Were they anybody's fault?
  Could you improve the work if you had to do it again?
- **You can write about performances you have been involved in – acting out your drama work for the class, doing a talk or a reading, etc**
  Did you work on your own or with other people?
  What went well? What went badly? What would you improve next time you do something like this?
- **You can write about any special conversations you have with your teacher**
  Did you start them, or did the teacher? What did you talk about?
  Was the conversation helpful? Will it help you to do better with your work in future?

Examiner's tip

Although there is no examination of Speaking and Listening, make sure that:

- you have covered all three of the En1 clusters of skills in the work you have done and that this is clearly shown on your record sheets;
- your teacher has seen you at your best – taking a variety of roles in a range of situations;
- if you have talked about reading or your use of language, that these discussions are also recorded as achievements against En2 and En3.

Chapter 3
Investigating talk

Some examination groups specify that part of your coursework should be a piece of non-fiction writing. Trying out some of the activities in this section will have shown you that talk is a very interesting area to research. It is all around you and most people have quite a lot to say about it. Here are a few possible topics and practical tips for getting started on a Talk Project, which you could write up for your coursework folder.

3.1 Talk project one: Baby talk

If there is a small child in your family, observing and writing about the way children learn words and begin to put them together into sentences is a fascinating study.

It is still a mystery to linguists who study language acquisition quite how children do learn to talk: in the first four years of life, a child learns a vocabulary of about 2000 words, and a complex set of grammatical rules, without any difficulty. You only have to think how difficult you probably find it to learn a foreign language to appreciate the achievement.

Background information

Between about four months and a year old, babies experiment with sounds by cooing (vowel sounds) and babbling (repeated consonant and vowel sounds like Ba-ba-ba.) Towards the end of this time, they only make sounds that they hear in the language spoken by those around them.

At about a year old, babies begin to communicate with single words: but they don't just name things. By using intonation like that of the adults around them, they make their single words into questions or commands, as well as statements. This is called the Holophrastic stage by linguists, because the one word is a 'whole' sentence in meaning.

When they are one to two years old, toddlers begin to put two words together. They are beginning to develop a kind of grammar. Usually, they have a set of phrases in which one word remains, but the second word may be varied, e.g. 'all-gone dinner', 'all-gone teddy', 'all-gone daddy'.

Between about two and four years old, children learn masses of new words and begin to work out all kinds of rules to do with meaning of words and the grammatical patterns that combine them into sentences. This is probably the most interesting age to study, because children make mistakes, though they are not so much mistakes as evidence that they are thinking hard about the rules of language.

One example of this is what linguists call 'over-extension': this occurs when a child has worked out a language rule, but uses it too widely. You will notice this where children over-extend the meaning of a word (e.g. calling all men 'Daddy' or all four-legged animals 'pussy').

You will also notice over-extended grammatical rules. For example, you will hear three-year-olds talking about 'mouses' and making up verb past tenses like 'I holded', though they would have been using the words 'mice' and 'held' at two years old. These changes are sure signs that the child is almost at the final stage of learning to talk.

By about five years old, the miracle has happened, and the child is speaking English, using the same rules as any adult speaker, though still with many more words to learn.

Putting this into practice

Try doing at least two of the following, and write up your findings.

1. Construct a questionnaire for parents or carers of young children, and collect examples of the kinds of early words and sentences their children said. Ask them about how they helped their child to learn to talk; whether they used special games and activities; how they altered their normal way of speaking to communicate with the child.
2. Tape record a child once a month for a period of six months, and see what progress in language development has taken place.
3. Transcribe a short extract of conversation between a child and one of its parents which demonstrates some of the signs of development shown above.
4. Listen carefully to the special way the adult talks to the child and consider how adult talk plays a part in helping the child to progress towards an adult use of English.

3.2 Talk project two: Speech and writing

We all seem to learn to talk with little difficulty, but learning to write does not come nearly so naturally. First attempts at writing are often written speech. As we become older, we learn to write in a more sophisticated way - based more on the patterns of what we read than the talk we hear. In fact, a problem unskilled writers have to overcome is to make their written work sound less like speech. If your teacher ever says your writing is 'too colloquial', this is the point he or she is trying to make - it is too much like spoken English.

So, how do spoken and written English differ? Doing some first-hand research into this can make an interesting project and can also help you become a better writer, since you will be more aware of the characteristics of good writing.

Putting this into practice

Work through the following activities, then write up your findings.

1. Begin by comparing these two descriptions of a memorable moment (for some football fans at least) in 1989:

> great play by Mike Newell ... that's Nevin's cross ... Sharp ... a goal ... of real first division pedigree ... Nevin found by Newell ... and Sharp in turn picked out by the cross ... the ball to the far post will always work if it's well delivered ... and you've got a brave forward on the end of it ... and of its type that's a classic for Everton ... and for Graham Sharp.

> ... over the advancing Leighton.
>
> Both Everton's goals had been well constructed, though neither compared with the third after 54 minutes. Newell initiated the move by setting Nevin free on the right. The cross, delivered to the far post, was met by Sharp, who, despite a challenge, was able to head the ball beyond Leighton.
>
> United responded ...

Which of these was a television commentary? (And how can you guess it was not on the radio?) Which came from the *Observer* newspaper? (And how can you guess it was probably not from a tabloid newspaper?)

Below is a list of features which are typical of either speech or writing. Sort out into two columns which ones apply to each of the above descriptions:

- Immediate/after the event;
- Uses a wide range of vocabulary / uses a smallish, repetitive vocabulary;
- Is constructed in sentences / consists of single words, or phrases, strung together with a limited range of connecting words;
- Permanent / transient;
- Emotional / reflective;
- Contains general words, slang and contracted words / is expressed using more precise and formal words;
- May contain dialect words and expressions / is standard English;
- Uses punctuation to break words into sense groups / uses pauses and intonation to group words;
- Is unedited and unpolished / is carefully constructed and worked on.

❷ Collect some contrasting pieces of speech and writing of your own choice. Tape some friends telling you anecdotes – then ask them to write the story down. Compare a real piece of conversation you have taped and transcribed with an extract from a written playscript. Video-tape a weather forecast, and compare the way it is expressed with the forecast in the newspaper. Transcribe a sports commentary taped from the radio, compare the same moment transcribed from a video-recorded television commentary and then see which is more like a newspaper report.

❸ Interview people about what they think is the difference between speech and writing – and see if what they tell you is accurate when compared with your own research.

3.3 Talk project three: Girl talk/boy talk

Linguists have done a great deal of research into the differences between the way males and females talk, either when they are together in mixed gender groups, or when they are in groups of their own gender.

Background information

Some major findings of the research include:

- In single gender groups, women are inclined to be cooperative and supportive of what each other says, whilst men are more likely to be competitive: they compete for talking time and compete to be the one who is right (or funniest).
- In mixed groups, men talk more (and more loudly!) than women, and women listen more than men.
- In mixed groups, men tend to be 'task-focused' (i.e. they want to get the job done quickly), while women tend to be 'relationship-focused' (i.e. they want to include people in the group and make them feel valued).

- In mixed groups, men interrupt women more than they interrupt other men. (Though remember the two different types of interruption mentioned on p.39.)
- In general, men talk more about facts, while women talk more about feelings.

Putting this into practice

Try doing at least two of the following and write up your findings.

1. Construct a questionnaire to find out whether a variety of people of different ages are aware of these differences, or whether they believe they are true from their own experience.
2. Tape some conversations, of mixed-gender and single-gender groups. Design a record sheet for collecting statistical evidence which either proves or disproves that these differences do exist.
3. Transcribe some short extracts which show definite evidence of the above differences, or definite evidence of the exact opposite.

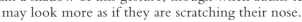

3.4 Talk project four: Body language

'It's not what you said, it's the way you said it!' How often have you heard someone say that?

Talk is more than just words. Part of our meaning is expressed by our faces. The way we stand or sit and the way we arrange our arms and legs may also be part of the message. We are not always aware that we are doing this. The intonation we use can either emphasise or contradict the literal meaning of the words we say.

There are many things about body language that even very small children understand. They know the difference between a smiling and an angry face. But they will not know that what gives them away when they are not telling the truth is that, without thinking about it, they cover up their mouth with their hands. Even adults may retain a shadow of this gesture, though when adults tell a lie, it may look more as if they are scratching their nose.

Background information

One basic distinction is between **open** and **closed** body language. When people who trust each other are talking together, they tend to sit or stand with their arms spread and their legs uncrossed. If they are agreeing with each other, they may even 'mirror' each other's position. This is **open** body language.

Closed body language is shown by tightly folded arms and crossed legs. This might demonstrate lack of trust, disagreement, dislike or nervousness.

Seating yourself so that you are physically higher than the person you are talking to is a way of indicating power (how often has a teacher told you off while you're sitting and they are standing?). Leaning on, or

putting your feet on, objects is an unconscious way of saying, 'I own this'. Putting your hands on your hips, or your thumbs in your belt, is a way of looking wider and larger and is an aggressive gesture. Avoiding eye contact is a sign of mistrust. Making eye contact with someone's face is a normal expression of social interest. Looking them up and down usually signifies a more intimate interest!

Putting this into practice

Try doing the following, and write up your findings. Ideally, you need a video-recorder to tape people in conversation and to study their body language, though you could try taping and drawing stick diagrams of interesting positions people adopt during a conversation.

1. Listen carefully to the intonation used on the tape. Do you spot any instances where intonation contradicts the words? Transcribe some extracts where this seems to be happening.
2. Find out how well other people can read body language: you could show them some of the pictures in this book and see how they would interpret those gestures or positions.

3.5 Talk project five: Varieties of English

You will already have found that people hold all kinds of opinions about accents and dialects. You could research how this may affect their attitudes towards others.

Putting this into practice

Try doing at least two of the following and write up your findings.

1. Construct a questionnaire that will help you find out about 'language biographies'. What factors influence the kind of accent or dialect people speak? (You may well be able to do this with your own family. If you have moved around the country, you may find that everyone in your family speaks with a slightly different accent. Accounting for these differences would be a good project.)
2. Conduct a survey on people's attitudes to their own accent, those of other areas and the RP (Received Pronunciation) accent. Find out how aware they are of modifying their accent or dialect in different situations.
3. If you live in an area where some people are bilingual or multilingual, this can be the basis for a fascinating project. Find out what languages people speak; when, where and to whom they speak them; and what purposes they use their different languages for. Find out which languages they can *write*, as well as speak: does it make a difference if a language is *only* spoken?
4. Tape the interviews you carry out. Transcribe extracts of conversation which highlight interesting discoveries.

3.6 Writing a transcript of spoken English

Taking a few sensible precautions when taping saves a lot of frustration: carry spare batteries if you are using a portable recorder, so it does not stop taping in the middle of your best interview. Make a copy of any tape you are going to transcribe, as winding tapes backwards and forwards can make them break. Do not try to transcribe more than a few minutes of talk – it is very time-consuming.
Use conventional transcription symbols like these:

=	one speaker follows another with no pause
[	two speakers talk at the same time
(.)	very brief pause
: :	a lengthened sound
word	a word with strong stress
°word°	a word said quietly
↑word↑	rising intonation
↓word↓	falling intonation

Chapter 4
What makes a good reader?

Danesh is a good reader. He loves Roald Dahl and can read his favourite books out loud with very few mistakes. He likes looking up information from the books in the school book corner and has just finished making his own book about different kinds of dinosaur. He even used a junior encyclopedia for some of the information, though he found that rather difficult to understand. His teacher expects him to get a level 3 in his Key Stage 1 tests.

Kylie is a good reader. She belongs to the local library and has read every single book it has by Enid Blyton. Recently she has started reading Nina Bawden's novels and is surprised by how different they are from each other, 'not like *The Famous Five*'. She reads comics and newspapers at home. She worries about the environment and is doing a lot of research about pollution that is damaging the ozone layer. In school she has just produced a poster to persuade her classmates not to use aerosols. She found some information in her older sister's science text book that she included in this. Her teacher says she is heading for a level 5 in her Key Stage 2 tests.

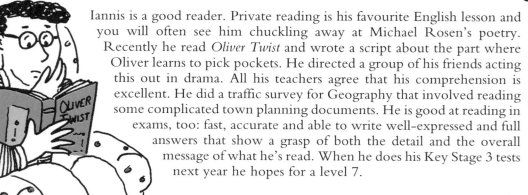

Iannis is a good reader. Private reading is his favourite English lesson and you will often see him chuckling away at Michael Rosen's poetry. Recently he read *Oliver Twist* and wrote a script about the part where Oliver learns to pick pockets. He directed a group of his friends acting this out in drama. All his teachers agree that his comprehension is excellent. He did a traffic survey for Geography that involved reading some complicated town planning documents. He is good at reading in exams, too: fast, accurate and able to write well-expressed and full answers that show a grasp of both the detail and the overall message of what he's read. When he does his Key Stage 3 tests next year he hopes for a level 7.

Waynetta is a good reader. She knows she is. She always has been. She likes reading. She reads a lot. She finds it easy. She took the extension paper at Key Stage 3 and was quite disappointed that she wasn't graded on it. What she wants to know is how she can prove it and make sure she is awarded the high grade she's sure she deserves for her GCSE.

4.1 Building on what you know

The very fact that you are reading this book shows that you are already an experienced and skilful reader. Not only do you know how to decode the words on the page, you also have enough experience of reading to know about the different purposes reading may serve.

You did not pick up this book simply to pass the time: it would hardly count as light entertainment. But you know that it contains some information which will be useful to you. You may have started off by **scanning** the contents page to get a general idea of what the book is about. No doubt there will be some sections that you already feel you know enough about, so you will **skim-read** those. Some parts will contain information you don't know, so those will need close reading. Some parts may be difficult to understand, so you'll find yourself **back-tracking** and **re-reading** to make sense of what is being said.

You will have been developing all of these skills right the way through school. You read without much effort and take it for granted, just like your ability to talk. You may find it hard to imagine what more there is to learn about reading during the two years of your GCSE course.

Reading for GCSE English

Your skills as a reader contribute 40% to your final assessment. Work that you do during your English course will be worth 10%. This work may be oral or written. The other 30% of your mark will depend on how well you perform in the written exam at the end of your course.

This section aims to show you the five areas of skill which will be assessed by your English teacher and the GCSE examiner. It also includes some 'Putting this into practice' assignments to back up the work you do in English and to help you prepare for the final exam. These will demonstrate what it is you need to be able to do to reach the higher grades.

Some of the skills you develop will merge into the skills you need to succeed if you also take English Literature. Some of these skills will also help you become a more efficient reader for the purposes of other subjects you are studying in school.

Examiner's tip

Obviously, it's perfectly possible to be a very good reader and never say or write a word about what you have read, but that would hardly allow your teacher to assess your ability. If you wish to demonstrate that you are a good reader, you will have to use your Speaking and Writing skills to show it, so you will need to read this section in conjunction with Sections Two and Four to do your best.

This book, on its own, will not turn you into a good reader. Good readers READ. They read books and newspapers and magazines. They think about what they read. They watch films, plays and television in the same thoughtful manner.

If an extract printed here interests you, follow it up: take the book out of the library. Change the newspaper you read. Take a look at that magazine where the interesting article was published and see what else it has to offer.

xaminer's tip

›e a better reader, get reading habit. Keep a k by the bed and read ›spapers and magazines ılarly.

4.2 What do I need to know how to do?

These are the skills GCSE English assesses:

- reading and interpreting a range of texts;
- writing (and talking) about literary texts;
- writing (and talking) about non-fiction and media texts;
- using reading skills to find and make use of information from different sources;
- understanding how writers use language.

1 Your experience of, and enthusiasm for, reading a variety of writing

You will need to show that you are able to read and understand a good selection of books: novels, poetry, plays, autobiographies, diaries, travel books, and that you have enough reading background to say what you like and dislike about them. You also need to show that you can understand factual texts like leaflets, and media texts such as magazines and films. Some of these texts should be from other cultures. For example, you might read a story from the Caribbean, or a newspaper article about the conflict in Bosnia.

2 Your ability to respond to and interpret literary texts

This could involve talking to your class about a book you have read or producing a piece of writing about it. To reach the higher grades, your work must show you know the book in detail and also that you understand the author's approach to writing, so you need to comment on style and technique as well as the 'story' of a book. Coursework on one of Shakespeare's plays is compulsory for all GCSE English students. You also have to do coursework on some prose or some poetry written before this century by a writer listed in the English National Curriculum (e.g. Charles Dickens, Charlotte Brontë or William Wordsworth, Christina Rossetti). Finally, you have to show, both in coursework and the examination, that you have read some prose or poetry written since 1900 by a major writer.

xaminer's tip

‹ out for collections of ›teenth-century stories ›elp you get started.

3 Your ability to evaluate and analyse non-fiction and media texts

This means that you need to develop critical reading skills which will enable you to analyse and explain. For example, how an advertisement or a pamphlet uses language to persuade the reader to a particular point of view. Media texts include films, radio and television programmes as well as written pieces.

4 Your ability to use written texts to find and make use of information

This may involve you going off to the library to do some independent work to back up what you're studying in class. You need to show that you know how to use all kinds of factual sources, from an encyclopaedia to a computer database, and that you can bring the information you discover together in a piece of work of your own: a talk for your class, or a written project.

Examiner's tip

The same study skills apply to reading in English and English Literature.

5 Your ability to show you understand how writers use language in texts

This involves showing that you understand the various techniques used by writers: from explaining how a poet uses literary devices like similes and alliteration, to explaining the effect of layout and presentation in a persuasive pamphlet. It could involve talking about the way Shakespeare's language differs from present-day English.

Whichever syllabus you are following, your English course will aim to help you develop all of these skills and your coursework will contribute to your final grade. It would be difficult to assess the whole range of your reading or your research skills in an examination, so your coursework will help to show what you can do in those areas. The final exam will test your ability to read and interpret literary texts (the second skill area) on one paper and will also test your ability to evaluate factual or media texts (the third skill area) on the other paper. Exactly what kind of text the questions will be about varies from exam board to exam board.

For example, all of the exam boards specify that you must study poetry, but London Examinations and NEAB specifically test that in the exam. NEAB does not test your ability to read media texts in the exam, but instead uses factual and informative texts, as one piece of coursework is a media project. The exam boards also have different rules about whether your reading grade may be assessed by speaking and listening coursework.

More details about the requirements of the different syllabuses are shown in Section 1. Your teacher will give you guidance about the contents of your coursework folder and the skills you will need to practise to prepare for the particular exam you will sit.

If you are taking English Literature GCSE as well as English, you will find that the skills needed to interpret literary texts and to comment on how language is used are also relevant to your Literature studies. English coursework on Shakespeare and on writers from before and after 1900 may usually be used as Literature coursework, provided it meets any special requirements in your Literature syllabus.

Chapter 5
Extending your independent reading

You are a unique individual. No one else has had a life exactly like yours. No one else has shared every one of your experiences and feelings. No one else will have shared your experience of reading either. You will have your own personal tastes and preferences. You will have read a great deal that you have forgotten about. You will have read (and re-read) certain things which are not just memorable, but actually part of you: part of the way you think and understand the world around you.

Reading is a very personal and private activity: often it's just you, alone with a book. All kinds of thoughts go through your mind as you are reading and these are yours and yours alone. Even when you read with your class in school, every single one of you will be thinking your own unique thoughts about the book, because each of you will be making sense of it according to your different experiences in life and different histories as readers.

Your development as a reader is a lifelong journey. During your GCSE course, your teacher has the responsibility of finding out how far you have already got, encouraging you and guiding you further along your own personal route, then assessing the point you have reached at the end of the course.

The journey is your own. If you're already a keen reader, this part of your English work will often be very enjoyable, even though some of it might be challenging. If you are starting out from a point where you know that reading is not something that you would choose to do for fun, or, at least, not the kind of reading your English teacher wants you to do, then you have some hard work ahead of you. What you need to remember is that your own personal route may be different, but you'll find it if you put the effort into searching for it.

5.1 Where am I now?

Complete this questionnaire to find out exactly what type of reader you are.

What kind of reader are you?

1 When did you last read a book?
(a) ages ago
(b) within the last month
(c) within the last week

2 Who was it by?
(a) I don't know
(b) I can't remember
(c) I can tell you

3 What was it about?
(a) I don't know
(b) I sort of know
(c) I can tell you in detail

4 Why did you read it?
(a) told to read it at school
(b) given it as a present
(c) I wanted to

5 Did you finish it?
(a) no
(b) I pretended I had
(c) yes

6 Did you enjoy it?
(a) not at all
(b) it was okay
(c) yes

7 Do you have a favourite author or authors?
(a) no
(b) I used to have
(c) yes

8 How many books do you own?
(a) one or two
(b) at least five
(c) ten or more

9 If someone gave you a £5.00 book token today would you...?
(a) try to sell it for £2.50
(b) have a vague idea of what you might buy
(c) buy something you know that you want to get

10 How do you read newspapers and magazines?
(a) look at the pictures
(b) flip through and read what catches my eye
(c) start at the front and read all the way through

11 What reading do you do in other subjects?
(a) as little as possible
(b) what I'm told to
(c) I use reading to find extra information

12 Do you have a hobby or interest which encourages you to read?
(a) no
(b) I have had in the past
(c) yes

13 Do the rest of your family read much?
(a) no
(b) occasionally
(c) regularly

14 When did you last visit your local library?
(a) can't remember
(b) in the last year
(c) in the past month

How did you score?

If most of your answers were (c)s: you're probably too good to be true! Seriously though, it shows that you have the reading habit and enjoy reading – two vital things. You need to make sure that you don't get 'stuck' in one reading groove and always be on the lookout for new reading matter.

If most of your answers were (a)s: you don't enjoy reading and you don't see any point in doing it. Overcoming that feeling has got to be your starting point in becoming a reader. You may find reading difficult as well. Finding the right books to get started with is going to be your next problem: your teacher should be able to advise you.

If most of your answers were (b)s: you're a lazy reader but you know what's involved in being a responsive reader. You need to find a few really good stories to read and then start to enjoy reading for its own sake.

This section focuses on your development as an independent reader of all kinds of texts. Let's start with a snapshot of your reading over the past year. What kinds of reading have you done? What kind of use have you made of all the different places you might go to find books to read?

This year I have read:

	Town Library	Home	School Library	School (English)	School (other)	Bookshop	Friend, etc
Folk tales							
Myths and legends							
Animal fiction							
School fiction							
Family fiction							
Adventure fiction							
Historical fiction							
Fantasy fiction							
Science fiction							
Romance fiction							
Poetry							
Plays							
Short stories							
Auto/biography							
Non-fiction							
Picture books							
Comics/Comic books							
Magazines							
Newspapers							
Stories, etc. by other pupils							

Tick the boxes which show **what** you read and **where** you got the book from. Now take a look at the gaps.

- You may have read masses of books, but realise when you are filling in the chart that they all fall into one category. If you are hooked on a certain type of bestseller, like horror or romantic fiction, extending your reading range will mean branching out into a much wider variety of reading.

- There may well be types of books you haven't read this year. Is this because you've tried them and don't like that kind of literature? Or is it a type of reading you have never tried at all? Extending your reading range will involve having another attempt, or a first attempt at types of reading you don't normally do.
- You may find that almost all your reading has been done in your English lessons. Extending your range will mean taking more responsibility for your own reading and taking advantage of some of the other sources of reading material.

A quick activity like this has its uses, but it doesn't provide the kind of information your teacher would need to assess your reading skills. That requires more detailed information about which books you have been reading and what you thought of them.

Putting this into practice

If you are at the beginning of your GCSE course, now is a good time to take stock of where you are up to and how you got there.

Get together with a friend, or better still two or three friends, and discuss the questions below. If you can, include both boys and girls in the discussion: the similarities between your development as readers will be useful in reminding you of books you may not remember on your own; the differences will show you just how individual every reader is and may help you spot areas of reading experience that, so far, you have missed out.

1. Before you started reading, did you like looking at picture books? Did you have stories read to you or told to you at home, or at play group? What do you remember about the ones you liked and the ones you disliked? Do you think watching television had any effect on your early experiences of stories?
2. When you learnt to read, how did you learn – at home or at school? What do you remember about the first books you read for yourself? What sort of reading (comics, etc) did you do at home at this age?
3. As your reading developed, which books do you remember particularly enjoying between the ages of 7 and 11? What else did you read? (Newspapers, encyclopaedias, cereal packets?) Which books do you remember from school?
4. Reading now. You have matured a great deal over the past three or four years – is this reflected in the things you read?
5. Which books have you read at home which were important to you? What else do you read at home?
6. What about the influence of television and video? Does it stop you reading (many adults say it does!) or encourage you to read?
7. What about the books you studied during Key Stage 3 at school? Try to cover plays and poems as well as novels and stories.
8. What do you want to read next? What do you hope to get out of your English course?

Examiner's tip

This assignment would make a useful introduction to a Key Stage 4 Reading Journal. If you haven't kept a reading journal previously, further advice about keeping a record of your reading on p.85 will help you to do this.

5.2 Where do I go from here?

Your GCSE course will seek to build on the reading you have already done. Unless you are a prolific reader, you are bound to come into contact with some types of book you had never read at all before the course started.

The wider your own range of reading, the better you will cope with the books you have to study in your English lessons. Areas of reading you will need to cover, particularly if there are currently gaps in your experience of reading, include the following:

- Modern novels and short stories written for adults
- Classic works written by great authors from the past
- Playscripts (from before *and* after 1900)

- Poetry (from before *and* after 1900)
- Literary non-fiction (like autobiography, travel writing, and letters and journals)
- Media texts
- Literature from other cultures

This chapter will give you examples of some of the different types of text you will read during your GCSE course. It will also show you how to approach reading coursework assignments and examination questions which test your reading skills.

5.3 Modern novels and short stories written for adults

The past twenty years has seen an explosion of fictional writing aimed at the teenage reader and it is quite likely that a great deal of your reading so far, both in and out of school, has been of this sort. Names you probably know will include Judy Blume, Jan Needle, Nigel Hinton and Jan Mark.

xaminer's tip

CSE, expect to have to books written for adults.

Now you are embarking on GCSE, you will be expected to extend your reading to include a much wider range of prose fiction, including books that were not written with younger readers in mind. You may already have read quite a number of adult books and it can come as a surprise when your English teacher tells you that, although James Herbert and Jackie Collins, for example, write extremely popular and readable stories, these are not counted as 'literature'. Part of what you need to learn as a reader is what is considered to be worth reading for the purposes of study. Your GCSE course will introduce you to many major writers and well-known books, plays and poetry.

One of the main differences between popular best sellers and literature is that the main purpose of best sellers is to entertain the reader: to amuse, excite or to shock. They don't usually set out to challenge the way the reader thinks about the world. Good literature sets out to make you think. The author will be attempting to put across a serious point. Of course, good literature can also be humorous, entertaining and shocking. It may even use the same genres as the best-seller: romances, science fiction and detective stories can all be found in books which are generally agreed to be 'great' literature.

Another thing that might surprise you is that 'modern' can mean anything written this century, not just in the last ten years or so. You would certainly find that some books written during the early 1900s seem almost as difficult to read and as far away from the world you live in as the 'classic' novels of earlier centuries. Even so, authors such as D. H. Lawrence, James Joyce and Virginia Woolf still count as modern writers. Writers like these will certainly be worth reading, but are probably not the best starting point if your experience of reading so far has been confined to teenage and popular fiction.

The extracts that follow are taken from three modern novels and one complete short story. They all make a point about how children are educated in the values of a particular society: how children learn to 'fit in'. Each one is, in some way, concerned with 'learning the rules', 'discipline' or 'punishment'. Apart from that, each of the books is very different.

Putting this into practice

As you read each extract, consider the following questions:

1. Who speaks the text? Is it a first-person ('I') or third-person ('he'/'she') narrative? Is the author adopting the omniscient (all-knowing) perspective, or is there one character whose thoughts and feelings you are invited to share?
2. What genre of fiction is this? Is it realistic, or does it have elements of fantasy? Is the author adapting autobiographical experience in his or her writing, or is this a world of the imagination?

3 Which of the characters do you sympathise with? How does this affect your opinion of the experience the extract describes?

4 Is the message of the extract clear, or would you need to read more of the book to check your first impressions? What thoughts about education has it made you have? Does it remind you of anything you have experienced yourself?

5 Think about the style of writing. Was the extract difficult or easy to read? Was the vocabulary used simple or complex? Did the author use much description or dialogue to help narrate the events?

6 Which did you enjoy reading most, and why? Would you want to read the rest of the book, or look for other books by any of these writers?

Brave New World by Aldous Huxley

Aldous Huxley wrote this novel in 1932. It tells of a future world, where science is used to create order. Huxley's other great novels include *Eyeless in Gaza* and *Point Counterpoint*. He also wrote short stories and travel books.

In this extract, the Director of Hatcheries and Conditioning (the D.H.C.) is explaining to a group of students how Delta-type babies are educated for their future. There are five ranks of people in this society, named after letters of the Greek alphabet. Alphas are superior and Epsilons are inferior. Deltas are the group above Epsilons.

M. Foster was left in the Decanting Room. The D.H.C. and his students stepped into the nearest lift and were carried up to the fifth floor.

INFANT NURSERIES. NEO-PAVLOVIAN CONDITIONING ROOMS, announced the notice board.

The Director opened a door. They were in a large bare room, very bright and sunny; for the whole of the southern wall was a single window. Half a dozen nurses, trousered and jacketed in the regulation white viscose-linen uniform, their hair aseptically hidden under white caps, were engaged in setting out bowls of roses in a long row across the floor. Big bowls, packed tight with blossom. Thousands of petals, ripe-blown and silkily smooth, like the cheeks of innumerable little cherubs, but of cherubs, in that bright light, not exclusively pink and Aryan, but also luminously Chinese, also Mexican, also apoplectic with too much blowing of celestial trumpets, also pale as death, pale with the posthumous whiteness of marble.

The nurses stiffened to attention as the D.H.C. came in.

'Set out the books,' he said curtly.

In silence the nurses obeyed his command. Between the rose bowls the books were duly set out – a row of nursery quartos opened invitingly each at some gaily coloured image of beast or fish or bird.

'Now bring in the children.'

They hurried out of the room and returned in a minute or two, each pushing a kind of tall dumb-waiter laden, on all its four wire-netted shelves, with eight-month-old babies, all exactly alike (a Bokanovsky Group, it was evident) and all (since their caste was Delta) dressed in khaki.

'Put them down on the floor.'

The infants were unloaded.

'Now turn them so that they can see the flowers and books.'

Turned, the babies at once fell silent, then began to crawl towards those clusters of sleek colours, those shapes so gay and brilliant on the white pages. As they approached, the sun came out of a momentary eclipse behind a cloud. The roses flamed up as though with a sudden passion from within; a new and profound significance seemed to suffuse the shining pages of the books. From the ranks of the crawling babies came little squeals of excitement, gurgles and twitterings of pleasure.

The Director rubbed his hands. 'Excellent!' he said. 'It might almost have been done on purpose.'

The swiftest crawlers were already at their goal. Small hands reached out uncertainly, touched, grasped, unpetalling the transfigured roses, crumpling the illuminated pages of the books. The Director waited until all were happily busy. Then, 'Watch carefully,' he said. And, lifting his hand, he gave the signal.

The Head Nurse, who was standing by a switchboard at the other end of the room, pressed down a little lever.

There was a violent explosion. Shriller and even shriller, a siren shrieked. Alarm bells maddeningly sounded.

The children started, screamed; their faces were distorted with terror.

'And now,' the Director shouted (for the noise was deafening), 'now we proceed to rub in the lesson with a mild electric shock.'

He waved his hand again, and the Head Nurse pressed a second lever. The screaming of the babies suddenly changed its tone. There was something desperate, almost insane, about the sharp spasmodic yelps to which they now gave utterance. Their little bodies twitched and stiffened; their limbs moved jerkily as if to the tug of unseen wires.

'We can electrify that whole strip of floor,' bawled the Director in explanation. 'But that's enough,' he signalled to the nurse.

The explosions ceased, the bells stopped ringing, the shriek of the siren died down from tone to tone into silence. The stiffly twitching bodies relaxed, and what had become the sob and yelp of infant maniacs broadened out once more into a normal howl of ordinary terror.

'Offer them the flowers and the books again.'

The nurses obeyed; but at the approach of the roses, at the mere sight of those gaily-coloured images of pussy and cock-a-doodle-doo and baa-baa black sheep, the infants shrank away in horror; the volume of their howling suddenly increased.

'Observe,' said the Director triumphantly, 'observe.'

Books and loud noises, flowers and electric shocks – already in the infant mind these couples were compromisingly linked; and after two hundred repetitions of the same or a similar lesson would be wedded indissolubly. What man has joined, nature is powerless to put asunder.

'They'll grow up with what the psychologists used to call an "instinctive" hatred of books and flowers. Reflexes unalterably conditioned. They'll be safe from books and botany all their lives.' The Director turned to his nurses. 'Take them away again.'

Still yelling, the khaki babies were loaded on to their dumb-waiters and wheeled out, leaving behind them the smell of sour milk and a most welcome silence.

One of the students held up his hand; and though he could see quite well why you couldn't have lower-caste people wasting the Community's time over books, and that there was always the risk of their reading something which might undesirably de-condition one of their reflexes, yet... well, he couldn't understand about the flowers. Why go to the trouble of making it psychologically impossible for Deltas to like flowers?

Patiently the D.H.C. explained. If the children were made to scream at the sight of a rose, that was on grounds of high economic policy. Not so very long ago (a century or thereabouts), Gammas, Deltas, even Epsilons had been conditioned to like flowers – flowers in particular and wild nature in general. The idea was to make them want to be going out into the country at every available opportunity, and so compel them to consume transport.

'And didn't they consume transport?' asked the student.

'Quite a lot,' the D.H.C. replied. 'But nothing else.'

Primroses and landscapes, he pointed out, have one grave defect: they are gratuitous. A love of nature keeps no factories busy. It was decided to abolish the love of nature, at any rate among the lower classes; to abolish the love of nature, but *not* the tendency to consume transport. For of course it was essential that they should keep on going to the country, even though they hated it. The problem was to find an economically sounder reason for consuming transport than a mere affection for primroses and landscapes. It was duly found.

'We condition the masses to hate the country,' concluded the Director. 'But simultaneously we condition them to love all country sports. At the same time, we see to it that all country sports shall entail the use of elaborate apparatus. So that they consume manufactured articles as well as transport. Hence those electric shocks.'

'I see,' said the student, and was silent, lost in admiration.

Second from Last in the Sack Race by David Nobbs

David Nobbs wrote this novel in 1983. It tells the story of the childhood of Henry Pratt in Yorkshire during the 1930s and 1940s. Nobbs is best known for having created the television character Reginald Perrin. His novels are never likely to be judged amongst the greatest works of literature, but they do fall into a category where popular fiction begins to merge into literature.

In this extract, young Henry has just passed his eleven-plus examination and, along with a few of his friends, has started at the local Grammar School.

“ Another September. Another beginning. Henry got off the Thurmarsh tram at the stop before the terminus. The grammar school was in Link Lane, next to the fire station.

Boys were converging on the school from all sides, in black blazers and black-and-yellow-striped ties. The new boys stood out among the scruffy stream like barristers in a public bar.

The school building was long, brick, many-windowed, uninspired but also unforbidding. He was looking for Martin Hammond, but found only Norbert Cuffley. Although he didn't want to be seen as an ally of such an outrageous goody, they clung together in that vast strangeness.

He caught sight of Martin Hammond in the school hall. The boys sat in rows, with the younger boys at the front. The masters filed in, and sat facing the boys. The hubbub subsided, and the headmaster, Mr E. F. Crowther, entered.

They stood and sang a hymn. They sat and the headmaster intoned a prayer. Henry also noticed Milner and Trellis from Brunswick Road. He was surprised to find that he was feeling quite excited.

Mr E. F. Crowther addressed the school. Mr Quell stifled a yawn.

'Welcome back, old boys. Welcome to Thurmarsh Grammar, new boys,' began Mr E. F. Crowther. 'You see before you our staff, as fine as body of men as can be found… in this building.'

Mr Crosby had heard this joke twenty times before, but he still laughed exaggeratedly at it.

'Thurmarsh. It is not perhaps a name that resounds throughout the educational world. It is not an Eton or a Harrow. But is it any the worse for that?' Mr E. F. Crowther paused, as if defying some miserable urchin to say 'yes'. Nobody did. Nobody ever had. 'I am proud to be headmaster of Thurmarsh Grammar,' he continued at last. 'Perhaps I am biased, because I am Thurmarsh born and Thurmarsh bred.'

'And Thurmarsh bread is very nice when it's fresh,' whispered Henry to Norbert Cuffley. He hadn't expected to say it. It just came to him. He was a budding humorist, an emerging character, and he felt exhilarated. Besides, it terrified Norbert Cuffley.

The headmaster paused, and looked in his direction. Careful, Henry.

'In the great war that strained the civilised world almost to breaking point,' resumed Mr E. F. Crowther, 'Old Thurmarshians have been up there beside Old Etonians and Old Harrovians. I am sure that in the battle to rebuild our nation and take up once again our rightful place in the forefront of history, there will once again be Thurmarshians in the van.'

'The bread van,' whispered Henry.

The headmaster turned towards him.

'Did somebody speak?' he asked.

Oh, miserable and aptly-named Pratt.

'Who spoke?' thundered the headmaster.

The room resounded to the loud silence of six hundred boys. You could have heard an earwig breathe.

'The whole school will stay in for one hour, unless somebody owns up,' said Mr E. F. Crowther.

'It were me, sir,' said Henry in a small voice.

'Stand up,' commanded Mr E. F. Crowther.

Henry stood up.

'Who are you?' said Mr E. F. Crowther.

'Pratt, sir.'

There was laughter.

'Silence,' said Mr E. F. Crowther. 'There is nothing funny about a boy's name. People who find names funny are puerile. You're new, aren't you, Pratt?'

'Yes, sir.'

'You have passed your eleven-plus, and are therefore considered fit to come here rather than fester away in a secondary modern school,' said Mr E. F. Crowther. 'Allow us to share the epigrammatical delight of your secret discourse, Pratt, and help us to judge whether we find you fit.'

'Sir?'

'What did you say?'

His mind was a blank. He could think of nothing except the truth.

'The bread van, sir.'

'The bread van, Pratt?'

'Yes, sir. Tha said tha hoped there'd be Thurmarshians in the van. I said "the bread van".'

'Are you related to Oscar Wilde, by any chance, Pratt?'

'No, sir.'

'I thought not. You're an imbecile, Pratt. What are you?'

'An imbecile, sir.'

'You will come and see me in my study after school.'

'Yes, sir.'

After the day's chaotic activities were over, and a relatively ordered basis for the future had been established, Henry made his way uneasily towards the headmaster's study.

'Good luck, bread van,' said a senior boy, whom he met in he corridor.

He knocked.

'Come in,' said Mr E. F. Crowther.

He entered.

Mr E. F. Crowther sat behind a large desk on which there were several piles of papers arranged on spikes. His study was airy. The walls were liberally festooned with rosters and graphs. The room stated, 'Things get done here. We are plain, practical men, concerned with achievement, not pretension.'

'Good afternoon, Pratt,' said Mr E. F. Crowther.

'Good afternoon, sir,' said Henry.

'Thought up any more little gems, Pratt?'

'No, sir.'

'A pity. I've had a hard day. I was looking forward to being entertained.'

Mr E. F. Crowther picked up his cane, then let it fall onto the top of his desk.

'Can you furnish me with any arguments that might persuade me not to cane you, Pratt?' he enquired.

'Yes, sir.'

The headmaster raised his eyebrows in eloquent surprise.

'Then do so.'

'I were excited, sir.'

'It's "I was excited," Pratt. You'll have to learn to speak grammatically here. After all, it is the grammar school.'

'I *was* excited sir.'

'Why?'

'Coming to Thurmarsh Grammar, sir.'

Mr E. F. Crowther gave Henry a searching glance. He prided himself on his searching glances. Sometimes, he was so keen on making sure that his glance was searching that he forgot to look for the thing for which he was searching.

'I must warn you that I have the sole franchise for all sarcasm uttered between these four walls,' he said.

'Please, sir?'

'Are you seriously telling me that you said "the bread van" because you were excited about coming to Thurmarsh Grammar?'

'Yes, sir.'

Mr E. F. Crowther leant back in his chair. Behind him, a hazy autumn sun shone. There was a beam of dust in the air.

'Explain,' he said.

'Well, sir, I didn't like it that much at Brunswick Road because it were... it *was* mainly Reading, Writing and Arithmetic, with just a bit of Geography and that. I were... I *was* looking forward to learning all the different subjects, like, like History and French and that, and with seeing all the older boys and everything, I thought about everything I was going to learn and how after I left school I might get on in t'world and be summat, and I felt like my life was just starting at last, and I gor over-excited, sir. I'm only eleven.'

The headmaster stared at Henry with his mouth slightly open.

'Try to stay excited,' he said, 'but try not to get so carried away with your enthusiasm that you say "the bread van" while I'm talking. Run along now.'

'Yes, sir. Thank you, sir.'

The Fifth Child by Doris Lessing

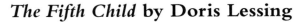

Doris Lessing wrote this novel in 1988. The story concerns the problems of a family bringing up a strange, violent child called Ben. Doris Lessing is one of the great writers of the twentieth century. Since she started writing in the 1950s, her range of published work has been vast, from philosophy to science fiction. *Martha Quest* (a novel based on her experiences of growing up in Africa) and her short stories are also a good introduction to her writing.

In this extract, Ben has just started school. Earlier in the story his parents, fearing his effect on their four older children, put him into a psychiatric hospital but later removed him because he was desperately unhappy there. Ben's only friends are an adolescent motorbike gang who take him to school and pick him up every day.

After Ben had been at school for a month, and there had been no unpleasant news, she [his mother] asked his teacher how he was getting on. She heard, to her surprise, 'He's a good little chap. He tries so hard.'

Towards the end of the first term she was summoned on the telephone by the headmistress, Mrs Graves. 'Mrs Lovatt, I wonder if you...'

An efficient woman, she knew what went on in her school and that Harriet was the responsible parent of Luke, Helen, Jane, and Paul.

'We all find ourselves at a loss,' said she. 'Ben is really trying very hard. He doesn't seem to fit in with the others. It's hard to put one's finger on it.'

Harriet sat waiting – as she had done, it seemed to her, far too often in Ben's short life – for some kind of acknowledgement that here might be more than a difficulty of adjustment.

She remarked, 'He has always been an oddball.'

'The odd man out in the family? Well there's usually one, I've often noticed it,' said affable Mrs Graves. While this surface conversation went on, the sensitised Harriet was listening for the other, parallel conversation that Ben's existence compelled.

'These young men who come and collect Ben, it's an unusual arrangement,' smiled Mrs Graves.

'He's an unusual child,' said Harriet, looking hard at the headmistress, who nodded, not looking at Harriet. She was frowning, as if some annoying thought were poking at her, wanting attention, but she did not feel inclined to give it any.

'Have you ever known a child like Ben before?' Harriet asked.

This risked the headmistress saying, 'What do you mean, Mrs Lovatt?' And in fact Mrs Graves did say 'What do you mean, Mrs Lovatt?' but quickly, and then, to stop Harriet telling her, she funked it with, 'He is hyperactive, perhaps? Of course that is a word that I often feel evades the issue. To say a child is hyperactive does not say very much! But he does have this extraordinary energy. He can't keep still long – well, a lot of children can't. His teacher has found him a rewarding little boy because he does try, but she says she has to put more effort into him than all the rest put together.... Well, Mrs Lovatt I'm glad you came in, it has been a help.' And as

"Harriet left she saw how the headmistress watched her, with that long, troubled inspection that held unacknowledged unease, even horror, which was part of 'the other conversation' – the real one.

Towards the end of the second term, she was telephoned: Would she come in at once, please? Ben had hurt someone.

Here it was: this is what she had dreaded. Ben had suddenly gone berserk and attacked a bigger girl in the playground. He had pulled her down, so that she fell heavily on the asphalt, bruising and grazing her legs. Then he had bitten her, and bent back her arm until it broke.

'I have spoken to Ben,' said Mrs Graves, 'He doesn't seem to be remorseful in any way. You might even think he doesn't know he did it. But at that age – he is six, after all – he should know what he is doing.'

Harriet took Ben home, leaving Paul to be picked up later. It was Paul she wanted to take with her: the child had heard of the attack, and was hysterical, screaming that Ben would kill him, too. But she had to be alone with Ben.

Ben sat on the kitchen table, swinging his legs, eating bread and jam. He had asked if John would come here to pick him up. It was John he needed.

Harriet said, 'You hurt poor Mary Jones today. Why did you do that, Ben?'

He seemed not to hear, but tore lumps of bread off with his teeth, and then gulped them down.

Harriet sat down close to him, so that he could not ignore her, and said, 'Ben, do you remember that place you went to in the van?'

He went rigid. He slowly turned his head and looked at her. The bread in his hand was trembling: he was trembling. He remembered, all right! She had never done this before – had hoped she would never have to.

'Well, *do* you remember, Ben?'

His eyes had a wild look; he could have jumped down from the table and run off. He wanted to, but was glaring around into the corners of the room, at the windows, up the staircase, as if he might be attacked from these places.

'Now listen to me, Ben. If you ever, ever, ever hurt anyone again, you'll have to go back there.'

She kept her eyes on his and hoped that he could not know she was saying inwardly, But I'd never send him back, never.

He sat shivering like a wet, cold dog, in spasms, and he went through a series of movements, unconsciously, the vestiges of reactions from that time. A hand went up to shield his face, and he looked through the spread fingers as if this hand could protect him; then the hand fell, and he turned his head away sharply, pressing the back of the other hand to his mouth, glaring in terror over it; he briefly bared his teeth to snarl – but then checked himself; he lifted his chin, and his mouth opened, and Harriet saw that he could have emitted a long animal howl. It was as if she actually heard this howl, its lonely terror…

'Did you hear me, Ben?' Harriet said softly.

He slid down off the table, and thumped his way up the stairs. He left behind him a thin trail of urine. She heard his door shut, then the bellow of rage and fear he had been holding back."

Girl by Jamaica Kincaid

This is a short story taken from a collection of short stories called *At the Bottom of the River*. The writer is from the Caribbean and the stories were first published in 1985. In this story, the learning which takes place is the kind which goes on at home rather than in school.

Because this kind of story is literature from another culture, you may find some of the ideas, and the vocabulary used to describe the ideas, unfamiliar, unless you are lucky enough to have family or friends who are familiar with the life, language and writing of the Caribbean. A discussion with a friend about any difficulties you encounter in understanding this story, and using a dictionary to check the meaning of unfamiliar words will give you practice in evaluating how the writer's use of dialect contributes to the story.

“Wash the white clothes on Monday and put them on the stone heap; wash the color clothes on Tuesday and put them on the clothesline to dry; don't walk barehead in the hot sun; cook pumpkin fritters in very hot sweet oil; soak your little cloths right after you take them off; when buying cotton to make yourself a nice blouse, be sure that it doesn't have gum on it, because that way it won't hold up well after a wash; soak salt fish overnight before you cook it; is it true that you sing benna in Sunday school?; always eat your food in such a way that it won't turn someone else's stomach; on Sundays try to walk like a lady and not like the slut you are so bent on becoming; don't sing benna in Sunday school; you mustn't speak to wharf-rat boys, not even to give directions; don't eat fruits on the street – flies will follow you; *but I don't sing benna on Sundays at all and never in Sunday school*; this is how to sew on a button; this is how to make a button-hole for the button you have just sewed on; this is how to hem a dress when you see the hem coming down and so to prevent yourself from looking like the slut I know you are so bent on becoming; this is how you iron your father's khaki shirt so that it doesn't have a crease; this is how you iron your father's khaki pants so that they don't have a crease; this is how you grow okra – far from the house, because okra tree harbors red ants; when you are growing dasheen, make sure it gets plenty of water or else it makes your throat itch when you are eating it; this is how you sweep a corner; this is how you sweep a whole house; this is how you sweep a yard; this is how you smile to someone you don't like too much; this is how you smile to someone you don't like at all; this is how you smile to someone you like completely; this is how you set a table for tea; this is how you set a table for dinner; this is how you set a table for dinner with an important guest; this is how you set a table for lunch; this is how you set a table for breakfast; this is how to behave in the presence of men who don't know you very well, and this way they won't recognize immediately the slut I have warned you against becoming; be sure to wash every day, even if it is with your own spit; don't squat down to play marbles – you are not a boy, you know; don't pick people's flowers – you might catch something; don't throw stones at blackbirds, because it might not be a blackbird at all; this is how to make a bread pudding; this is how to make doukona; this is how to make pepper pot; this is how to make a good medicine for a cold; this is how to make a good medicine to throw away a child before it even becomes a child; this is how to catch a fish; this is how to throw back a fish you don't like, and that way something bad won't fall on you; this is how to bully a man; this is how a man bullies you; this is how to love a man, and if this doesn't work there are other ways, and if they don't work don't feel too bad about giving up; this is how to spit up in the air if you feel like it, and this is how to move quick so that it doesn't fall on you; this is how to make ends meet; always squeeze bread to make sure it's fresh; *but what if the baker won't let me feel the bread?*; you mean to say that after all you are really going to be the kind of woman who the baker won't let near the bread?”

5.4 Literary non-fiction

Not all literary writing is fictional. Throughout your GCSE course, you will be expected to extend the range of your reading to cover a variety of books where writers are writing about their own experience in a literary way.

The extracts which follow are intended to show you what kind of writing is included in this category and, possibly, to introduce you to some types of writing you have not read before. Most of these books would fit the description of having been written for adults, and some were written before this century.

Literary non-fiction includes autobiographies, biographies, travel writing and also more intimate kinds of writing, such as personal letters and private diaries. The range of styles and different levels of formality in these kinds of writing varies enormously, as you will see in the examples which follow.

1 Autobiography

The story of a writer's own life is more like a novel than most other types of literary non-fiction. In fact, some novels have similarities with autobiographies: *Jane Eyre*, for example, is written as if it were an autobiography. *Second From Last in the Sack Race* has its origins in David Nobbs's own childhood in Yorkshire, though many of the events in the book are obviously fiction and there is a great deal of exaggeration for humorous effect which would be out of place in a genuine autobiography.

The extracts which follow are taken from three twentieth-century autobiographies. Each is an account of the writer's childhood experiences, growing up in relatively deprived circumstances. For all three authors, their account of how they received the education which equipped them to become writers in later life is an important aspect of their life story. School, home and friends played different parts for each of the three.

Putting this into practice

As you read the extracts, consider the following questions:

1. Who were the people who had the most influence on the education of these writers and what was the effect of the influence?
2. How important does their reading seem to have been in influencing the development of their English skills?
3. What differences do you notice in the style of writing of the three extracts? Can you detect in each one where the writers make use of dialect words and phrases remembered from the place they grew up in? How and where do they do this? Is it effective to mix standard English and dialect in this way?

Lark Rise to Candleford by Flora Thompson

Flora Thompson (who calls herself Laura in her autobiographical writing) tells of her childhood and young adulthood in an Oxfordshire village during the closing years of the nineteenth century. The book was written in 1945. In this extract, she tells of the memories she has of her final years at her village school and of her teacher, Miss Shepherd.

> But the most memorable day for Laura was that on which the Bishop came to consecrate an extension of the churchyard and walked round it in his big lawn sleeves, with a cross carried before him and a book in his hands, and the clergy of the district following. The schoolchildren, wearing their best clothes, were drawn up to watch. 'It makes a nice change from school,' somebody said, but to Laura the ceremony was but a prelude.
>
> For some reason she had lingered after the other children had gone home, and the schoolmistress, who, after all, had not been invited to the Rectory to tea as she had hoped, took her round the church and told her all she knew of its history and architecture, then took her home to tea.

“ A small, two-roomed cottage adjoining the school was provided for the schoolmistress, and this the school managers had furnished in the manner they thought suitable for one of her degree. 'Very comfortable', they had stated in their advertisement; but to a new tenant it must have looked bare. The downstairs room had a deal table for meals, four cane-bottomed chairs of the type until recently seen in bedrooms, a white marble-topped sideboard stood for luxury and a wicker armchair by the hearth for comfort. The tiled floor was partly covered with brown matting.

But Miss Shepherd was 'artistic' and by the time Laura saw the room a transformation had taken place. A green art serge cloth with bobble fringe hid the nakedness of the deal centre table; the backs of the cane chairs were draped with white crocheted lace, tied with blue bows, and the wicker chair was cushioned and antimacassared. The walls were so crowded with pictures, photographs, Japanese fans, wool-work letter-racks, hanging pincushions, and other trophies of the present tenant's skill that, as the children used to say: 'You couldn't so much as stick a pin in.'

'Don't you think I've made it nice and cosy, dear?' said Miss Shepherd, after Laura had been shown and duly admired each specimen of her handiwork, and Laura agreed heartily, for it seemed to her the very height of elegance.

It was her first invitation to grown-up tea, with biscuits and jam – not spread on her bread for her, as at home, but spooned on to her plate by herself and spread exactly as she had seen her father spread his. After tea, Miss Shepherd played the harmonium and showed Laura her photographs and books, finally presenting her with one called *Ministering Children* and walking part of the way home with her. How thrilled Laura was when, at their parting, she said: 'Well, I think we have had quite a nice little time, after all, Laura.'

But, at the time of that tea-drinking, Laura must have been eleven or twelve, one of Miss Shepherd's 'big girls' and no longer an object of persecution. By that time the play was becoming less rough and bullying rarer, for the older children of her early schooldays had left school and none who came after were quite so belligerent. Civilization was beginning to tame them.

But, even in her earlier days, her life was easier after Edmund began school, for he was better-liked than she was; moreover, he could fight, and, unlike most of the other boys, he was not ashamed to be seen with his sister.

Often, on their way to school, Laura and he would take a field path which led part of the way by a brook backed by a pinewood where wood-pigeons cooed. By leaping the little stream, they could visit 'the graves'. These were two, side by side, in the deepest shade of the pines, and the headstones said: 'In Memory of Rufus' and 'In Memory of Bess'. They both knew very well that Rufus and Bess had been favourite hunters of a former owner of the estate; but they preferred to think of them as human beings – lovers, perhaps, who in life had been used to meet in that deep, mysterious gloom.

On other days they would scramble down the bank of the brook to pick watercress or forget-me-nots, or to build a dam, or to fish for minnows with their fingers. But, very often, they would pass along the bank without seeing anything, they would be so busy discussing some book they had read. They were voracious readers, although their books were few and not selected, but came to them by chance. There were the books from the school library, which, though better than nothing to read, made little impression upon them, for they were all of the goody-goody, Sunday-school prize type. But their father had a few books and others were lent to them, and amongst these were a few of the Waverley Novels. *The Bride of Lammermoor* was one of the first books Laura read with absorbed interest. She adored the Master of Ravenswood, his dark, haughty beauty, his flowing cloak and his sword, his ruined castle, set high on its crag by the sea, and his faithful servant Caleb and the amusing shifts he made to conceal his master's poverty. She read and re-read *The Bride* and dipped into it between whiles, until the heathery hills and moors of Scotland became as real to her as her flat native fields, and the lords and ladies and soldiers and witches and old retainers as familiar as the sober labouring people who were her actual neighbours.

At seven years old *The Bride* made such an impression upon her that she communicated her excitement to Edmund, himself as yet unable to read, and one “night in their mother’s bedroom they enacted the scene in the bridal chamber, Edmund insisting that he should be Lucy and Laura the bridegroom, although she had told him that a bridegroom was usually one of his own sex.

‘Take up your bonny bridegroom!’ he cried, so realistically that their mother came running upstairs thinking he was in pain. She found Laura crouching on the floor in her nightdress while Edmund stood over her with a dagger which looked very much like his father’s two-foot rule. No wonder she said, ‘Whatever will you two be up to next!’ and took *The Bride of Lammermoor* away and hid it.

Then a neighbour who had bought a bundle of old books for a few pence at a sale lent them *Old Saint Paul’s*, and the out-house door was soon chalked with a cross and the wheelbarrow trundled round the garden to the cry of ‘Bring out your dead!’

Between the ages of seven and ten, Laura became such a confirmed reader that, when other books failed, she would read her father’s dictionary, until this disappeared because her mother thought the small print was bad for her eyes. There was still the Bible, which could not be forbidden, and she spent many an hour over that, delighting in the Old Testament stories of the Pillar of Fire, and of Ruth and Esther and Samuel and David, and of Jonah and the whale, or learning by heart the parables in the New Testament to repeat at Sunday School. At one time she had a passion for the Psalms, not so much from religious fervour as from sheer delight in the language. She felt these ought to be read aloud, and, as she dare not read them aloud herself, lest she should be overheard, she would persuade Edmund or some other child to read them with her, verse and verse about.

Once, when Edmund was upstairs in bed with measles and her mother was out, she and another girl were having a fine time imitating the parson and clerk reading the Psalms in church, when Edmund, who could hear all that was going on downstairs, called out to ask whose Bible Alice was using. She was using his and when Edmund had his suspicions confirmed he was so enraged that he dashed downstairs in his nightshirt and chased Alice all down the garden to the gate. If his mother could have seen him out of doors with his spots, in his night shirt, brandishing his Bible and threatening the retreating Alice, she would have been horrified, for measles patients were then told that they must not put so much as a hand out of bed or the spots would ‘go inward’ and the simple measles would turn to black measles, when they would probably die. But no one saw him and he returned to his bed, apparently not a ha-penny the worse for his airing.

A little later, Scott’s poems came into their lives and Edmund would swing along the field path to school reciting ‘The way was long, the night was cold’, or stop to strike an attitude and declaim,

Come one, come all this rock shall fly
From its stern bases soon as I,

or wave Laura on with ‘Charge, Chester, charge! On, Stanley, on!’ At that time their conversation when alone together was tinged with the language of their favourite romances. Sometimes Edmund would amuse his sister and himself by translating, when a battered old zinc bucket became ‘ye antique pail’, or a tree slightly damaged by the wind ‘yon lightning-blasted pine’, while some good neighbour of theirs whom they could see working in the fields would have given Edmund what he would have called ‘a darned good bommicking’ if he had heard himself referred to as ‘yon caitiff hind’.

Sometimes they tried their hand at writing a little verse themselves. Laura was guilty of a terrible moral story in rhyme about a good child who gave his birthday sixpence to a beggar, and Edmund wrote a poem about sliding on the ice with the refrain ‘Slide, glide, glide, slide, over the slippery pond’. Laura liked that one and used to sing it. She also sang one of her own, beginning, ‘The snowdrop comes in winter cold’, which ran, with a stanza for every flower, through the seasons, and to which she added yet another stanza every time she saw or remembered a flower hitherto neglected. One day her mother asked her what that ‘unked thing’ she was trying to sing was about, and, in an unguarded moment, she brought out the scraps of paper on which it was written. She did not scold or even laugh at her folly; but Laura could feel that she was not pleased, and, later that evening, she lectured her soundly on her needlework. ‘You can’t *afford* to waste your time,’ she said, ‘Here you are, eleven years old, and just look at this seam!’”

A Ragged Schooling by Robert Roberts

The writer tells us of his growing up in the slums of Salford during the early 1900s. The book was written in 1974. In this extract he describes an incident remembered from his final years at school, at a time when most children finished their education at fourteen years old.

“During my last two years at school I acted as ‘number one’ monitor, which meant release on most days from lessons, a freedom rather irksome, since learning drew me still. I lackeyed for the headmaster, running his errands, seeking truants, checking lists and, of course, going off every Monday afternoon with the leather bag. Through a riveted reading each week of the *Magnet* magazine some of us boys were aware of the profound respect that the scholars of Greyfriars College registered for their headmaster, that revered sadist, Dr Locke; but I felt none for mine, or the school either. Without scruple I read all correspondence and confidential notes, picking up a deal of curious information, which was distributed for the interest and amusement of classmates. This way they got early warning of the visits of His Majesty's Inspectors. We noticed then how our teachers developed the jitters, how they suddenly became more anxious, patient, friendly, pumping us with answers to questions which, it was hoped, the dreaded HMIs would ask on ‘Judgement Day’. And the great ones duly arrived, putting the fear of God into everyone on the staff. But *we* loved them! Like Dutch uncles they went round the classes, treating us with a sort of old-world courtesy, always enquiring, and making us feel that, in school at least, girls and boys were the people who mattered. Among these men were some of the pioneers who dragged the elementary education system ‘kicking and screaming’ into the twentieth century. They came, and their questions ranged far and wide. ‘Where, my boy,’ asked one inspector, addressing Sydney Carey in Standard V, ‘is the city of Rome?’

‘On the Ganges!’ Syd told him. (In geography Sydney put most places on that holy river, a weakness due to our possession of Empire.) The great man looked sad, and our teacher, Miss Bethel, bit her lips.

‘Sir!’ I shouted, shooting up an arm. ‘Capital of Italy, sir! Called the Eternal City!’ The old gentleman gobbled with pleasure and spoke to his colleague. I then proceeded to paint the lily! ‘Also known as the ‘*Internal* City’, sir, because it's chockful of underground passages and caves and cellars where all them early Christians lived!’

Now this was news to them. They smiled together, murmured a moment, then the elder turned. ‘Well, hardly, my boy, hardly. But a very good answer indeed!’ I fell back on my laurels and Miss Bethel shot me a lovely smile.

They moved among us like visiting royalty. All canes disappeared, and after several days of gentle but effective buzzing about our hive they summed it all up. Later the Head and some of his minions got their roasting, a cooled-off version of which appeared in the school log afterwards. Certain members of the staff were ‘incompetent’, ‘unintelligent’, ‘unqualified’, ‘unimaginative methods used; teaching conditions – appalling’.

Once a chief inspector came with an assistant who had visited us on an earlier occasion. In the aftermath old Rowley, the Head, looked, I thought, more shaken than usual. He stood by his desk after school closed and seemed to be in deep trouble. Putting books away, I busied about with both ears cocked. How pleasant it was to see the mighty humbled! The inspectors, I gathered, were deeply disturbed at his scholars' inability to express themselves. We appeared to lack something, mentioned several times, called ‘oral facility’. I rolled the words over in my mind and, later, asked my mother about it all. ‘They can't talk!’ she said. The inspectors added that we had responded to their questions either not at all or in broken, ungrammatical sentences. ‘Most disturbing!’ Moreover we had been drilled, it seemed, into a sort of slavish passivity: the teacher addressed us pupils and we did nothing but sit and listen, and altogether there was no health in us. The chief inspector put his fist somewhere in the region of the master's chest, then brought it towards his own, spreading his fingers. ‘Draw it *out*!’ be said. ‘Understand?’ Rowley nodded dumbly. Expanded vocabulary, fluency, self-assurance, that's what they were after! Our Head defended himself weakly, pointing out the kind of children he had to deal with – 'the homes they come from…' But his critics now showed impatience; they had visited similar schools to ours and found the pupils far more articulate. Something had to be done, and that quickly. In among the ruck of words that followed I heard Rowley say emphatically that he too had boys who… and he called me over. This lad, for instance, from Standard VII…

The chief inspector gazed down on me kindly. 'I didn't see you, my boy, in the top class!'

'No, sir,' I said. 'I was washin' out Standard VI's inkwells all afternoon.' He then asked me about the family – how my father earned his living. Did my parents take a newspaper and read books?

'My mother reads all sorts,' I told him. 'History books, story books – everything. I'm in the liberry.'

'And do you talk at home?' the other inspector asked, 'in the family – conversation?'

'We've a shop, sir. It's talkin' all day!'

'Ah, well, now!' he said. 'That's understandable! Now can you tell me the meaning of the word "articulate" – ar-tic-u-late?'

'Able to speak well, I think, sir – express yerself, like?'

'Excellent! Thank you, my boy!'

Old Rowley was beaming. 'You can go now!'

The new regime to increase verbal flow and stimulate self-assurance began the very next week under the direction of a phthisic young Scotsman. In the hall Mr Mackie always made great show and taught us well, but behind a classroom door away from the Head's surveillance he fell at once into a coma of indifference, and precious little instruction any of us got. But now the heat was on. According to the log book, His Majesty's Inspector required clear evidence, next time round, of an improvement in 'oral facility'. In any case, our school was to be the subject of a special report to the Board of Education. Fortunately, Mr Mackie had a brainwave: we would establish, he said, a 'moot', of which the old Anglo-Saxons had been very fond. We knew about the Anglo-Saxons. In our moot, problems of the day would be thrashed out. 'Everyone will be allowed,' he said, 'to stand up in front of the class and say just what they like. But no reading! Talk! Self-expression! That's what I want! The Anglo-Saxons didn't read!'

Mr Rowley, much enthused, came and set the first moot point, chalking it up on the board – 'Children should go to school until they are fifteen.' 'But write a composition on it beforehand,' he told us, 'then you'll have plenty of thoughts to go at when it comes to the public speaking. You can be *for* this, or against it, just as you wish.'

I turned out an essay of several pages wildly in favour of the proposal, and Mackie chose me at once as a protagonist. Unfortunately, in spite of threat or cajolery, he couldn't find a single other pupil willing to stand before the class and put the opposing, or indeed any, point of view, and this not for want of ideas but through fear alone. Free speech didn't come easily to children kept down at home and in the classroom. Just before the time for debate arrived, however, at which Mr Rowley himself would preside, the teacher dragooned a terrified girl off the back row. 'After Robert has finished his address,' Mackie told her, '*you* say a few words. Just a sentence or two, if that's all you can manage, but say *something*!' Having chatted the theme over with my mother the night before, I got on the box provided and did my three-minute stint without trouble. Rich people, I remember saying, sent their children to schools and colleges until they were twenty-one, so there must be something good in it. We would become doctors and teachers and chemists and explorers – things like that, if we went to school until we were fifteen. I was all for it.

Although Mackie had informed us that the audience was quite free to heckle or clap, they heard me out in dead silence. But both adult listeners seemed very pleased; the Head even patted my shoulder. 'Well, well!' said Mr Mackie. 'Very well spoken indeed! You almost convinced me! I've a story book at home for you – a little present. Now, Weeton!' (They dispensed with Christian names at school, even for girls.) My opponent, Lily Weeton, a pallid girl with plaits, came out and stepped on the box. Her words were few but explosive. 'I think,' she said, 'we should gerrout to work at fourteen and fetch some money in for us parents.' Then she stepped off the box to a thunderclap of applause, cheering and clog-stamping that rocked the school.

Bubbling excitement, our 'electorate' now went to the poll, and the headmaster, acting as returning officer, announced the result in professional style:

Roberts, Robert 2
Weeton, Lily 48

Storming cheers again for the victor. Eddie Franklin and a girl friend had given me a sympathy vote, but nevertheless admitted to being intellectually with the opposition. 'Even Mackie was against me!' I complained to my mother that evening.

'Humph!' she said. 'Shows how much sense *he's* got!'

I Know Why the Caged Bird Sings by Maya Angelou

The writer tells of her childhood during the 1930s in the small American town of Stamps, Arkansas. She had been abused as a child and had stopped talking. Mrs Flowers, described earlier in the book as the 'aristocrat' of the Black community in Stamps, befriends Marguerite (Maya's full name) and this extract tells of her attempts to encourage the little girl to talk again.

There was a little path beside the rocky road, and Mrs Flowers walked in front swinging her arms and picking her way over the stones.

She said, without turning her head, to me, 'I hear you're doing very good school work, Marguerite, but that it's all written. The teachers report that they have trouble getting you to talk in class.' We passed the triangular farm on our left and the path widened to allow us to walk together. I hung back in the separate unasked and unanswerable questions.

'Come and walk along with me, Marguerite.' I couldn't have refused even if I wanted to. She pronounced my name so nicely. Or more correctly, she spoke each word with such clarity that I was certain a foreigner who didn't understand English could have understood her.

'Now no one is going to make you talk—possibly no one can. But bear in mind, language is man's way of communicating with his fellow man and it is language alone which separates him from the lower animals.' That was a totally new idea to me, and I would need time to think about it.

'Your grandmother says you read a lot. Every chance you get. That's good, but not good enough. Words mean more than what is set down on paper. It takes the human voice to infuse them with the shades of deeper meaning.'

I memorized the part about the human voice infusing words. It seemed so valid and poetic.

She said she was going to give me some books and that I not only must read them, I must read them aloud. She suggested that I try to make a sentence sound in as many different ways as possible.

'I'll accept no excuse if you return a book to me that has been badly handled.' My imagination boggled at the punishment I would deserve if in fact I did abuse a book of Mrs Flowers'. Death would be too kind and brief.

The odors in the house surprised me. Somehow I had never connected Mrs Flowers with food or eating or any other common experience of common people. There must have been an outhouse, too, but my mind never recorded it.

The sweet scent of vanilla had met us as she opened the door.

'I made tea cookies this morning. You see, I had planned to invite you for cookies and lemonade so we could have this little chat. The lemonade is in the icebox.'

It followed that Mrs Flowers would have ice on an ordinary day, when most families in our town bought ice late on Saturdays only a few times during the summer to be used in the wooden ice-cream freezers.

She took the bags from me and disappeared through the kitchen door. I looked around the room that I had never in my wildest fantasies imagined I would see. Browned photographs leered or threatened from the walls and the white, freshly done curtains pushed against themselves and against the wind. I wanted to gobble up the room entire and take it to Bailey, who would help me analyze and enjoy it.

'Have a seat, Marguerite. Over there by the table.' She carried a platter covered with a tea towel. Although she warned that she hadn't tried her hand at baking sweets for some time, I was certain that like everything else about her the cookies would be perfect.

They were flat round wafers, slightly browned on the edges and butter yellow in the center. With the cold lemonade they were sufficient for childhood's lifelong diet. Remembering my manners, I took nice little lady-like bites off the edges. She said she had made them expressly for me and that she had a few in the kitchen that I could take home to my brother. So I jammed one whole cake in my mouth and the rough crumbs scratched the insides of my jaws, and if I hadn't had to swallow, it would have been a dream come true.

As I ate she began the first of what we later called 'my lessons in living'. She said that I must always be intolerant of ignorance but understanding of illiteracy. That some people, unable to go to school, were more educated and even more intelligent than college professors. She encouraged me to listen carefully to what country people called mother wit. That in those homely sayings was couched the collective wisdom of generations.

When I finished the cookies she brushed off the table and brought a thick, small book from the bookcase. I had read *A Tale of Two Cities* and found it up to my standards as a romantic novel. She opened the first page and I heard poetry for the first time in my life.

'It was the best of times and the worst of times...' Her voice slid in and curved down through and over the words. She was nearly singing. I wanted to look at the pages. Were they the same that I had read? Or were there notes, music, lined on the pages, as in a hymn book? Her sounds began cascading gently. I knew from listening to a thousand preachers that she was nearing the end of her reading, and I hadn't really heard, heard to understand, a single word.

'How do you like that?'

It occurred to me that she expected a response. The sweet vanilla flavor was still on my tongue and her reading was a wonder in my ears. I had to speak.

I said, 'Yes, ma'am.' It was the least I could do, but it was the most also.

'There's one more thing. Take this book of poems and memorize one for me. Next time you pay me a visit, I want you to recite.'

I have tried often to search behind the sophistication of years for the enchantment I so easily found in those gifts. The essence escapes but its aura remains. To be allowed, no, invited, into the private lives of strangers, and to share their joys and fears, was a chance to exchange the Southern bitter wormwood for a cup of mead with Beowulf or a hot cup of tea and milk with Oliver Twist. When I said aloud, 'It is a far, far better thing that I do, than I have ever done...' tears of love filled my eyes at my selflessness.

On that first day, I ran down the hill and into the road (few cars ever came along it) and had the good sense to stop running before I reached the Store.

I was liked, and what a difference it made. I was respected not as Mrs Henderson's grandchild or Bailey's sister but for just being Marguerite Johnson.

Childhood's logic never asks to be proved (all conclusions are absolute). I didn't question why Mrs Flowers had singled me out for attention, nor did it occur to me that Momma might have asked her to give me a little talking to. All I cared about was that she had made tea cookies for *me* and read to *me* from her favorite book. It was enough to prove that she liked me.

❷ Travel writing

Travel writing is a very particular type of autobiography, dealing with the experiences of the writers on journeys to places far away fom home: the people they meet, the ways of life they observe, and their thoughts about the differences between their usual way of life and the lives of others.

Putting this into practice

The following extracts come from two books which tell of the travels of English writers in the Middle East. Both writers seem fascinated by the changes to the traditional Arab way of life which have come about because of money from oil and the fact that this has brought the people of these countries into contact with western society. Not all the changes are necessarily seen as good.

❶ As you read the extracts, look particularly at what the writers learn by listening to the people they meet. Both writers highlight the separation of men and women which is required by those who follow Islam. They show how this affects the daily lives of the people they meet and they consider the positive and negative aspects, both now and in the future.

❷ Try to come to some conclusions of your own about what each writer has to say.

A Traveller on Horseback by Christina Dodwell

This is an account of the writer's travels through Turkey and Iran. It was written in 1987 and is particularly interesting because there are not very many women travel writers. In this extract, she writes of her stay in Tehran and is thinking about how Khomeni led a backlash against western values and tried to reintroduce a traditional Muslim way of life. Because she is a woman, she actually manages to talk to some Iranian women about their views and attempts to make it clear to her readers that opinions about separation and modest dress are by no means clear cut.

“I had grown to love awakening at dawn out on the *talar*, and hearing all the horses slowly waking up and whinnying soft greetings as we washed and made coffee. And I adored my morning rides on the big white mare, those spacious horizons, and the scent of crushed sage under hoof.

But after a week I noticed that the river level was dropping. It would soon be totally dry. The wheat had ripened and I could hear its seed-heads clicking and rattling in the breeze, and the crack as the ears popped open. It was time to move pasture. We loaded all our gear, the saddlery, and some last sacks of vegetables for market into the jeep and left. Narcy teased me about their house in Tehran with its washing machine and cook. It was difficult to imagine him and Louise in a house, they had been such happy nomads.

There were many military road blocks because some trouble had flared up with insurgents in the mountains. Above the forest we re-crossed the Elburz Mountains, whose peaks you can still see from the main street in Tehran. The Firouz house is in the centre of the city with its own private shady garden, an old building with some of the comforts of life, but no bedsteads. Here, as before, we laid our sheets out on floor-pads.

During the Revolution when Louise and Narcy came back to Tehran they were arrested and put in prison. ‘But that's nothing special,’ Louise had said. ‘Most people went to prison for a while.’ Many people had also been killed. Louise was in solitary confinement for two weeks, which ended when she went on hunger strike. Narcy was jailed for two months. Louise came back to the house which had been sealed and was in chaos, with slogans like ‘Death to America’ scrawled in lipstick and excrement. One of the slogans, written in lipstick, has been left in place, as part of the decor.

One morning we wandered around the local antique shops. I especially liked the miniatures, in some the figures were stepping out of the picture on to their paper surround. Whenever I went out of the house I had to put on my scarf and *mantau*.

It felt absurd to be dressing up as if for an English winter, the blazing heat surprised me every time. We also went to the bazaar which has an astonishing number of gold shops. I wondered who keeps them in business, there were few shoppers. Gaggles of merchants seemed to be selling to each other.

Traffic in Tehran is maniacal. Men drive cars just like they drive donkeys, leaving the thinking to the donkey. And since donkeys are driven at maximum speed, so are their vehicles, while traffic lights flash, all three lights at once, seeming more for decoration than for traffic control.

One day in a carpet shop I got into conversation with a man who spoke out frankly saying that the Iranian people made a mistake over installing Khomeni, though he admitted that he was among those who had wanted the Revolution. 'We all wanted it to come; if only the Shah hadn't hidden the facts of life from us.' Illogically, he added, 'It was wonderful when the Shah was here.' This line about how great things were under the Shah was one I heard many times as people were forgetting their earlier hardships in the light of the present ones. But they say there won't be another revolution, because Khomeni sends all the troublemakers to be killed in the fight against Iraq.

As for women, the Shah's twin sister and his wife had championed women's rights, and in the sixties they won emancipation into a male-dominated society, with equal pay laws following in the early seventies, but it's all rather irrelevant since a working wife is still an insult to her husband.

During the previous Shah's time, the wearing of the *chadoor* had been made illegal. The effect was as shattering for some women as to insist that all western women walk down the high street in a bikini.

Now of course the *chadoor* or *mantau* is compulsory. Actually I don't think the women mind as much as their liberated sisters would want them to. They quite enjoy wearing one as a means of flirtation, sometimes wearing little underneath, and it gives the plain girl the same start as the beauty. Their natures are lovely; and kinder, more generous people would be hard to find.

Being female meant I could associate freely with Iranian women, and over the full course of my journey I talked with an enormous number, whose background varied from local bus passengers to the wealthy upper class. Segregation of men and women applies in all spheres, even the beaches are segregated, and on the female beach the women still have to wear a *chadoor* or *mantau*. It would be terrifying to swim in such a garment. A wife cannot play tennis with her husband, unless the court is private and not overlooked by public buildings. Iranian women who resisted covering up risked having acid sprayed in their faces.

It was time for me to move on; my visa was half expired so I bought a ticket on the public bus to Kerman which is 1,000 kilometres south-east of Tehran.

Arabia Through the Looking Glass by Jonathan Raban

This is also an account of the writer's travels to several Middle Eastern countries. In this extract, he travels out from the capital city of Abu Dhabi, which is very rich and very westernised, to a small village. Here he talks to a man who is trying to preserve the old way of life and protect his family from what he sees as dangerous changes.

Just six years ago, the old man said, counting the years off on his fingers, their life had been very different from this. They had spent the summers in a mud fort a few miles down the road – quarters they shared with many other families. Then, for the winter, they had driven their sheep and camels south to Muscat, where they lived in tents. It had not been like this at all: they had been very poor; there had been no television, no motor cars. Now – he praised Allah and Sheikh Zayed – they had this fine house; they had 'a.c.'; life was very good; they wanted for nothing. He remembered when Al Ain had been only an oasis in the desert: now it was a fine city, with a Hilton hotel. (It also had a hotel called the 'Rolex'; the names of famous wristwatches are potent symbols in this part of the world.)

In the shadow beyond where we were sitting, I saw a woman's face pressed against the mosquito mesh of a door frame. When she saw me looking at her her face dissolved back into shadow.

“ Did he not, I asked, think that with the coming of the city there would come other, bad things? Could a close family like his own survive in a world of tall buildings and superhighways?

His family would always stay together, he said. His eldest son, who was not here today, was an engineer; he had trained in Beirut and London. When he was away, he had written home every week. When he returned, he was still obedient to his father. The power of the bedu family was very strong; I must understand that. The city was good, the motor car was good; how one used these things depended on the character of the people.

'But,' I said, 'you have a television —'

'Two!' he interrupted me. He had two televisions: one for the women and one for the men.

'On television you see what goes on in cities in the West, like London and New York. You see the violence in the streets, the break-up of families; aren't you frightened that something like that can take place here?'

Television, said the old man, was a great teacher. One learned much about distant countries from it. There was much to praise in England and America.

While the father talked, I looked at the young men to see if their faces showed any flicker of scepticism or dissent. I thought that I caught the occasional hint of a smile – but perhaps that was only because I expected to find one there. When I addressed questions to them, it was the old man who nearly always answered on their behalf, finishing sentences which they had begun. His youngest son wanted to be a doctor. I said that to be a doctor he might have to train far away: the boy said that he would come home to his family every Friday. *Every* Friday, said the old man; theirs was a close family, and it was unthinkable for anyone not to be home on Friday.

Sitting among the leaves, sipping coffee and smelling incense and eucalyptus, I tried to threaten them with another world of thuggery, isolation and family breakdown. The more I talked, the more unreal the words sounded in my own head. The men and the boys listened politely while I spoke of marooned wives in tower blocks and juvenile delinquency. Nothing like that, they assured me, would ever happen here. It was obvious that they thought I was telling improbable travellers' tales. Yet they had come much further than I had. Six years away from being desert nomads, they were talking confidently about careers in engineering and medicine; one member of the family had already worked in Europe and the Lebanon; they gave every sign of having adapted gracefully to a life in which Modern Tissues, the Range Rover, the twin-tub washing machine, two televisions, floral Thermos flasks, air travel and the local Hilton were taken perfectly for granted. The veiled women fluttered behind dark screens: I wondered how many more years it would take for them to emerge, and what the consequences would be then. At present their exclusion from this male domain of freedom, ambition and machines was vital: the blithe way in which the bedu men were able to talk about the future depended on keeping the women in the past.

The old man said that he would like to show me his farm. He led me around the edge of the women's quarters – still inside the walled box – to a well. Beside the well, on a patch of earth just a few feet square, he was growing oranges, mangoes, dates, grapes and olives. They were clustered so thickly together that it was like standing in a shadowy greengrocer's shop, with fruits entwining with each other on their stalks.

I said that it seemed to me to be a miracle of intensive agriculture. He must be a very talented gardener to make so many things grow so richly in so small a space. He smiled self-deprecatingly, showing his two teeth, and said I must not compliment him: I should instead praise Allah and Sheikh Zayed.

As we drove away I looked back at the village through the car window. Its streets were just as empty, its dice-like houses just as small and squat, as they had seemed when we arrived. It gave away nothing to the world about what was going on inside. Its farms and leafy courtyards were well-kept secrets. The family I had met had gone through an extraordinary revolution. They had been suddenly exposed to the full blast of twentieth-century manners and things. Other people in other places had simply been smashed by the impact: half of Africa has been devastated by the gale damage. Here, though, it was different. The bedu had met the century head-on, but they had been able to deal with it in the family, protected by thick walls of breezeblock and cement. It seemed much the safest and most graceful way. ”

3 Letters and journals

Some writing which ends up published in books was never originally written with that intention. Many people write letters to their friends, or keep journals for their own private thoughts. These are particularly interesting when they are kept by writers who also produced more polished writing for public consumption.

Putting this into practice

1. Compare the two journal entries. Does the fact that Hopkins was writing notes for his own personal use, whilst Dorothy Wordsworth was writing an account she intended to share with her brother, make a difference to the way the diarists express their ideas?
2. What similarities and differences can you see between the descriptions Hopkins includes in his journal and those in the poem? (His choice of adjectives and use of imagery deserve attention.)
3. Consider how William Wordsworth takes ideas for his poem from Dorothy's journal and note what he adds to make it something more than an account of a memory from childhood.

Gerard Manley Hopkins

Hopkins is most famous for his poetry which was written during the second half of the nineteenth century, but he also kept a journal where he recorded details of things he observed whilst out walking in the countryside. These detailed descriptions and comparisons are very similar to those found in his poetry.

> “*Oct. 19*– I was there again with Purbrick, at the scaffolding which is left as a mark of the survey at the highest point. We climbed on this and looked round: it was a fresh and delightful sight. The day was rainy and a rolling wind; parts of the landscape, as the Orms' Heads, were blotted out by rain. The clouds westwards were a pied piece – sail-coloured brown and milky blue; a dun yellow tent of rays opened upon the skyline far off. Cobalt blue was poured on the hills bounding the valley of the Clwyd and far in the south spread a bluish damp, but all the nearer valley was showered with tapered diamond flakes of fields in purple and brown and green.
>
> *Nov. 8* – Walking with Wm. Splaine we saw a vast multitude of starlings making an unspeakable jangle. They would settle in a row of trees; then, one tree after another, rising at a signal they looked like a cloud of specks of black snuff or powder struck up from a brush or broom or shaken from a wig; then they would sweep round in whirlwinds – you could see the nearer and farther bow of the rings by the size and blackness; many would be in one phase at once, all narrow black flakes hurling round, then in another; then they would fall upon a field and so on. Splaine wanted a gun; then 'there it would rain meat' he said. I thought they must be full of enthusiasm and delight hearing their cries and stirring and cheering one another.
>
> *Nov. 11* – Bitter north wind, hail and sleet. On the hills snow lying and the mountains covered from head to foot. But they could scarcely be seen till next day, at Blandyke, which was fine and clear. I went with Mr Hughes up Moel y Parch, from the top of which we had a noble view, but the wind was very sharp. Snowdon and all the range reminded me of the Alps: they looked like a stack of rugged white flint, specked and streaked with black, in many places chiselled and channelled. Home by Caerwys wood, where we saw two beautiful swans, as white as they should be, restlessly steering and 'canting' in the water and following us along the shore: one of them several times, as if for vexation, caught and gnawed at the stone quay of the sluice close under me.”

Pied Beauty

Glory be to God for dappled things –
For skies of couple-colour as a brinded cow;
For rose-moles all in stipple upon trout that swim;
Fresh-firecoal, chestnut-falls; finches' wings;
Landscape plotted and pieced – fold, fallow, and plough;
And all trades, their gear and tackle and trim.
All things counter, original, spare, strange;
Whatever is fickle, freckled (who knows how?)
With swift, slow; sweet, sour; adazzle, dim;
He fathers-forth whose beauty is past change:
Praise him.

Dorothy Wordsworth

In the early 1800s, Dorothy and William Wordsworth went to live in the Lake District. Dorothy kept a journal for her brother which was almost like a letter to him. She too recorded details of things she saw on country walks (one of the most famous entries in the journal is where she describes seeing the daffodils which are the subject of one of the best known of all English poems), though she also records details of her life and conversations with her brother, inspiring some poetry which you might not otherwise guess had its origins in autobiographical experience.

[*March 14th,*] *Sunday Morning.* William had slept badly – he got up at nine o'clock, but before he rose he had finished *The Beggar Boys*, and while we were at breakfast that is (for I had breakfasted) he, with his basin of broth before him untouched, and a little plate of bread and butter he wrote the Poem to a Butterfly! He ate not a morsel, nor put on his stockings, but sate with his shirt neck unbuttoned, and his waist coat open while he did it. The thought first came upon him as we were talking about the pleasure we both always feel at the sight of a butterfly. I told him that I used to chase them a little, but that I was afraid of brushing the dust off their wings, and did not catch them. He told me how they used to kill the white ones when he went to school because they were Frenchmen. Mr Simpson came in just as he was finishing the Poem. After he was gone I wrote it down and the other poems, and I read them over to him. We then called at Mr Olliff's – Mr O. walked with us to within sight of Rydale – the sun shone very pleasantly, yet it was extremely cold. We dined and then Wm. went to bed. I lay upon the fur gown before the fire, but I could not sleep – I lay there a long time. It is now halfpast 5 – I am going to write letters – I began to write to Mrs Rawson. William rose without having slept – we sate comfortably by the fire till he began to try to alter *The Butterfly*, and tired himself – he went to bed tired.

To a Butterfly

Stay near me – do not take thy flight!
A little longer stay in sight!
Much converse do I find in thee,
Historian of my infancy!
Float near me; do not yet depart!
Dead times revive in thee:
Thou bring'st, gay creature as thou art!
A solemn image to my heart,
My father's family!
Oh! pleasant, pleasant were the days,
The time, when, in our childish plays,
My sister Emmeline and I
Together chased the butterfly!
A very hunter did I rush
Upon the prey: – with leaps and springs
I followed on from brake to bush;
But she, God love her, feared to brush
The dust from off its wings.

5.5 Literature from other cultures

One requirement of the Programmes of Study for National Curriculum English is that you should read texts about other cultures and by writers from other cultures. If you have worked your way through these extracts, you will have encountered writers like Jamaica Kincaid, Doris Lessing and Maya Angelou, in addition to accounts by two travel writers of their contact with the Muslim culture of the Middle East.

The books you are required to study in school, and the pre-released materials upon which your final examinations are based, will also include some texts from other cultures.

The WJEC and London Examinations syllabuses both ask for a piece of coursework which reflects the reading of texts from other cultures. If you are studying English Literature, your work has to show understanding of the cultural context of texts from other cultures.

If literature from other cultures interests you, this is something you could follow up in your independent reading, since all the other categories of texts listed on pp.63–4 could well include literature set outside England, or written by writers who have grown up in other parts of the world where English is an important, if not the first, language.

5.6 Writing about independent reading

So far this section will have given you some idea of the variety of reading you might undertake during your GCSE course, in addition to the books you study in class. Even if you wanted to, it would hardly be possible for you to do a detailed assignment on every one of the books. In order for your teacher to assess you, you will need some written proof that you have read a range of books. One of the examining groups, NEAB, suggests that you use a record of your reading as the starting point for an interview with your teacher about what you have read. This would count as a Reading coursework assignment.

5.7 Recording reading

Your school may have prepared forms for you to use to record your reading. These may simply record factual details of the books you have read:

Title:	____________	Title:	____________
Authors/Editors:	____________	Authors/Editors:	____________
Publishers:	____________	Publishers:	____________
First published:	____________	First published:	____________
I.S.B.N. :	____________	I.S.B.N.:	____________
Date begun:	____________	Date begun:	____________
Date completed:	____________	Date completed:	____________
Where from?	____________	Where from?	____________
Book No.:	____________	Book No.:	____________

or may have space for you to make a short comment on your book:

Title:	______________	Title:	______________
Author:	______________	Author:	______________
Date finished:	______________	Date finished:	______________
Comments:	______________	Comments:	______________
Star rating:	☆ ☆ ☆ ☆ ☆	Star rating:	☆ ☆ ☆ ☆ ☆

5.8 Keeping a reading log

In Section Two you will have read about the advantages of keeping a written log of your speaking and listening activities. Keeping a detailed log of your reading is useful for similar reasons. It will be more than just a record of titles and dates. Your comments may also allow your teacher to assess your 'response' skills and possibly your understanding of written language.

If you are reading a difficult and lengthy book, you will find it useful to 'think on paper' as you go along. Spontaneous thoughts and feelings of that kind will help you sort out your ideas in preparation for more formal assignment writing.

Examiner's tip

If you haven't kept a reading log before, it is often difficult to decide how best to do it. Here are some ideas for the kind of comments you may wish to write.

- When you choose a book you can write about your first thoughts. Look at the picture on the cover and the blurb on the back. Who is the author? What is the title? What attracted you to the book? What do you think it will be about?
- You can give a very brief summary of the story – just a paragraph about the important events (the plot) in each chapter.
- You can say what you think might happen next.
- You can compare one part of the book with another – or compare it with other similar stories – or a television or film version. You can ask questions about the book. What is going through your mind as you read? What do you what to find out about the story?
- You can write about the people in the book. What are they like? How do you feel about them? Do you sometimes want to give them advice, or criticise the way they behave, or feel sorry for them? You can predict how you think they might have changed by the end of the story.
- You can write about what kind of book it is and how well you think the author is dealing with that type of story. What does the author do well, or badly?
- When you finish the book you can recommend it to other readers, or say why you wouldn't recommend it.
- You can talk about problems (and good bits) you found as you were reading it.

If you use these suggestions alongside the advice this section gives about interpreting literary texts and understanding language, you will be able to check whether the comments you write are demonstrating the skills listed in the assessment criteria. Such a record will be of use both to you and to your teacher.

This brief extract from a reading journal kept by Neil during the first year of his GCSE course gives a clear indication that his reading skills are of a very high level:

> 'Howard's End' – what can I say, comment would be superfluous – definitely the best book I have ever read. Poor Leonard Bast's fate was admirably conceived and well-executed, and the tragedy of this was balanced by the joy of Helen's reconciliation with her sister, and the growth of a family relationship between her and Mr. Wilcox. One only wishes that Leonard was alive to share in their happiness and equanimity (and to father the boy of course! but then Jackie would have to be out of the way – how unfortunate!)
>
> Now I am partaking of your counsel and resting Forster for a while before attempting the 'Passage'. [A PASSAGE TO INDIA]
>
> I am just going to start 'The Private Memoirs and Confessions of a Justified Sinner' (James Hogg). It is said to mark a peak in English (Scottish) Literature. It is 'a peculiar blend of mockery, disturbing frisson and black humour.'

- He talks to his teacher about his independent reading and follows up suggestions made.
- He has read – and enjoyed – a very challenging novel on his own.
- He shows a sensitive response to the plot of *Howard's End*.
- At the end of the extract, he shows that he is able to comment on the approach of another author (James Hogg) to his next chosen book.
- Even in this short extract, a range of reading is obvious.

Chapter 6
Writing about literary texts

6.1 Responding to literary texts

When you undertook the activities outlined in the 'Putting this into practice' assignments in Chapter 5, not only were you increasing your range of reading, you were also showing how well you responded to what you had read. A discussion of your thoughts or your written answers would have allowed your teacher to compare your performance with the grade criteria for English.

Let's take a look at the grade criteria for an A and a C which you will find in every board's syllabus.

Grade A (for En 2 Reading)

Candidates articulate and sustain their responses to texts, developing their ideas and referring in detail to aspects of language, structure and presentation. They identify and analyse argument, opinion and alternative interpretations, making cross-references where appropriate. They make apt and careful comparison within and between texts.

Grade C (for En 2 Reading)

Candidates show understanding of the ways in which meaning and information are conveyed in a range of literary and non-literary texts. They give personal responses to literary texts, referring to aspects of language, structure and themes in justifying their views. They select and summarise a range of information from different sources.

Examiner's tip

In the examination you are expected to respond to a range of texts, and you must be able to discuss the language of literary texts to gain a C grade or higher. You need to develop a vocabulary to talk about special techniques writers use to communicate their ideas. You will need to be able both to identify the techniques being used and discuss how they work. This is especially important when you are writing about poetry, and that includes the poetry of Shakespeare's plays.

Literary techniques

Below are some of the special techniques used by writers, especially poets.

- **An image** is a kind of picture, as the name suggests, but in a poem it is a picture made of words, comparing one thing with something else. You use your imagination to work out the comparison so you may share the poet's mental picture.
- **A simile** is a particular kind of image, where one thing is said to be the same *as* or *like* something else. You will be told by the writer what is being compared with what so this comparison is easy to follow and work out:

  They collapsed like rubber dinghies with the plugs pulled out.
  (from *The Lesson* by Roger McGough)

- **A metaphor** is a more complex sort of image where one thing is actually said to be something else. Metaphors are more difficult to unravel than similes because you have to work out exactly what is being compared with what – and the things they have in common:

  Seagulls in a loose V-formation
  Fly in squadrons…
  (from *Sanctuary* by Duncan Forbes)

- **Personification** is a kind of image where an object is described as if it is alive, able to move and to change rather as the poet's view of it changes:

  I am the tree
  creaking in the wind
  outside in the night
  twisted and stubborn.
  (from *I am the Tree* by Dennis Brutus)

- **Alliteration** is where several words in a line of poetry begin with the same sound – although not necessarily the same letter:

  The stuttering rifle's rapid rattle
  (from *Anthem for Doomed Youth* by Wilfred Owen)

- **Onomatopoeia** is where the words reflect or create the sound they describe:

  …the air cracks
  above rooftops cracking striking
  rockets guffawing before stuttering…
  (from *Suddenly the Air Cracks* by Gabriel Okara)

- **Assonance** is where several words in a line, or few lines, of a poem contain the same vowel (a, e, i, o, u) sound. Often this is used to capture a particular mood.

  Voice, when it came,
  Lipstick coated, long gold-rolled
  Cigarette holder pipped.
  (from *Telephone Conversation* by Wole Soyinka)

6.2 Preparing to write about texts

You will notice that in the grade descriptions and the more specific grade criteria for English there are many phrases like: 'referring to aspects of the text'; 'referring to details to support their views'; 'referring in detail to aspects of language.'

To gain a high grade for Reading, you need to have read your literary texts very thoroughly and you need to be able to pick out the bits of them which will be evidence of a real understanding of all the necessary areas.

To help you do this, you will need to learn how to annotate your texts using underlining or highlighting (to make the important details stand out) and brief marginal notes (which will remind you of the reasons why you thought that particular detail was significant).

This skill is essential if you are to make the best use of anthologies or other pre-released material, and it is also useful in helping you cope well with unseen texts under examination conditions.

When you have to write coursework assignments on complex texts such as a Shakespeare play or a poem, annotation helps you read more closely.

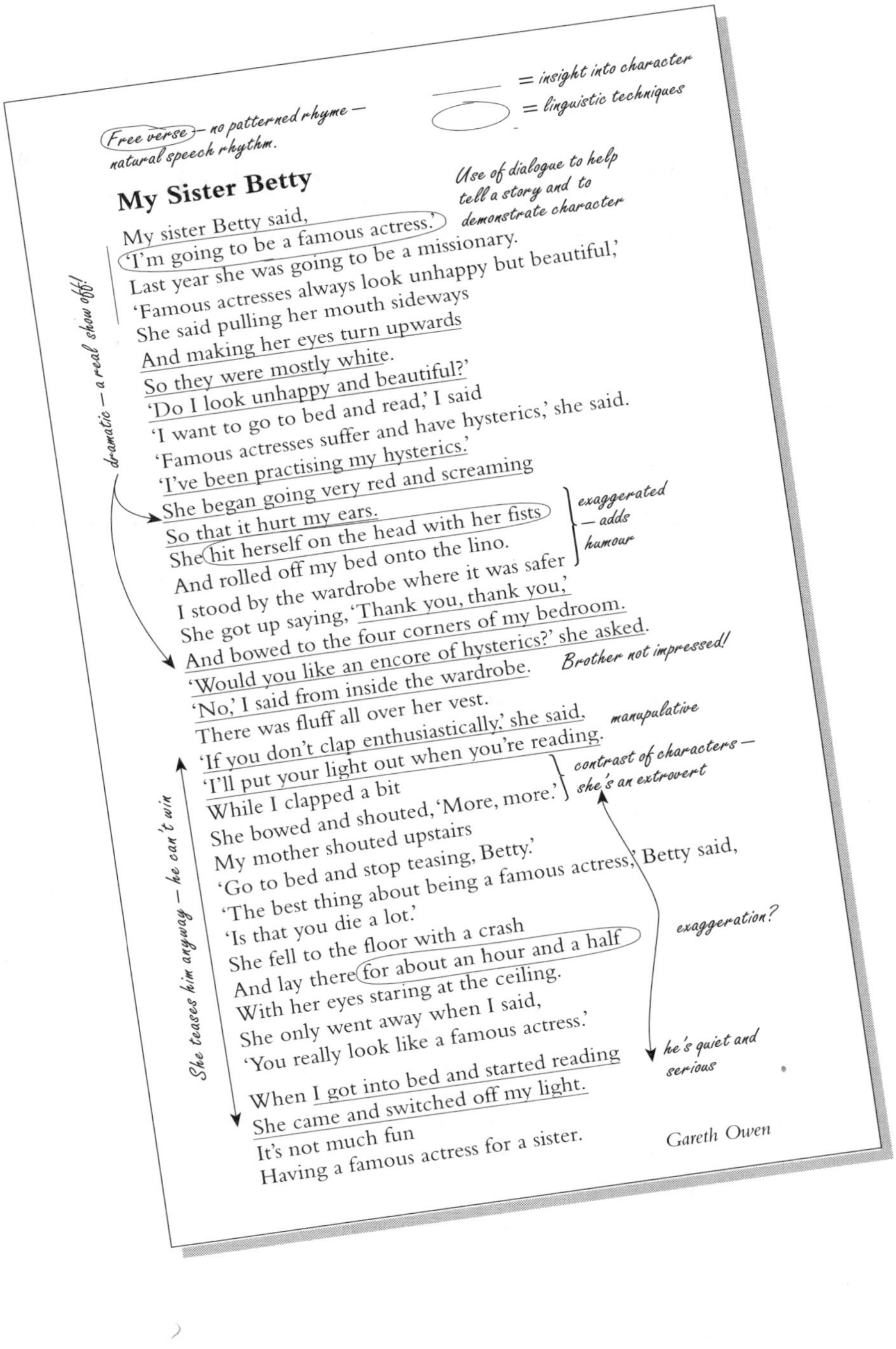

My Sister Betty

My sister Betty said,
'I'm going to be a famous actress.'
Last year she was going to be a missionary.
'Famous actresses always look unhappy but beautiful,'
She said pulling her mouth sideways
And making her eyes turn upwards
So they were mostly white.
'Do I look unhappy and beautiful?'
'I want to go to bed and read,' I said
'Famous actresses suffer and have hysterics,' she said.
'I've been practising my hysterics.'
She began going very red and screaming
So that it hurt my ears.
She hit herself on the head with her fists
And rolled off my bed onto the lino.
I stood by the wardrobe where it was safer
She got up saying, 'Thank you, thank you,'
And bowed to the four corners of my bedroom.
'Would you like an encore of hysterics?' she asked.
'No,' I said from inside the wardrobe.
There was fluff all over her vest.
'If you don't clap enthusiastically,' she said,
'I'll put your light out when you're reading.'
While I clapped a bit
She bowed and shouted, 'More, more.'
My mother shouted upstairs
'Go to bed and stop teasing, Betty.'
'The best thing about being a famous actress,' Betty said,
'Is that you die a lot.'
She fell to the floor with a crash
And lay there for about an hour and a half
With her eyes staring at the ceiling.
She only went away when I said,
'You really look like a famous actress.'
When I got into bed and started reading
She came and switched off my light.
It's not much fun
Having a famous actress for a sister.

Gareth Owen

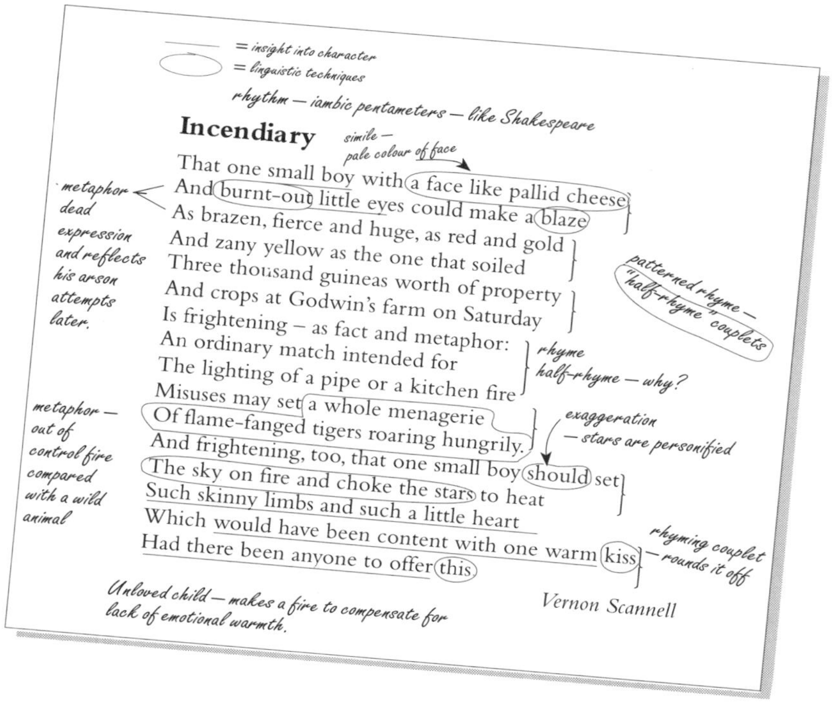

Incendiary

That one small boy with a face like pallid cheese
And burnt-out little eyes could make a blaze
As brazen, fierce and huge, as red and gold
And zany yellow as the one that soiled
Three thousand guineas worth of property
And crops at Godwin's farm on Saturday
Is frightening – as fact and metaphor:
An ordinary match intended for
The lighting of a pipe or a kitchen fire
Misuses may set a whole menagerie
Of flame-fanged tigers roaring hungrily.
And frightening, too, that one small boy should set
The sky on fire and choke the stars to heat
Such skinny limbs and such a little heart
Which would have been content with one warm kiss
Had there been anyone to offer this.

Vernon Scannell

6.3 Writing response and literature assignments

There are two types of written work you are likely to be asked to do on your literary reading: you may be asked to **analyse** the text or you may be asked to **extend** it.

Analysing the text

You could write an analysis of the literary qualities of the text. This could be a character study, a description of the main themes and ideas in the text, or a review and appreciation of it. For all of these you would be looking into the text and referring to it for ideas and examples.

Extending the text

You could write something imaginative based on the text. This might well be a piece of empathic writing where you imagine that you are a character in the novel or where you set another story against a similar background. Or it could be a story set somewhere else, but with a similar plot and themes.

The first thing with both these options is that the relationship between what you write and the original must be evident. This is especially important if you are aiming for a high grade. It is also important that you show your ability to write in detail about your personal response to what you have read.

The second thing to ensure is that the you are not just retelling the story. If you write about the text's literary qualities, it is important that you write about aspects of relationships, themes and the plot in detail rather than ramble on about them in general. In an examination, take care to choose a question which will help you to show an understanding of more than just the storyline. If it is a coursework assignment where you have an opportunity to negotiate you own task, it will be worth your while to discuss this with your teacher and to get his or her approval before you begin to write.

xaminer's tip

›se coursework
›nment and examination
›tions that let you show
› you know.

Basic principles for literature essays

Once you have completed your reading and decided on a task then your next problem is what to write. Hopefully, all your years of English lessons will help you and you will have no problem, but it is worth underlining some fundamental principles, whether you are writing coursework, or answering an examination question.

1. Remember to refer to everything you know and have been told about planning and drafting writing. Coursework needs to be re-drafted to gain the best possible marks.

2. Make sure you start with an introduction which shows you have read and understood the title. If it is based on your reading of a particular book or books, mention the titles and authors' names here. Make sure that you don't start with a conclusion which just gives your opinions: that should wait until the end.

> Whilst we were reading Laurie Lee's autobiographical account of his childhood, 'Cider With Rosie', as a class, I read several other accounts of childhood, some biographical and others autobiographical. For my assignment, I intend to compare Marjory, the child whose story is told in 'No End to Yesterday' by Shelagh Macdonald with Laurie, from 'Cider With Rosie'.

3. Once that's clear in your mind, don't be afraid to think about and state your own ideas. Examiners would rather read some fresh ideas expressed in your own words than any amount of second-hand facts and copied information.

> I thoroughly enjoyed reading 'No End to Yesterday' because sometimes it was extremely funny and at others, very sad indeed. I felt I had much more in common with Marjory than I did with Laurie because some of the mischief she was involved in reminded me of experiences I had had myself, like the time she was, quite wrongly, accused of stealing.

4. When you want to say something, try to begin by making a point, then develop the point by making clear what you mean. Finally, give an example, if possible, to back up what you are saying.

> Marjory's friendship with her cousin, Teddy, is very close. It is probably important to her because she lives with her grandparents, so she does not have the close relationship with a parent Laurie Lee had with his mother. Marjory and Teddy do everything together. One of the most memorable parts of the book tells of the time they developed a secret plan to kill their grandmother.

5 Introduce your examples and quotations clearly and decisively. Make it clear exactly why you are using them and what you are trying to show.

The main reason Marjory's grandmother is so strict with her is that she fears Marjory will grow up like the mother who deserted her. It is almost as if she blames Marjory for this:

'The child should be grateful. Naughty? Wicked! We took her from the gutter; gave her a home.' This is very typical of the way she talks to others about her granddaughter.

6 Think hard about how to order your ideas into a complete piece. The sequence of ideas and paragraphs is very important if a reader is to make sense of what you write. The writing must seem to flow almost effortlessly from point to point.

... thus you can see the contrast between the happiness of Laurie's earliest memories of family life and Marjory's confusion and misery.

The contrast continues into their accounts of school life: whilst Laurie does not seem to have been particularly interested in school work, Marjory here finds the happiness lacking at home...

7 Be original. Give your own views and say 'I think this...' or 'I believe that...' but always be sure to back your opinion with evidence and detail.

8 Finish your piece with a neat conclusion. Examiners want to know where you are going and what you have achieved, found out or proved in the writing. If you are not too sure then don't expect them to be!

Although 'Cider with Rosie' and 'No End to Yesterday' both tell of children growing up in the nineteen twenties, they offer many contrasts in the picture of childhood they present to their readers. Laurie's childhood in the country seems to have been a time of carefree innocence, whilst Marjory, growing up in London, has to come to terms with adult experiences from a very early age. Although the stories were very different, I enjoyed each in its own way.

Examiner's tip

Show the examiner that you can read challenging and difficult texts, but relate these to others which you know and like, so that your writing stems from genuine interest and enthusiasm.

Choose a task which will show what you can do when you are working to the best of your ability. Don't make life easy for yourself by choosing the simple option.

As you write, make sure you introduce your own ideas, but back them up by reference to examples and ideas from what you have read.

6.4 Writing empathically

When you write in an **empathic** way you show that you have a shared understanding of the situation in which the characters you are describing find themselves.

Suppose your friend breaks up with a partner after a long relationship. You feel sorry for him or her but maybe you think that the break-up is best in the long run. You are kind and reassuring. In this case you are being sympathetic towards your friend, you have feelings of sympathy. On the other hand, if you cried all day with your friend and told each other that is was all the partner's fault then you would be sharing what he or she was feeling rather than just responding. Your reaction would be empathic – sharing the other person's feelings, rather than having a reaction towards them. Psychologists, social workers and even teachers feel that they should sometimes empathise with the people they deal with. They imagine what it would be like to be in the patient's or in the pupil's shoes. They believe that this understanding can help them to do their jobs better.

Empathic writing works in just the same way. You show understanding of a situation, not by commenting on it from the outside but by trying to be part of it and imagining that you are in that situation yourself. Apart from English, History is a subject where empathic writing is commonly used. Imagining what it would be like to be bombed during the London Blitz may tell you more about what people had to put up with than being told that so many tons of explosives were dropped in a single night.

So, with novels, stories, plays and poems it is possible to respond empathically to what you have read. How would this work in practice on the pieces of writing you have looked at already in this section?

This poem, *The Choosing*, by Liz Lochhead, is a first-person narrative poem: it is written from the poet's point of view as 'I', 'me', so it encourages the reader to feel empathy with the experience she describes.

The Choosing

We were first equal Mary and I
with the same coloured ribbons in mouse-coloured hair,
and with equal shyness
we curtseyed to the lady councillor
for copies of Collins' Children's Classics.
First equal, equally proud.

Best friends too Mary and I
a common bond in being cleverest (equal)
in our small school's small class.
I remember
the competition for top desk
or to read aloud the lesson
at school service.
And my terrible fear
of her superiority at sums.

I remember the housing scheme
where we both stayed.
The same house, different homes,
where the choices were made.

I don't know exactly why they moved, but anyway they went.
Something about a three-apartment
and a cheaper rent.
But from the top deck of the high-school bus
I'd glimpse among the others on the corner
Mary's father, mufflered, contrasting strangely
with the elegant greyhounds by his side.

He didn't believe in high-school education,
especially for girls,
or in forking out for uniforms.

Ten years later on a Saturday –
I am coming home from the library –
sitting near me on the bus,
Mary
with a husband who is tall,
curly haired, has eyes
for no one else but Mary.
Her arms are round the full-shaped vase
That is her body.
Oh, you can see where the attraction lies
in Mary's life –
not that I envy her, really.

And I am coming from the library
with my arms full of books.
I think of the prizes that were ours for the taking
and wonder when the choices got made
we don't remember making.

Suppose you decided to write a letter from Liz Lochhead to another old friend from the same primary school, but whose life was now more like the poet's. If your version of the day's events told about how she had met her old friend, Jennifer, in the supermarket and how they had had a wonderful chat about how well they had both done since they last saw each other, where they went for their holidays and how they still had so much in common, you can see that, here again, you would be showing absolutely no understanding of what you had just read. Read the letter below and see how it reflects the ideas in the poem.

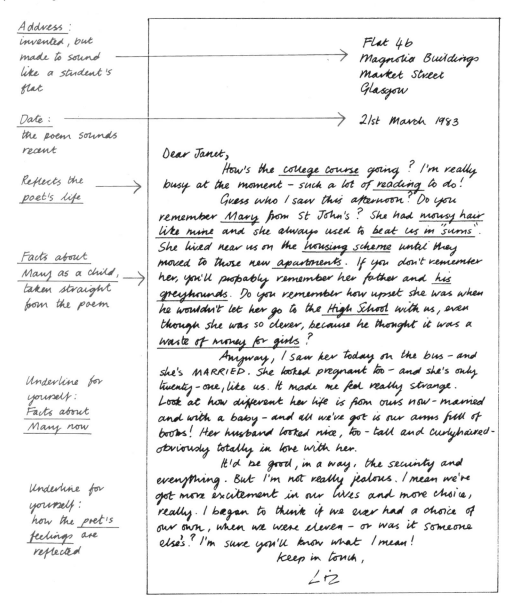

Address: invented, but made to sound like a student's flat →

Flat 4b
Magnolia Buildings
Market Street
Glasgow

Date: the poem sounds recent →

21st March 1983

Dear Janet,

Reflects the poet's life →

How's the college course going? I'm really busy at the moment – such a lot of reading to do!

Facts about Mary as a child, taken straight from the poem →

Guess who I saw this afternoon? Do you remember Mary from St John's? She had mousy hair like mine and she always used to beat us in "sums". She lived near us on the housing scheme until they moved to those new apartments. If you don't remember her, you'll probably remember her father and his greyhounds. Do you remember how upset she was when he wouldn't let her go to the High School with us, even though she was so clever, because he thought it was a waste of money for girls?

Underline for yourself: Facts about Mary now

Anyway, I saw her today on the bus – and she's MARRIED. She looked pregnant too – and she's only twenty-one, like us. It made me feel really strange. Look at how different her life is from ours now – married and with a baby – and all we've got is our arms full of books! Her husband looked nice, too – tall and curlyhaired – obviously totally in love with her.

Underline for yourself: how the poet's feelings are reflected

It'd be good, in a way, the security and everything. But I'm not really jealous. I mean we've got more excitement in our lives and more choice, really. I began to think if we ever had a choice of our own, when we were eleven – or was it someone else's? I'm sure you'll know what I mean!

Keep in touch,

Liz

The poem is actually about the distance which has grown between the two girls' lives. The poet looks at the way the different attitudes of the two families towards their daughters' education has resulted in these two girls, who were so alike at primary school, ending up with hardly anything in common at all.

The title of the poem is worth thinking about, because the 'choice' was not really made by them but by their circumstances.

These thoughts are reflected in a good empathic piece of writing, which would show how you were on the bus on the way home from the library and how it made you feel to see how Mary had changed and your opinions about the contrasts in the lives you were each leading now. This letter is responding to what was in the poem. The writer is sharing Liz Lochhead's feelings about the situation and transporting herself into it.

Look at the annotations which show how the beginning of the empathic letter relates to the first half of the poem. Try to add your own annotations, showing where the same happens in the second half.

Good empathic writing is not difficult as long as you have a clear understanding that the writing is trying to show your response to the text in another way. Therefore, what you write must have a close relationship to the original. Think hard about the points of contact between your writing and the original text – there should be plenty between them.

Examiner's tip

When you are faced with an empathic writing task, ask yourself these questions when you draft your work.

- Have I captured the atmosphere and feeling of the original text?
- Have I said things about the characters which reveal my understanding of them and their feelings as well as saying what they are like?
- Have I noted details from the text and used them in my writing? Have I made sure that nothing in my writing contradicts details which are in the text?
- When writing about poetry, choose a poem which interests you and a task which gives you plenty to write about.
- When writing about plays, see your task through an audience's eyes.
- When writing empathically, concentrate on making clear connections with the original piece of writing.

Chapter 7
Writing about classic texts

The National Curriculum makes it compulsory for every student of GCSE English to study a play by Shakespeare and either some poetry or some prose written before 1900 by a great English writer. Every examination board specifies that a piece of your English coursework should show your understanding of a Shakespeare play. Some syllabus options also require a piece of English coursework based on pre-twentieth century prose writing (which means either a novel or at least one short story). If you are also taking English Literature, then you may find that you are preparing classic texts for examination answers as well as for coursework.

It is possible that you will find texts like these challenging both to read and to write about for a variety of reasons. This section aims to give you some general help in approaching writing tasks on classic texts, or, indeed, any work of literature which you are finding complex. It is worth reminding you that there is no substitute for reading (and re-reading) the book in order to make your own personal sense of it. You may find that study guides on specific literary texts are helpful, but do remember that your own ideas in your own words are what is required when you write about literature.

Examiner's tip

If you find older texts difficult to understand, rather than making the lazy excuse that a book is 'too hard' or 'boring', see if you can identify what causes you problems, and find ways to help yourself:

The problem	Some solutions
The story is difficult to follow.	Two main reasons for this: either the sheer length of the text, or because the story-line is complex. Watching a film or video version may help – especially of a Shakespeare production. (*Caution*: Novels may be adapted so the film story-line differs from that of the book.) Read (or watch, or listen to) a 'potted version' – such as the *Shakespeare Animated Tales*, an audio-tape or an abridged version. Chapter or scene summaries in a study guide may also help sort out confusions about the story-line.

The problem	Some solutions
There are many characters with strange names and I get really confused about who is who.	Try to visualise characters in your head as you read – or even sketch them. Note down names and a few specific details for each character as a quick reference guide.Draw family trees to sort out different generations and family relationships. (Useful for long nineteenth-century novels.)
It's so slow-moving and full of description that I'm tempted to miss chunks out – then I find I've missed an important event and it doesn't make sense.	Bear with this. In the days before film, television and photography, readers and theatre audiences had far fewer mental images of different places. They did not expect thrill-a-minute action of the kind that keeps you on the edge of your seat during a film. Appreciate this as part of the style of writing. Practice will help you read more patiently and thoughtfully. Descriptions are often very important for atmosphere or even symbolism.
The English is very different from modern English – there are words no one uses any more. The way words are put together is different from modern speech, too.	On a first read, don't expect to understand every single word – as long as you follow what is happening and why. Film, video, audio-taped versions or a live production can help here. English which is hard to read is often easier to follow when you hear it. Read the words out loud to yourself or with a friend. Bring the text alive. When you are preparing to write and you have identified important quotations you want to use as evidence, make use of notes in your book (or a good dictionary) to check difficult words and phrases. (Language changes over time – words alter in meaning, or even disappear.) Take an interest in what you learn. Shakespeare, in particular, is a challenge to read because he uses a vocabulary about ten times larger than most of us use when we write. Also, he is not trying to imitate everyday speech – his important characters speak in verse. Literary techniques (see p.88) mean you have to think to understand his English.

7.1 Writing about Shakespeare's plays

If you recently completed Key Stage 3, you will already know how much work is necessary to prepare yourself to write about one of Shakespeare's plays in an examination. You will probably also have completed coursework about the play you studied. Writing GCSE coursework about another Shakespeare play will not be too different, though you may find that you are expected to show a more detailed knowledge of the events of the whole of the play and to comment on the language in more depth than was required in Year 9.

Shakespeare and GCSE coursework

Shakespeare wrote over thirty plays and your teacher is allowed to choose any of these for your GCSE English coursework, except that you are not allowed to hand in coursework based on the play you studied in Year 9. If you are taking GCSE English

Literature, you may double enter the coursework you produce for English, provided that the assignment meets any special requirements. For example, some boards expect Literature assignments on Shakespeare to show that you understand the historical context of the play. This chapter will give you an example of how to find out and write about information which shows you understand some ideas and beliefs people had in the sixteenth and seventeenth centuries, when Shakespeare wrote his plays.

Shakespeare – live

It is important to remember that Shakespeare wrote his plays to be watched in the theatre. If you are lucky enough to see a live performance of the play you are studying, think carefully about the choices the director has made, about the actors playing the parts, how they speak their lines, how they move, how they are dressed. Think about the effect the play has on you sitting there in the audience, the emotions you feel, the moments you find most gripping, any shocks and surprises you experience – and this can happen even with a play you know very well indeed.

If you cannot find a live theatre production, then a film adaptation or a video of a stage production, or even a radio or audio-taped performance, will help you to make better sense of the play. The more different interpretations you see and hear, the more sense you will make of the lines printed on the page. Always take opportunities to mention relevant details about productions you have seen, especially if you are writing about a topic like the effect a character has on the audience, or the way a particular atmosphere is built up during the play.

English coursework assignments will allow you to show your understanding of the play you are studying; however, the following questions on *Macbeth*, taken from English Literature examinations, will give you an idea of how some tasks encourage you to discuss aspects of performances you have seen.

- What do you think of the way Macbeth behaves and speaks in Act Five Scene Five? How do you think an audience would respond to this part of the play?

  WJEC (specimen)

- Explain how Shakespeare creates the sense of evil in the play. You may wish to consider: the atmosphere and settings of evil; the words spoken about evil; the changes in the character of Macbeth and Lady Macbeth during the play; the murders; the influence of the witches.

  SEG (specimen)

- Choose two scenes which you think would have a strong impact on an audience. Briefly explain what happens in these scenes and say why you think they will have an impact.

  WJEC (specimen)

Examples of questions on the play you are studying can be found on old examination. papers. A study guide on your particular play will also have some examples of essay questions, as well as other helpful information about the play and its playwright.

7.2 Case study: an assignment on *Macbeth*

This unit outlines the steps you might take when you have to write a piece of coursework on your Shakespeare text, particularly if it is an assignment which requires some background historical or cultural research.

The task set

- Discuss ideas and beliefs about the role of king which people held at the time *Macbeth* was written. Explain how your understanding of these ideas influences your judgement of Macbeth's character.

Where to begin

1. Remind yourself how many kings are mentioned in the play: Duncan, then Macbeth. And don't forget about Edward, the English King, or Malcolm who becomes King of Scotland at the end or Banquo's descendants who will be kings in the future.

2. Go through the play and select five or six short sections which focus on what kings do – or should do.

3. Think of performances you have seen – and remind yourself how these kings were presented on stage.

4. Research some history. You should discover that, in Shakespeare's England, everyone believed strongly in Christianity. This had a radical effect on what they thought about the role of king. They believed that kings were chosen, by God, to represent God's power on earth. They believed that breaking any of the ten commandments was a sin against God. They believed that the Devil tempted people to do evil – and that evil-doers would be punished by death and an eternity in Hell. Some people also truly believed that the Devil gave supernatural powers to witches, who worshipped him instead of God.

   One more historical fact you might discover is that Guy Fawkes attempted to blow up the Houses of Parliament, intending to kill King James I, in 1605, the same year Shakespeare wrote *Macbeth*. James I was also terrified of witches.

5. Think about how your research alters your ideas about the play. How would the evil Macbeth commits have been judged at the time? (In a way, he takes God's own powers into his hands by making himself King. By killing Duncan, he is not just committing the crime of murder, he is sinning by putting God on earth to death.) What do you now think about the witches and Lady Macbeth and their role in tempting him? *Macbeth* was first performed with King James in the audience. How do you imagine he reacted to the events and ideas in the play?

6. Now annotate the information you have collected (take a look at p.101 to see the kind of points you should be looking for.)

7. Now start to write. Remember the advice about writing literature essays given on pp.90–2.

8. Make a plan of points you want to include. For example:

   Para. 1 – Intro – 'Macbeth' written almost 400 years ago – set in a Christian world – belief that kings were God's chosen representatives on earth. 4 kings in the play – 3 real ones, and Macbeth who becomes king by killing Duncan. (Banquo's heirs??)

   Para. 2 – Malcolm's speech, where he lists the virtues of a good king – compare Duncan – justice and generosity – appearance in RSC play – white hair and robe – looks like God. (Why doesn't he fight with his army?? Too old? or too gentle to kill?)

   Para. 3 Compare Duncan with mentions of saintly King Edward (the Confessor) of England. Both good kings. Fit to represent God's will.

   Para. 4 Contrast with Macbeth – he shouldn't be King anyway – tempted into the sin of killing D by witches and wife ('spirits that tend on mortal thoughts') – so they are doing the Devil's work. Is Macbeth evil – or just weak?

   Para. 5 Reactions to killing of Duncan – Macduff 'sacrilegious murder' – others see the SIN aspect. Macbeth just afraid of being found out. He is immoral.

   Para. 6 Macbeth as king ('blood will get blood') – evil, dangerous tyrant – compare with Malcolm's list of his supposed sins – also how many of 7 deadly sins does Macbeth commit?

   Para. 7 The role of king can never really be Macbeth's – he got it by sin – God did not choose him. 'Borrowed clothes' – underlined on stage by king's empty robe. And the vision of Banquo's kingly descendants. Macbeth in black – looks more like his own hired murderers.

   Para. 8 Malcolm – the real king – chosen by his father – God's choice – puts things right at the end – justice – healing – ('by the grace of God')

Writing about Shakespeare?

You can find information from:

the play script

Act 1 Scene 3

Dun. Welcome hither.
I have begun to plant thee, and will labour
To make thee full of growing. Noble Banquo
That hast no less deserv'd, nor must be known
No less to have done so, let me infold thee
And hold thee to my heart.
Ban. There if I grow,
The harvest is your own.
Dun. My plenteous joys,
Wanton in fulness, seek to hide themselves
In drops of sorrow. Sons, kinsmen, thanes,
And you whose places are the nearest, know
We will establish our estate upon
Our eldest, Malcolm, whom we name hereafter
The Prince of Cumberland; which honour must
Not unaccompanied invest him only,
But signs of nobleness, like stars, shall shine
On all deservers. From hence to Inverness,
And bind us further to you.

Duncan rewards the good – he loves his subjects

Act 3 Scene 6

Lord. The son of Duncan
From whom this tyrant holds the due of birth,
Lives in the English court, and is receiv'd
Of the most pious Edward with such grace
That the malevolence of fortune nothing
Takes from his high respect; thither Macduff
Is gone to pray the holy King upon his aid
To wake Northumberland and warlike Siward,
That by the help of these—with Him above
To ratify the work—we may again
Give to our tables meat, sleep to our nights,
Free from our feasts and banquets bloody knifes,
Do faithful homage and receive free honours—
All which we pine for now. And this report
Hath so exasperate the King that he
Prepares for some attempt of war.

A Scottish Lord compares the evils of the tyrant Macbeth with the goodness of Edward, the English King

reference books

E GUNPOWDER PLOT

605, a group of
tholic gentlemen tried
kill James I by blowing
p the Houses of
Parliament with barrels of
gunpowder hidden in the
cellar. The plot was
discovered, and one of the
leaders Guido (or Guy)
Faukes (third from the
right) was tortured and
executed.

King James I

- dictionaries
- encyclopedias
- history books
- books about Shakespeare's plays

Sin (sin), sb. **1.** A transgression of the divine law and an offence against God; a violation (esp. wilful or deliberate) of some religious or moral principle. **b.** *transf.* A violation of some standard of taste or propriety 1780. **2.** Without article or pl. Violation of divine law; action or conduct characterized by this; a state of transgression against God or His commands OE. **1.** Plenary remission of their synnes 1524. At present, for my sins, I live in a village of the plain BORROW. *The seven deadly sins;* The Seven curs'd deadly Sins…Pride, Envy, Sloth, Intemp'rance, Av'rice, Ire, And Lust 1711.

135 THE HOUSE OF STUART

James often employed the title of King of Great Britain (in the preamble to the Authorized Version of the Bible, for example), but his official style by which he was proclaimed was 'King of England, Scotland, France and Ireland, Defender of the Faith', and another hundred years would elapse before the words 'Great Britain' officially became part of the royal style and title.

Having escaped from the control of the cottish lords and clergy, James was determined o exert his authority as ruler in his new ingdom. In order to do this he began t ropound the theory of the 'divine right kings', maintaining that the king was abo he law and answerable only to God. He nough of a statesman, however, not to his claims too far. He did not con Parliament head-on when they consi efused to vote him extra funds, but tu other ways of raising money. He insti order of Baronets, a new hereditar between knighthood and the peerag the dignity for £1,080.

In 1605 an attempt by Catholic to blow up the King and Parliame ning on 5 November was d luding Gui

anti-Cat felt am voted Purit refo bro th r

productions of the play

The empty King's robes – a shadow over Macbeth's life

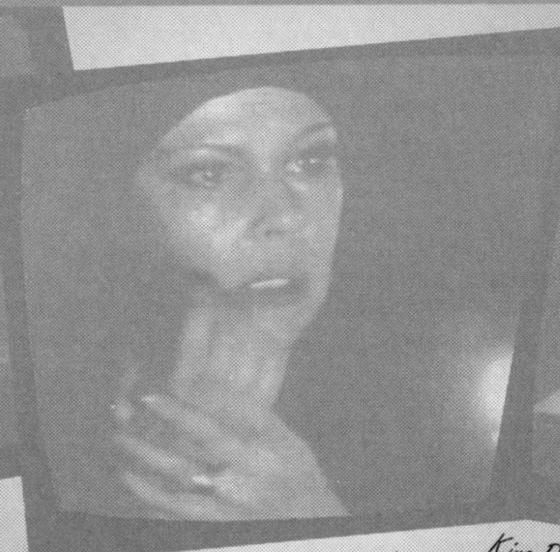
Lady Macbeth 'washing her hands'

King Duncan – white and God-like

Para. 9 — Conclude — focus on Macbeth as king compared with other true kings — I judge him more harshly — evil, not just easily led. He did the Devil's work by killing Duncan — deserved to die just for that (and so did Lady Macbeth) — what he did afterwards made it even worse.

9 Draft, read and re-draft your essay. Here are some extracts based on the notes above.

An opening paragraph

Shakespeare wrote 'Macbeth' in 1605, in the early years of the reign of James I, himself a Scottish king, who had just survived Guy Fawkes' attempt at assassination. It must have pleased King James that the play showed Macbeth punished by death for the assassination of King Duncan, also supporting his belief that witches were real, evil and dangerous. In 'Macbeth', Shakespeare presents us with ideas about kingship which are less easy for a modern audience to understand than they would have been for James I and his subjects. He is writing about a world where there was a shared belief in the Christian ideas of Good and Evil. In his world, a king was believed to be chosen by God to rule in God's place on earth. In 'Macbeth', we see four kings exercise their power: Duncan, Malcolm and Edward of England are shown to rule wisely and justly in God's place; Macbeth, however, is a usurper whose reign of terror damages all of Scotland. By the end of the play, the modern audience will judge Macbeth more harshly, if the play is put into this historical perspective.

Examiner's tip

Note how you can weave in factual research as well as outlining the topic you have been asked to discuss in your essay. We can see where this assignment is heading.

Paragraphs 2 and 3: Good kings

Hidden away in a long and complicated discussion, when Macduff tries to persuade Malcolm to return to Scotland to fight Macbeth, is a list of 'king-becoming graces' which Malcolm says he lacks. These include: 'justice, verity, temperance, stableness, bounty, perseverance, mercy, lowliness, etc.' Our immediate impression of his father, King Duncan, at the beginning of the play, is that these are the exact qualities which make him a king truly ruling in God's place. He is just, and also generous, for he punishes traitors, like the Thane of Cawdor who has been fighting against his army, and rewards those who are deserving, like the hero of the battle, Macbeth:

'Go pronounce his present death
And with his former title, greet Macbeth.'

He is 'stable', too, for he seems to be more disappointed in the behaviour of the rebel than seeking angry revenge. In the Royal Shakespeare Company production, Duncan is even presented as a physically God-like figure, with his long white robe and white hair.

Just as saintly is the description we later hear of King Edward of England who, amongst other God-like qualities, is able to cure the sick just by touching them:

'Such sanctity hath heaven given his hand.'

Examiner's tip

Note how the use of quoted evidence shows a detailed knowledge of the text and how comments explaining the significance of the quotations demonstrate an understanding of Shakespeare's English. The mention of a performance makes a relevant point.

Paragraph 7: Macbeth

By the end of Act 4, we are in no doubt that Macbeth is the complete opposite of saintly figures like Duncan and Edward. Macduff, learning of the slaughter of his innocent family, describes Macbeth with the metaphor 'hell-kite' – not just a vicious and greedy bird of prey, but an evil bird of the Devil. He was not chosen by God, neither is he able to carry out the role of God on earth. He is 'dress[ed] ... in borrowed robes', to adapt his own surprised words when he was given the title Thane of Cawdor. In the Royal Shakespeare Company production, this point is made visually by the presence of the empty golden robes of the king hanging in the background of many events in the middle of the play. There is no real king. If Macbeth wears the robes, he is only dressing up. In his black costume, Macbeth looks more similar to the killers he hired to murder his friend Banquo than a servant of God.

Examiner's tip

Note how this paragraph shows close analysis of the language of the play – including its poetic imagery – and also demonstrates an understanding of how a stage production can help to make concrete sense of abstract ideas.

A concluding paragraph

My first reading of the play, from a modern viewpoint which did not take into account the Christian background of the play, left me with some feelings of sympathy for Macbeth as a weak but ambitious man led on by clever and manipulating women. Violent behaviour had won him honours on the battlefield. How was he to see that it was no way to become or be a king? I felt he was still a fine brave soldier at the end of the play, but that he had lost his way in life. However, once I began to understand the Christian idea of kingship and how the Devil is seen as the influence tempting humans into sin and evil, I began to judge Macbeth much more harshly. Banquo warned him early on how dangerous the witches were, but he took no notice. He is more troubled by being caught for killing Duncan than he seems to be by the knowledge that, by this act of sacrilege, he has become an agent of the Devil and condemned himself to hell. He had no right to the throne or the crown of Scotland. He is evil. He commits the most deadly of sins. In the world of the play, he deserves not only death but eternal damnation. King James I would have approved of the lesson this play teaches to any would-be assassins plotting against his life, and its warning about witchcraft.

Examiner's tip

Note how the final paragraph sums up a personal response – here explaining a change of opinion. It also looks back at the way the essay was introduced and neatly rounds off the discussion of the title. Overall, these extracts from an assignment demonstrate that the candidate's appreciation of the social, historical and cultural context of *Macbeth* affects his or her appreciation of the play. The knowledge is skilfully integrated into the essay. If the rest of the essay were of this standard, it would gain a very high grade.

⑩ If you are studying *Macbeth*, you could now try to flesh out the notes for the remaining paragraphs of this essay. If your Shakespeare play is another text, adopt this approach when you deal with assignments which require research into historical or cultural background.

7.3 Writing about pre-twentieth century novels and short stories

Many GCSE English candidates will find that an assignment based on a classic story or novel is a compulsory part of their coursework. Those who are also studying English Literature, depending on which syllabus they are following, may also find that this assignment has to be a comparison. To do the assignment well, you will need to select the texts carefully so that there are some similarities which makes it possible to compare the two. They could be of the same genre (e.g. both detective stories) or they could explore similar themes (e.g. childhood experiences.) There will also need to be some clear-cut differences so you are able to discuss contrasts (e.g. how the characters of the heroines differ or how the authors present different attitudes to war).

If your assignment is to be assessed for English Literature as well as English, in addition to demonstrating understanding of social and historical aspects of texts, you are also expected to show an understanding of the literary tradition. This means that you know how different types of literary writing have developed particular forms and features over time. It could involve you in writing about how one author's work has influenced writers who followed, or how different authors have worked within, and developed, genres of writing.

7.4 Case study: an assignment on *Jane Eyre*

This section takes you through the steps you might find useful when you have to write a piece of coursework on a prose text, particularly if it is an assignment which requires you to compare texts and/or to discuss literary traditions.

The task set

- What are the characteristics of a romantic novel? In your discussion, you should compare *Jane Eyre* with at least one other prose text you have read, explaining how far your chosen texts are typical of the romance genre.

Where to begin

❶ Select other texts to write about. It would be difficult to define typical characteristics of a genre if you had only ever read one story. If you need another classic text, you could choose one of the love stories told in a novel by Jane Austen, such as *Pride and Prejudice* or *Persuasion*. If reading two long novels seems too time-consuming, then you could choose a short story. You could even discuss older traditional folk and fairy tales which centre around the story of love overcoming obstacles and leading to 'marriage and happy ever after', like *Cinderella*, provided that you are also discussing enough texts to cover the examination board requirements.

If you need to choose a modern text, you could take a novel like *Rebecca* by Daphne du Maurier. You could look to see if there is a love story in your anthology. Something 'realistic' rather than 'romantic', like *Tea in the Wendy House* by Adèle Geras, would enable you to develop contrasts. Provided that you have shown that you have read enough texts of recognised literary value to fulfil your examination board's requirements, you could even choose to discuss a modern popular romance like those published by Mills and Boon.

Publishers and film-makers make millions of pounds each year from romantic stories. Often these bear little relation to real life, and the portrayal of women is often negative. But writers have discovered that certain themes are likely to capture the public imagination.

1 The characters
The hero is supposed to be tall, dark and handsome. Ideally he should have a responsible job: doctors are good because they care about people, but business-men and airline pilots can also be romantic.

The heroine tends to be an independent woman who knows her mind, but also "knows her place". She tends not to be weak, but she can be vulnerable. It is a bonus if she can help her man with his career—nurses, secretaries and air hostesses all make excellent heroines in these stories:

2 The meeting
Love at first sight does not make for much of a story. The classic love story always has its fair share of doubts and conflicts. Initially the heroine may find the hero arrogant and unfeeling, or some terrible event in the past may make her feel that she will never be able to find true love.

2a The setting
Hospital stories are extremely popular: publisher Mills & Boon devotes a whole section, Love On Call, to them. Historical settings, especially In the Regency period (1811–1820), are also popular. One new departure Is the contemporary romance starring career women and set in the world of high finance or advertlsIng. These stories are often set in the United States.

3 The affair
Slowly the two lovers find that they are only truly happy when they are with each other. The scenes when the hero and heroine realise they are in love are meant to be uplifting and make the reader feel glad to be alive.

4 The crisis
"The course of true love never did run smooth", as Shakespeare once said. At some point in the course of any great romance, the couple undergo a test of their love for each other. The heroine may see the hero comforting another woman or feel that the memories of the death of her childhood sweetheart are so painful that she can never marry another.

5 The happy ending
Eventually the couple decide to make a lifetime's commitment to each other. All the trials and tests of their courtship have been worthwhile and they can slip happily into married bliss.

5a The tragic ending
Many of the great literary love stories do not have happy endings. The stories of Dido and Aeneas, Romeo and Juliet, and Troilus and Cressida all end with the separation or death of the lovers.

2 Read about the genre as well as reading the texts you have chosen. The article from *The Guardian* above summarises some typical features of a modern love story. What more can you discover about how the great eighteenth- and nineteenth-century classic romantic novels helped to shape the popular modern romance?

A film version of your text, or any great film love story, will add to your ideas about typical features of the romance.

3 Select relevant extracts from your prose texts to provide evidence for your writing. In the following pages are extracts from three texts all dealing with an event which occurs in every love story: the moment when the hero asks the heroine to marry him.

As you read, consider the following questions:

- What similarities do you notice in the story-lines? Are there any obvious differences?
- Compare the major characters. What do they have in common and how do they differ? Look at the descriptions of strongly felt emotion and the way this is reflected in the dialogue spoken between the central couple in each extract.
- Compare the the setting of each of the extracts and consider how the writer uses it to create a particular atmosphere.
- Think about the different styles of writing and how these are similar because they are typical of romantic novels, but differ because the books were written at different times and for different readers.
- Which of the extracts do you feel is the most successful piece of writing? Which would be most likely to prompt you to go away and read the rest of the book? Why? (Be honest with yourself here: being able to recognise and talk about some of the difficulties of reading English written a long time ago is evidence that you are able to respond to the language of a text.)

Jane Eyre by Charlotte Brontë

Jane Eyre is one of the most famous love stories of all time. It was first published in 1846 and has always been the best known of Charlotte Brontë's novels. Even if you have not read the book, the story will probably be familiar to you through television and film adaptations. It has always been a popular set text for GCSE and could well be one which your teacher will choose for you to study in class.

The events which lead up to this extract are that Jane Eyre has been working at Thornfield Hall as a governess to Adèle, who is the ward of her wealthy employer, Mr Rochester. Jane has fallen in love with Mr Rochester, but believes that her dreams are hopeless as he seems to be planning to marry a lady of his own class, Blanche Ingram.

Here, Mr Rochester is testing Jane's feelings for him before he proposes to her. He has just suggested that she takes a post as governess to a family on Ireland. Jane is devastated

'I grieve to leave Thornfield: I love Thornfield: I love it, because I have lived in it a full and delightful life – momentarily at least. I have not been trampled on. I have not been petrified. I have not been buried with inferior minds, and excluded from every glimpse of communion with what is bright and energetic and high. I have talked, face to face, with what I reverence, with what I delight in – with an original, a vigorous, an expanded mind. I have known you, Mr Rochester; and it strikes me with terror and anguish to see I absolutely must be torn from you for ever. I see the necessity of departure; and it is like looking on the necessity of death.'

'Where do you see the necessity?' he asked suddenly.

'Where? You, sir, have placed it before me.'

'In what shape?'

'In the shape of Miss Ingram; a noble and beautiful woman – your bride.'

'My bride! What bride? I have no bride!'

'But you will have.'

'Yes – I will! – I will!' he set his teeth.

'Then I must go – you have said it yourself.'

'No: you must stay! I swear it – and the oath shall be kept.'

'I tell you I must go!' I retorted, roused to something like passion. 'Do you think I can stay to become nothing to you? Do you think I am an automaton? – a machine without feelings? and can bear to have my morsel of bread snatched from my lips, and my drop of living water dashed from my cup? Do you think, because I am poor, obscure, plain, and little, I am soulless and heartless? You think wrong! – I have as much soul as you – and full as much heart! And if God had gifted me with some beauty and much wealth, I should have made it as hard for you to leave me, as it is now for me to leave you. I am not talking to you now through the medium of custom, conventionalities, nor even of mortal flesh: it is my spirit that addresses your spirit; just as if both had passed through the grave, and we stood at God's feet, equal – as we are!'

'As we are!' repeated Mr Rochester – 'so,' he added, enclosing me in his arms, gathering me to his breast, pressing his lips to my lips: 'so, Jane!'

'Yes, so, sir,' I rejoined: 'and yet not so: for you are a married man – or as good as a married man, and wed to one inferior to you – to one with whom you have no sympathy – whom I do not believe you truly love; for I have seen and heard you sneer at her. I would scorn such a union: therefore I am better than you – let me go!'

'Where, Jane? To Ireland?'

'Yes – to Ireland. I have spoken my mind, and can go anywhere now.'

'Jane, be still; don't struggle so, like a wild frantic bird that is rending its own plumage in its desperation.'

'I am no bird; and no net ensnares me; I am a free human being with an independent will, which I now exert to leave you.'

Another effort set me at liberty, and I stood erect before him.

'And your will shall decide your destiny,' he said. 'I offer you my heart, my hand, and a share of all my possessions.'

'You play a farce, which I merely laugh at.'

'I ask you to pass through life at my side – to be my second self, and best earthly companion.'

'For that fate you have already made your choice, and must abide it.'

'Jane, be still a few moments: you are over-excited: I will be still too.'

A waft of wind came sweeping down tile laurel-walk, and trembled through the boughs of the chestnut: it wandered away – away – to an indefinite distance – it died. The nightingale's song was then the only voice of the hour: in listening to it I again wept. Mr Rochester sat quiet, looking at me gently and seriously. Sometime passed before he spoke; he at last said –

'Come to my side, Jane, and let us explain and understand one another.'

“

'I will never again come to your side: I am torn away now, and cannot return.'

'But, Jane, I summon you as my wife: it is you only I intend to marry.'

I was silent: I thought he mocked me.

'Come, Jane – come hither.'

'Your bride stands between us.'

He rose, and with a stride reached me.

'My bride is here,' he said, again drawing me to him, 'because my equal is here, and my likeness. Jane, will you marry me?'

Still I did not answer, and still I writhed myself from his grasp: for I was still incredulous.

'Do you doubt me, Jane?'

'Entirely.'

'You have no faith in me?'

'Not a whit.'

'Am I a liar in your eyes?' he asked passionately. 'Little sceptic, you *shall* be convinced. What love have I for Miss Ingram? None: and that you know. What love has she for me? None: as I have taken pains to prove: I caused a rumour to reach her that my fortune was not a third of what was supposed, and after that I presented myself to see the result; it was coldness both from her and her mother. I would not – I could not – marry Miss Ingram. You – you strange, you almost unearthly thing! – I love you as my own flesh. You – poor and obscure, and small and plain as you are – I entreat to accept me as a husband.'

'What, me!' I ejaculated, beginning in his earnestness – and especially in his incivility – to credit his sincerity: 'me who have not a friend in the world but you – if you are my friend: not a shilling but what you have given me?'

'You, Jane, I must have you for my own – entirely my own. Will you be mine? Say yes, quickly.'

'Mr Rochester, let me look at your face: turn to the moonlight.'

'Why?'

'Because I want to read your countenance – turn!'

'There! you will find it scarcely more legible than a crumpled, scratched page. Read on: only make haste, for I suffer.'

His face was very much agitated and very much flushed, and there were strong workings in the features, and strange gleams in the eyes.

'Oh, Jane, you torture me!' he exclaimed. 'With that searching and yet faithful and generous look, you torture me!'

'How can I do that? If you are true, and your offer real, my only feelings to you must be gratitude and devotion – they cannot torture.'

'Gratitude!' he ejaculated; and added wildly – 'Jane, accept me quickly. Say, Edward – give me my name – Edward – I will marry you.'

'Are you in earnest? Do you truly love me? Do you sincerely wish me to be your wife?'

'I do; and if an oath is necessary to satisfy, I swear it.'

'Then, sir, I will marry you.'

”

Runaway Nurse

This is an extract from a Mills and Boon romance: not a book you would be likely to study at school! However, it does make an interesting contrast with the other two extracts.

The story that leads up to this extract, which is from very near the end of the novel, tells of a nurse, Toni Hammond, who has gone to work in Australia to escape from an unhappy love affair. There, whilst working for Mrs Partridge, she has met and fallen in love with Doctor Grant Hammond. Unfortunately, he seems to be more interested in Sara and Celia than he is in her until, one night, they find themselves alone together.

“

She raised her eyes to his involuntarily, and met a look she did not recognise but which sent her whole being into a frantic turmoil. In a sudden convulsive movement he gathered her unresisting body into his arms and brought his mouth down hard on hers, persuading her lips apart with his, touching his tongue to hers, until she yielded completely and let her arms fold around his neck, her fingers sliding up into his hair until she was pulling his head down to hers, and pressing her body against his as hard as his was to hers. There was no stemming the rush of emotion as her pent-up feelings found relief in the violence of his kiss and in the close contact with the man she loved. She surrendered herself to the sweeping desire his nearness aroused and they swayed unsteadily on the carpet, almost overbalancing, until suddenly Grant groaned and released her.

'Toni…' His eyes were smouldering and the veins in his temples showed blue against his tanned forehead, showing her the extent of his emotion.

Then suddenly she remembered Celia and a wave of anger drowned her love. 'You didn't really run out of gas, did you?' she whispered in horrified realisation.

He smiled wickedly. 'For a minute back there in Jacaranda Street I thought you weren't going to fall for it!'

She backed away from him, outraged. 'How could you? How could you go on being the town playboy and flirt when…' Words failed her for a moment, but with a renewed burst of anger, she said tightly, 'I suppose it would have spoiled your record to let me go without first conquering me. Oh, Grant, I thought better of you than that, now…' Her disappointment in him welled up in tears. 'It isn't very fair to Celia, is it?'

He looked stunned at her vehemence. 'Toni, what on earth are you talking about?'

'You love Celia,' she stabbed at him accusingly. 'I know you were holding back because you were uncertain, but today after you saw that photograph of Annabel you felt completely free at last, didn't you?'

He wiped a hand across his brow and looked hard at her tearful and angry face. 'Yes, I do feel absolutely free now. But whatever gave you the idea I was in love with Celia?'

'You asked me,' she reminded him coldly, 'at that dinner party with Dolly and Tom and Sara what I would do if I loved someone and I wasn't sure if they loved me, or even that they were suitable. I thought you meant Sara… but you didn't, so the only other person it could possibly be was Celia.'

Grant was rocking back and forth with contained laughter which disconcerted her. What was the joke? So far as she was concerned it was no joke to kiss a woman the way he had just kissed her, when he was supposed to be in love with someone else. She was ashamed of herself for allowing him to get away with it. She just couldn't understand him.

'Your lapse just now was quite unforgivable,' she said primly.

He eyed her with grim amusement. 'Wasn't yours?' he countered and there was a light in his eyes that was not really mockery.

'Yes, it was,' she murmured, eyes downcast.

She felt his fingers under her chin, lifting it and forcing her to look at him again. He was smiling now, as he pushed her firmly on to the couch and then sat beside her.

'What I did just now,' he said, his face very solemn, very close to hers, 'told me something that I've been wanting to know for a long time but was afraid to ask.'

She held her lips tightly together and looked at him defiantly, determined to give nothing away, whatever he might think.

'Toni, don't try to deny it!'

She wriggled away from him, but he moved closer and laid a hand firmly across her knees so that she could not get up and run from him. The arm of the couch helped effectively to imprison her.

'I'm not denying anything,' she said coolly, staring at a threadbare patch in the carpet where someone had regularly rubbed the heels of their shoes restlessly. Had this been Grant's favourite place that she was now sitting in?

'Toni,' he said softly, 'you jumped to conclusions rather precipitately that night when I asked you what you'd do if you loved someone…'

'Well, you were always round at Mrs Partridge's,' she defended hotly, 'so naturally I thought – we all thought – that you came to see Sara. It seemed obvious that you didn't want to make a big thing of it because this time you were really serious.'

Laughter shook him again. 'Oh, what amateur detectives you were! And Sara, I'm afraid, indulging in a game of wishful thinking quite out of character for her.'

'Well, yes, she did realise that herself in the end. She wasn't hurt.'

"

'I'm glad,' he said, 'although I have to say it would have been her own fault if she had been. I never gave her the slightest encouragement, any more than I encouraged Celia to think I might be serious. Would you have me never take a woman out unless I were serious? Don't tell me you never go out with a man unless you are? What about Nolan?'

She was trapped. 'Yes, but... that night you said...'

'My dearest Toni – Celia was not the alternative I had in mind.' Her eyes opened wide. 'Then who...?'

He cupped her face in his hands and lightly brushed her lips with his.

'Who but you, my darling? Who else but you, love? It was you I was talking about, and for one unbelievable moment I almost thought... and then you went and said "Sara", and spoiled it.'

His words slid through her brain but did not stick. She couldn't believe she had heard him say 'love'. Not Grant, who despised her, mocked her, treated her curtly, brusquely, sometimes so contemptuously.

'But you never liked me from the start,' she protested, 'so how could you...?' Her words drifted away under the sweet tender pressure of his lips.

'How could I not? That was the whole trouble, my darling. The very first night I saw you, standing on Mrs Partridge's verandah, looking so pert in your nurse's uniform, yet so lost and alone, you did something to me that night that no woman had ever done before. You stirred some depth in me that had never been stirred before. But it was all wrong. You were too much like Annabel, even to your prestigious relatives. I didn't want to fall in love with you only to find that you'd turn out just like Annabel, using your vocation to catch a rich husband, leaving me with bitterness and regret – again. I was not going to be caught a second time.'

Slowly Toni's brain was taking it in, and a warm glow grew and spread through her, like taking a draught of mulled wine on a cheerless and chilly day.

'So you were horrid and sarcastic and very abrupt with me,' she murmured.

'I'm afraid I often was. I hated myself for it, but I had to cast you in the mould even if it didn't fit you, because I was afraid to be let down again.'

'And when you saw that photograph in the magazine today?'

He smiled ruefully. 'It was the final stone out of my shoe. Deep down I knew I was wrong about you, that you were not at all like Annabel – the night of the accident proved that – but there was a trace of bitterness lingering, the dregs of a feeling long since dead but not put to rest. Seeing her face put it finally to rest. I felt nothing, not even bitterness any more.'

'I know. I felt you were different. I thought it meant you now felt free to ask Celia to marry you. I was surprised you didn't rush straight off to see her after dinner, but then I remembered what you'd said that night and I thought you must be afraid she would say no.'

He touched his forehead to hers. 'Wrong again! I was dying to ask *you* to marry me but afraid you might say no. You didn't even like me, and with good reason, and also you'd said you were going back to Martin General for personal reasons which you said were a man – this Paul...'

'Very definitely past tense,' she said.

He looked puzzled. 'Then why wouldn't you stay and help out at the hospital? You made all my doubts about you come back by refusing to do that. It couldn't have been just because you disliked me.'

She smiled as he drew back and looked hard at her. 'Quite the opposite. Just as I ran away from Martin General because I couldn't bear working near Paul, I had to run away from here because I knew I couldn't bear being near you.'

He stroked her neck with his fingertips, a light gentle touch that sent shivers through her. 'Was it so awful then... at the first aid lectures...'

'Oh, Grant, you don't know how awful!'

'I do,' he said. 'It was agony for me, too, wanting you there, cursing you for the way you affected me, hating Nolan because I thought you were falling in love with him, wanting to kiss you every time we were alone together for more than ten seconds...'

'You did once,' she recalled wryly.

'And you nearly slapped my face!'

> She suddenly coloured. 'Grant, I always wanted to apologise for walking off the dance floor that night at the church hall. It was terribly rude of me.'
> He was laughing. 'It served me right for goading you. I think I began to realise that night that you were genuine, but I didn't dare believe it.'
> 'Did you suffer terribly? I felt I'd made a laughing stock of you.'
> 'There were a few giggles. The nurses up at the hospital were jubilant because the arrogant Doctor Thompson had been snubbed by a little English nurse – something they wouldn't have dared to do, you see.'
> 'You knew I was at the dance, didn't you? Did you go along specially so that you could upbraid me for leaving Mrs Partridge?'
> 'No. I called in to Mrs Partridge's and learned where you were. I was jealous as hell of Nolan. I just couldn't stop myself going along to see you, and then to stamp on my feelings I had to be horrid to you.'
> Toni leaned against him and his arm slipped comfortingly around her shoulders. 'And I never thought,' she murmured, 'I never once dared to hope…'
> 'How will you like being the wife of a country G.P.?' he asked, taking the tip of her ear-lobe between his lips.
> 'I don't see why I shouldn't.'

Tea in the Wendy House by Adèle Geras

This short story is a very different love story. Lynn and Graham have known each other all their lives. The story describes how adolescence brings changes as their friendship turns into a first romance and, eventually, to Lynn's becoming pregnant. In this extract, the night before her wedding, she thinks back to how she told Graham about the pregnancy, and even further back to a game of Mummies and Daddies in the primary school Wendy House.

> When I first found out I was pregnant, I tried to run away. I didn't really think at all, not about where I was going, nor about what I would do when I got there. I didn't take any money with me. I didn't pack anything. I just went as I was and got on the first train I could find. To Stoke-on-Trent. By the time I got there, I changed my mind. I phoned Graham at work. I was crying.
> 'Come and get me, Graham. I want to come home. Please come and get me. I haven't any money.'
> Graham didn't ask questions. He simply said: 'Stay there. Stay in the buffet. I'll be there. I'll come in Dad's car. I'll ring your mother. I'll tell her something, or she'll worry. Wait for me.'
> 'I'm waiting.'
> I drank three cups of vile, greyish coffee. They seemed to go on and on. Then Graham burst into the buffet, out of breath. He must have run all the way from the car park. He pushed his way through the tables to where I was sitting. He pulled me to my feet, and flung his arms around me and squeezed me as if he wanted to gather me right into himself, never let me go, and we stayed like that for a long time, not speaking, rocking to and fro. The other people all arond us must have thought – I don't know what they must have thought.
> 'Let's get out of here,' Graham said at last. 'Come and sit in the car.'
> We walked in silence to where the car was waiting. As we sat down, Graham said:'Please don't ever run away again, Lynn. Do you promise?'
> 'OK' I said. 'Don't you want to know why I did?'
> 'In a minute. I just want to say something first.'
> 'OK'
> 'I don't know how to say it. It sounds so bloody corny.'
> 'Go on.'
> 'Will you marry me?'
> I started laughing, and the laughter grew and grew, and Graham laughed too.
> 'I told you it was corny,' he said. 'But will you? Will you marry me?'
> 'It looks as if I have to,' I said.
> 'No you don't. But I wish you would.'
> 'Stupid! I do have to. Well, not have to exactly, but I'm pregnant, so it's just as well you asked me.'

> Graham said nothing. The laughter disappeared quite suddenly, out of the air.
> 'Don't tell me,' I said. 'You've changed your mind. I don't blame you. You really don't need to saddle yourself with a wife and baby at nineteen, you know. I can quite see where it would tie you down.'
> 'I'm bloody furious, if you must know,' he muttered , with exactly the same look he used to give me years ago if I jogged his elbow while he was making aeroplane models, or walked through his game of marbles, scattering coloured glass balls in all directions.
> I screamed at him: 'What gives you any right to be furious? You're the bloody father. Whose bright idea was it, anyway? Who wanted me so much that it hurt? Who was it told me all those things? All those LIES? Anyway, who needs you? I'll have this baby on my own, and you can go and get knotted, for all I care!'
> He put his head in his hands. 'You don't understand Lynn.' he whispered. ' You didn't understand. I'm not cross about the baby. I love you.'
> 'You said you were furious.'
> 'I was. I am. But not about what you think, Not about that,'
> 'About what, then?'
> 'About you running away. Away from me. When you should have been ... oh, I don't know, running to find me. Do you see?'
> 'I didn't know if you'd want me.'
> 'That's what makes me angry. That you didn't know that. Do you really think I didn't mean any of those things I said?'
> 'Well, I thought you did, at the time, but it could have been the white heat of passion, couldn't it? A madness produced by the nearness of my luscious body?'
> Graham laughed. 'It could. I suppose. But it wasn't. I love you, and I'll tell you something else.'
> 'What's that?'
> 'I'm quite pleased that you're pregnant.'
> 'I don't know if I am.'
> 'You'll be a lovely mum.'
> 'Is that all? A lovely mum? I used to have ambitions.'
> 'Really?'
> 'Yes. Trapeze artist, deep-sea diver, high-powered business woman, inspiring teacher – you name it, I've wanted it. I want to sing at La Scala and dance at Sadlers Wells.'
> "I don't think anyone can do both, can they?'
> 'Don't be so damned literal. You know what I mean.'
> Graham smiled. 'Yes, I know what you mean.' He started the car.
> 'We're going home.'
> 'What'll we tell them?'
> 'The truth.'
> 'Oh Lord. Really?'
> 'Yes, really. And Lynn? I want you to know something. I asked you to marry me before I knew... about the baby, I mean. I've always wanted to marry you.'
> 'Have you? Always?'
> 'Well, since I was about six.'
> 'You never said.'
> 'It just never came up before, that's all.'
>
> > Lynn and Mandy are having tea in the Wendy House.
> > 'I'm the mummy,' Lynn says and you're the little girl.'
> > 'I want to be the Daddy.' Mandy's mouth puckers up. Maybe she will cry.
> > 'Silly.' Lynn is scornful. 'Girls can't be Daddies. Boys are Daddies.'
> > 'We haven't got a boy.'
> > 'I'll get Graham.' Lynn runs to the climbing frame. Graham is hanging upside down by his knees from the top bar.
> > 'Graham,' she shouts. 'Come and play. Come and be a Daddy in the Wendy House.'
> > 'Don't want to.'
> > 'Come on.' She tickles him under the arms and he hits her and climbs down. She pulls him over to the Wendy House.
> > 'I don't want to be a stupid Daddy in a stupid Wendy House.'

'I've got cakes,' says Lynn."

'Not real cakes.'

'You can pretend they're real.' She pushes him on to a stool. 'You can pour out the tea if you like.'

'I'm the baby,' says Mandy.

'Can I put her to bed?' Graham asks Lynn.

'Yes.' Lynn looks at Mandy. 'Bedtime. Lie down over there.'

Mandy lies on the floor. Graham covers her with a blanket. 'Go to sleep, baby.'

Lynn and Graham sit on white stools, sipping pretend tea out of the red plastic cups. The light pours through the sunshiny curtain, and glitters on the glossy, white paint of the table. Inside the Wendy House, everything is bright and pretty. ”

4 Select extracts from your chosen texts which deal with other typical events: the first meeting of hero and heroine; events which drew them closer together; events, or other people, which seem to be obstacles in the path of their love; the way the story ends.

As you read these extracts more closely, think about how far your heroes and heroines fit the stereotyped pair of lovers.

5 Annotate your chosen extracts, paying particular attention to similarities and differences between older and more recent texts. This will help you to discuss the developing 'tradition' of the romantic story.

6 Make notes to collect together ideas you may include in your assignment. The headings in the article on p.105 could help here.

Characters:

Heroine — tells story from her viewpoint in all these examples — Jane Eyre and Lynn very much independent women — Jane especially so considering when the book was written — education and working for her living. NOT a stereotype — 'small and plain' — not the usual beauty. Proud and brave when she leaves after discovery of Bertha M. rather than be R's mistress. School for farmers' daughters — quite a feminist idea. Reader admires her. Lynn also has ambitions — glamorous dreams — but a REAL one to be a teacher. Independent — initial reaction to pregnancy is to run away and deal with it on her own. Even bossed Graham about in the Wendy House. Reader feels sorry for her. Toni — a stereotype — beautiful caring nurse — independent enough to hold out against Grant — quite spirited — until he tells her he loves her — then turns into a marshmallow. No doubt she'll help him in his career!

Hero Rochester — not conventionally handsome — a BYRONIC hero — like E. Brontë's Heathcliff. Rich — gentleman — nearest hero in these 3 to a Prince. Intelligent, sensitive etc, but a guilty, murky past, and the mad wife in the attic, is not typical. Ends up lame and blind. DEFINITELY not the typical hero by then. Graham — boring, responsible, works for a solicitor. Nothing here about what he looks like. Get the impression Lynn doesn't really fancy him. He's quite passionate — says he loves her and kisses her all over!! Dr Hammond — stereotyped tall, dark and handsome. Successful. Chased by loads of women. Description of kiss is so overdone it's more funny than romantic — veins throbbing in his temples, etc.

First meeting Rochester and Jane — him the Prince on his white charger (well, a brown horse) — but he falls and hurts himself — points forward to end where, again, he depends on J physically. Not very typical. G and L in the Wendy House — not at all typical - but first date to the Church Hall dance — first kiss — shaky legs — butterflies — more like love at first sight. Toni and Grant — usual across a crowded room, love at first sight.

Settings 'Jane Eyre' quite typical — the rich man's house — the grounds — the seasons — spring when it starts, summer when it blossoms, etc. Proposal in orchard. Adam and Eve. Symbols used as well as atmosphere. 'Wendy House' also a symbol — G and L playing at families end up in a little terraced house with the same curtain material - she still feels as if she's playing — and as if she's trapped. Real v. glamorous settings. Some Mills and Boon go for glamour — this one is more ordinary — cosy. Nothing symbolic.

The affair/crisis/ending (plot structure) Jane and Rochester a bit like Grant and Toni — she falls in love with him more and more each time they meet — OBSTACLES: he surrounded by other beautiful (but horrible) women — Blanche and Celia — then the proposal once misunderstanding cleared up. Grant and Toni — stereotype — happy ever after. Jane Eyre less typical — proposal, wedding ceremony — then discovery of bigger obstacle than the difference in their social positions — R is already married. Great shock only half way through book. Hundreds of pages before she goes back and the HAPPY ENDING. Graham and Lynn — pregnancy is not a typical feature of romances. Not an obstacle to marriage — but the story shows it could be an obstacle to love and happiness, especially for Lynn. Both these stories ask questions about what kind of married relationship will make a woman happy. Typical romances assume bliss is automatic once you get your man — Jane Eyre summarises life after as 'supremely blest'. Twentieth century stories might end with marriage, but do hint that life's problems continue after.

Thoughts and conclusions all these stories take the characters and plotting of a typical love story and then alter it a bit — to suit reality at the time, maybe. Why are love stories, happy and sad, so popular with women?? Mills and Boon is most stereotyped — even then Toni seems to want to carry on being a nurse after marriage — and the setting of the surgery shows what her future home might be like. 'Jane Eyre' turns stereotypes upside down — plain heroine, lame hero, the mad wife, ideas of 'equal' marriage — yet it's the most romantic of the lot (last chapter is unbelievable). 'Wendy House' is not romantic — hardly even a love story — more a comment on modern reality of woman's role in marriage and motherhood.

7 Draft, and re-draft your assignment. Take note of the advice about writing essays based on literary texts on pp.91–2.

Here are some extracts from an assignment, expanding some of the ideas in the notes above.

Introduction

From Greek Mythology to Mills and Boon, stories about passionate love, both happy and tragic, have always made compelling reading. It is not surprising that since fictional prose stories of the kind we call novels began to appear in the late seventeenth century, romantic tales have been amongst them. The novel was the first literary form to develop genres of writing which attracted large numbers of women readers and some authors began to specialise in writing these. Novels were certainly the first form of writing respectable women dared to publish. Stories about poor girls who overcome many obstacles to capture the heart and hand of a prince moved out of the magical, fairy-story world of Cinderella and were adapted to the real world of the women who read these novels. The three stories I have chosen to compare in my discussion of the characteristics of the romantic novel are all written by women and tell their stories largely from the female point of view. 'Jane Eyre' is the oldest, from the mid-nineteenth century. Adèle Geras' short story 'Tea in the Wendy House' and 'Runaway Nurse' (a Mills and Boon popular romance) are both fairly recent pieces of writing.

Examiner's tip

This introduction shows research into the origins of the romantic novel. It raises interesting ideas about women as readers and writers of literature. There is already promise that this assignment will demonstrate understanding of the literary tradition. It is made clear which texts will be discussed – and they seem to be appropriate and interesting choices for a discussion of the romance genre.

Characters – the romantic hero

The heroes of these three stories change in ways which take them further and further away from the perfect fairy-tale prince as nineteenth and twentieth century writers adapt the ideal to appeal to their readers. Rochester, in 'Jane Eyre', is a rich gentleman who owns land and property. He is cultured, well-travelled and intelligent, as a romantic hero should be: 'Who taught you to paint wind? There is a high gale in that sky, and on this hilltop. Where did you see Latmos?' he comments when Jane first shows him her artwork, demonstrating his sensitivity towards her paintings and alluding to his travels. He is quite at home discussing music, philosophy and literature with Jane, too. Yet he is not the conventional 'tall, dark and handsome' hunk, but short and stocky with craggy, 'granite-hewn' features. He is also not very moral. The story hints that he has had many lovers, before we even find out he is actually married. He is more of a Byronic hero (Byron, the poet, had a lame leg, despite which many women found him irresistible and fell under his spell as he travelled around Europe.)

Rochester is a contrast with Grant Hammond, who is more the handsome stereotyped lover, even down to the caring nature of his work as a doctor. Being a doctor in a novel always seems more glamorous than the real-life work would make you think. Graham is different again. He is caring and responsible and has a 'steady' job 'articled to a solicitor well-known in the town'. He can be extremely romantic, doubting that he 'will ever be able to stop' kissing Lynn. Unlike the reader's reaction to the others, though, we cannot help but share Lynn's mixed feelings. Graham sounds boringly middle-aged before his time. Will he really suit energetic, ambitious Lynn, who dreamt of being a trapeze artist and an opera singer, or is this a marriage heading towards the divorce court — as with half the real teenage marriages in today's world?

Examiner's tip

The three male characters are discussed with detailed evidence drawn from each text. Their similarities to and differences from the typical hero are clearly outlined, as are their differences from each other. The reference to Byron shows research into literary traditions. The style of writing here is generally very fluent – though I question the use of a word like 'hunk' in a formal essay!

Settings – atmosphere and symbolism

Settings play an important part in all three of the novels. The proposals take place against very different backgrounds, two of which have both atmospheric and symbolic significance. Rochester asks Jane to marry him in a conventionally romantic setting: a warm, scented summer evening in the 'shadowy orchard' of his stately home, Thornfield Hall. We are told the place is 'Eden-like', reminding us of the perfect place the first couple in the world inhabited — but also how they lost it because of their sin — which hints at the next unhappy development in this romance.

The station buffet at Stoke-on-Trent is less romantic, but, like Graham, it is everyday, real, mundane life. The Wendy House referred to in the title of the story is also an important setting because Lynn's memories of games in the bright, clean playhouse are what she tries to recreate when she hangs curtains with 'a lovely pattern of small yellow and white flowers' in the kitchen of her 'small, terrace house in a dingy street'. At the end of the story, Lynn dreams that she is imprisoned in the Wendy House, as, in a way, she is, so this setting is symbolic.

The setting described for Grant's proposal in 'Runaway nurse', surprisingly, is not romantic at all. Grant proposes in the 'comfortable old-fashioned and slightly shabby' living-room behind his surgery. Maybe the ordinariness of this setting is meant to convince the reader that such passionate love can be found in her own everyday world. It is different from the usual glamour of popular romantic fiction.

Examiner's tip

What is impressive here is that this candidate shows how places can be used as central symbols which contribute to the meaning of a story. Quoting and commenting on the reference to Eden in *Jane Eyre* is another example of knowledge of literary traditions. The ability to explore possible reasons for choice of less obvious settings is another pointer that this candidate is heading for a high grade. Detailed pieces of evidence have been selected from all three texts.

Concluding thoughts

The really intriguing thing all three of these stories have in common is not so much how they fulfil stereotypes of romantic fiction, but how each one sometimes defies cliché. Jane returns to find Rochester blind and physically damaged by a fire that destroyed his property, at the end of Charlotte Brontë's tale, yet only then agrees to marry him, now they are 'equal'. It is a happy ending, but not a stereotyped one. The kind of marriage Grant offers Toni as 'wife of a country GP' seems to assume her own independent career in nursing is over. Happiness is assured, of course, but the clichés of wealth and glamour are absent. Domestic cosiness is what Toni gets. The Wendy House demolishes even this promise of modern happiness. Lynn's reservations about happy home and family life leave the reader wondering what will happen to her and Graham. The 'happy ever after' stereotyped ending looks uncertain here. The endings of these stories help to demonstrate how writers seem to avoid completely stereotyped romance. Instead, they take the typical elements: characters, settings, events; then adapt them in the ways I've described in this essay to create more gripping and more believable stories.

Examiner's tip

The candidate has drawn some thoughtful conclusions about the development of the romance genre. Summarising the endings of the three stories to point out general similarities and differences makes for a neat assignment ending, still very much focused on the title. (Because this candidate has been so thorough, this could end up being a very lengthy piece of writing. It might be more manageable to take ONE aspect of romantic fiction – heroines, or the use of setting, or some typical features of plot development, and write about a more specific topic in rather more depth.)

8 If you are studying *Jane Eyre*, or another romantic novel, you could consider this final comment and take another look at the notes for this assignment on pp.104–5. Choose one aspect of the text to write about and plan and draft your own short assignment.

Any assignment which requires you to make comparisons between two or more prose texts, or to discuss aspects of literary tradition, would benefit if you follow the steps explained above.

7.5 Writing about poems

As part of your English GCSE you have to show that you have read and understood some poetry. This involves a piece of coursework if you are following MEG, SEG or WJEC syllabuses, or an essay in the examination if you are following NEAB or London Examinations syllabuses. It is likely that you will study poetry written both before and after 1900, especially if you are also entered for English Literature GCSE.

Whether you write about poetry in the examination or in coursework, some things are likely to be the same for everyone:

- You will be asked to compare at least two poems.
- You will have had the chance to read and discuss the poems in class – poetry on the examination paper will be taken from your anthology.
- In your writing you will be expected to show you understand the *language* used in the poem.
- You may also be asked to analyse and explain what poems say about *character* and *relationships* (if they are about people), *setting* (if they describe places), *themes* (the ideas and emotions expressed in the poems).

The skills you need to plan and write your assignment or examination answer are very similar to those you will use when you write about Shakespeare or prose texts, except that because poems are more condensed and concise, you may find you have to read more closely and think more carefully to find enough to say for a high grade. This will be particularly true in examinations where you are writing under timed conditions.

Putting this into practice

Try your hand at the following question, using the additional notes and advice given here to help you write your answer.

- **Study the poems *At Castle Boterel* and *Afterwards* by Thomas Hardy.**

  In both poems Hardy reflects on what has been important in his life. What impression does he convey about love, life and death in these poems? You should refer to his language and choice of words and the structure of the poems.

  London Examinations (specimen)

1. Both these poems, along with four other poems by Hardy, are ones you would have studied in advance before attempting this question in the examination. In the *London Examinations Anthology*, the poem *At Castle Boterel* is in a section called 'At the Crossroads' – with pieces of writing about decisive moments in life, like starting school or starting work. *Afterwards* is in a section called 'Love and Loss' – along with pieces of writing dealing with lovers who have been separated, either temporarily by one leaving, or permanently by death.

   Some notes have already been made on these poems. Add any more points you notice as you read.

At Castle Boterel

As I drive to the junction of lane and highway,
And the drizzle bedrenches the waggonette,
I look behind at the fading byway,
And see on its slope, now glistening wet,
Distinctly yet

dark/wet – dismal atmosphere – winter – old age
(waggonette) horse drawn cart

Myself and a girlish form benighted
In dry March weather. We climb the road
Beside a chaise. We had just alighted
To ease the sturdy pony's load
When he signed and slowed.

Spring – youth – dry/sunny
This is a memory
(chaise) horsedrawn cart

What we did as we climbed, and what we talked of
Matters not much, nor to what it led, –
Something that life will not be balked of
Without rude reason till hope is dead,
And feeling fled.

Love will last till his death

It filled but a minute. But was there ever
A time of such quality, since or before,
In that hill's story? To one mind never,
Though it has been climbed, foot-swift, foot-sore,
By thousands more.

personification short-but one of the most important things to happen in that place

Primaeval rocks form the road's steep border,
And much have they faced there, first and last,
Of the transitory in Earth's long order;
But what they record in colour and cast
Is – that we two passed.

timeless – very old
things are always changing

And to me, though Time's unflinching rigour,
In mindless rote, has ruled from sight
The substance now, one phantom figure
Remains on the slope, as when that night
Saw us alight.

Hope – things change, but the hill and the stones will always share his memory
personification – you can't rule Time – he is now somewhere else
But his memory of her lasts – she's a 'ghost' of his past – metaphor

I look and see it there, shrinking, shrinking,
I look back at it amid the rain
For the very last time; for my sand is sinking,
And I shall traverse old love's domain
Never again.

March 1913

The memory is powerful, even though he is now old.
metaphor – the egg timer – he is old and will die

Afterwards

When the Present has latched its postern behind my tremulous stay,
And the May month flaps its glad green leaves like wings,
Delicate-filmed as the new-spun silk, will the neighbours say,
'He was a man who used to notice such things'?

If it be in the dusk when, like an eyelid's soundless blink,
The dewfall-hawk comes crossing the shades to alight
Upon the wind-warped upland thorn, a gazer may think,
'To him this must have been a familiar sight.'

If I pass during some nocturnal blackness, mothy and warm,
When the hedgehog travels furtively over the lawn,
One may say, 'He strove that such innocent creatures should
Come to no harm,
But he could do little for them; and now he is gone.'

If, when hearing that I have been stilled at last, they stand at the door,
Watching the full-starred heavens that winter sees,
Will this thought rise on those who will meet my face no more,
'He was one who had an eye for such mysteries'?

And will any say when my bell of quittance is heard in the gloom
And a crossing breeze cuts a pause in its outrollings,
Till they rise again, as they were a new bell's boom,
'He hears it not now, but used to notice such things'?

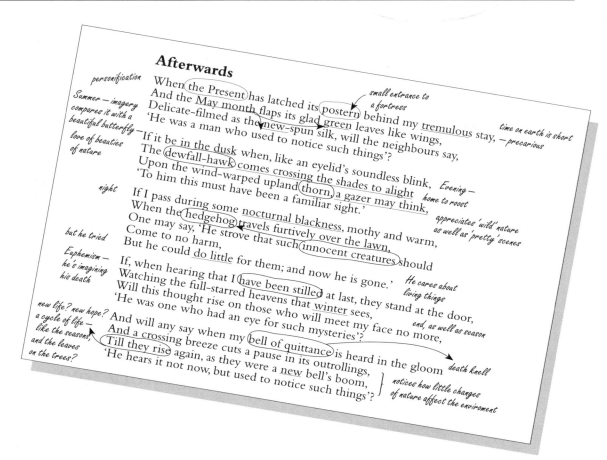

personification
small entrance to a fortress
Summer – imagery compares it with a beautiful butterfly
time on earth is short – precarious
love of beauties of nature
Evening – home to roost
night
appreciates 'wild' nature as well as 'pretty' scenes
but he tried
Euphemism – he's imagining his death
He cares about living things
end, as well as season
new life? new hope? a cycle of life – like the seasons, and the leaves on the trees?
death knell
notices how little changes of nature affect the enviroment

2 Plan what you will write in your essay. You have about 40 minutes to complete this task, so you will only be able to write about two sides of A4. You need to find maybe six distinct points to make about the poems. These notes for an essay should help with ideas.

1 Poems about an old man's memories – CB about a moment of closeness – love for a girl; A about love of nature. Both about how time changes things ceaselessly – yet both about the hope that something good remains for ever.

2 Knows he will soon die – but both poems are about hope – CB – riding up hill in a wagonette reminds him of a similar journey when he and the girl walked to 'ease' the horse. Now old – weather – 'drizzle', 'fading' (sounds melancholy) etc – youth symbolised by 'dry March'. But the memory is shared by the hill and the stones – they'll be there after he dies. A – describes thoughts about Nature which make it sound like a cycle – 'new', 'green' May moves through 'dusk' to 'winter night' – but at the end the death knell, interrupted by the breeze, begins again – 'they rise' – resurrection?? – new life – like the Spring every year.

3 Both poems personify time – very powerful – 'unflinching rigour' – 'The Present' closing him out of the castle which is life. Love of the world and nature on earth are important 'Earth's long order' in CB. He wants to be remembered for what he's loved – the girl – but lots more in A – noticing how beautiful Spring is – imagery – makes the leaves sound like the wings of a butterfly – silky – delicate; even caring about a vulnerable hedgehog. Message – he didn't do a lot, but he cared very deeply.

4 Philosophical – in CB imagines how long the hill and the 'primaeval' rocks have been there – and contemplates the mysteries of the stars in A – feelings of awe at huge concepts like this – make people seem small and 'tremulous'. Powerful language (find examples) – and alliteration – make his intense feelings clear.

5 Structure helps emphasise thoughts – both poems use similar pattern of alternate lines rhyming in 4/5 line stanzas – CB then has v. short end lines – about half the length of the other lines – push home important ideas e.g. 'we two passed', 'never again'. A has final lines which sum up each stanza with a spoken comment the poet would like made about him – epitaphs – things people will admire about his life – like his observation of small but important details.

6 Sum up: how he feels as he prepares to die – knows it can't be escaped – feels sad to miss wonderful things in life like love and nature – maybe a bit afraid of not being – no comfort from religion in these poems – reassuring himself that something of him will remain – memories – his and others. Searching for things to give him hope – like being part of a cycle like the seasons – and that some things he did in life were timelessly important like loving the girl and recognising beauty in the world.

3. Write up these notes as an examination answer. Time yourself – 40 minutes maximum.
   - Begin with an introduction – end with a conclusion – and paragraph the ideas in the middle of your essay.
   - Remember to quote evidence for each point you make. Set quotations out properly, in the original lines of the poem, and explain how they support your point.
   - Keep checking the wording of the question. Use the guidance to write a full answer.
   - Try to write about both poems in each paragraph. Bring out how they are similar – in ideas, language and structure – and how they differ.
   - If you know something about Hardy's life or other writing (poems, novels or stories) do mention it where relevant to your answer.
4. Read your finished essay through and correct any errors you spot.

7.6 Writing about other literary texts

You have read a great deal of advice about writing imaginatively about literature and about structuring analytical essays. Now you need to apply what you have learned to the texts you actually encounter as your GCSE course progresses.

You will use similar skills for both English and English Literature:

- as you prepare to write coursework or to answer examination questions on texts you have read beforehand;
- to deal with unseen literary texts which you read for the first time in the examination room;
- to write about modern or classic literature;
- to write about literature from any culture.

Chapter 8
Non-fiction and media texts

8.1 Finding and using information

At the beginning of this section, you were reminded of the skills you will already have developed as a reader before you began your GCSE English course. So far this section has been concerned mainly with the development of your intensive reading skills: your ability to read every word, to read in depth, to the extent that you can understand what's going on between the lines as well as what is actually stated on the page.

This chapter is concerned with a much wider variety of skills: the reading skills you adopt to extract factual information from a whole range of materials, from dictionaries and instruction manuals to radio progammes and computer databases. This type of reading is not exclusively to do with words, either: the ability to use an atlas, or to understand symbols like road signs, or the washing instructions on clothes labels would also be included amongst these reading skills.

It has been said that we live in an information society. We are surrounded by facts. In our lives we will only make use of a tiny fraction of the information (stored in books, in libraries, held on computer memory, etc) which surrounds us every time we walk down the high street, or which pours through our letter boxes and out of our televisions and radios every day. It is important, though, that we have the skills to find and use the fraction of that information that is necessary in our individual lives.

Putting this into practice

You will be able to see for yourself the huge variety of information skills you use in your daily life by keeping a record of every information text you come into contact with during one day.

Fill in the chart on p.120, using these notes to decide what to record in each column:

Text Give the title of the book or television programme, or a brief statement of the information the text contained, e.g. a 'special offer' poster in a supermarket.

By choice? Tick this column if you actually looked for the information on purpose. Put a cross if it was just something you happened to notice.

Approach? Did you read in detail, or watch with your full attention? Or did you skim-read to get the gist, or simply notice it was there, but decide it didn't need your attention?

Outcome? Did you do anything as a result of your reading? Did you use the information?

Your chart could end up looking a bit like this:

Text	By choice?	Approach?	Outcome?
Letter from time-share company	✗	Skim-read the beginning	Threw it in the bin
Radio weather forecast	✓	Listened carefully	Wore a coat
Poster about fleas in the vet's surgery	✗	Looked at picture Too far away to read writing	Bought flea collar for cat

You will probably find your chart fills up with an astonishing range of reading long before the day is out. Learning to read flexibly for different purposes is yet another language skill you will have developed without being particularly aware that you can do it.

But are you as good as you could be?

Do you ever miss out on useful information because you lack the skills needed to make a quick assessment of whether something may be useful to you or not? Are your 'information retrieval skills' (another name given to this aspect of study skills) good enough for the purposes of your school work? Can you use reference books to find the information you need to help you in your studies?

8.2 What do I need to know?

By Key Stage 4 you will be expected to know how to use anything arranged alphabetically. This could include:

- an index
- a dictionary
- an encyclopaedia
- a library classification system
- a phone book

You should also know how to search out the information you need in:

- an adult thesaurus
- contents pages of books
- texts that do not need reading from end to end, like this book, or the Highway Code
- pamphlets, catalogues and brochures
- a CD Rom

8.3 Writing about non-fiction texts

It is not enough, of course, simply to research information: you also need to have some proof, either spoken or written, to show what you have done with the information you have found out.

Your English examination may test some of the skills outlined above, in particular your ability to read a number of short non-fiction texts and to summarise information they contain. You will quickly realise that many informative texts also aim to persuade the reader.

To test how well you have read, an examination paper will have two sorts of activity: one where you answer short questions selecting and evaluating specific details; another where you make use of the information you have found and the techniques you have spotted in a piece of informative or persuasive writing of your own.

Examiner's tip

Techniques which contribute to a biased text:

- You may be asked to separate out facts from opinions: the writer may disguise personal views to make them look as if they are factual truth.
- Which information is included – and what seems to be left out?
- Is some of the information overstated or exaggerated ?
- Is the information presented using emotive vocabulary which tries to influence the feelings of the reader (e.g. words like 'shocking' and 'damage' make you disapprove; words like 'clean' and 'healthy' make you approve)?
- Are type-faces or pictures chosen to emphasise certain parts of the information?
- Does the style of writing draw the reader in (e.g. a very chatty style, addressing the reader as 'you', asking direct questions, giving orders, etc)?

Putting this into practice

Below is a practice examination paper for you to try. Read the two articles carefully and then answer all the questions, spending an hour on each section.

SECTION A: 1 hour

1 Use the fact sheet and the article to summarise the main effects of the grounding of the oil tanker, M.V. Braer, and the action taken as a result.

Now look at the WWF fact sheet.

2 How does this fact sheet try to persuade you to write to the Minister of Transport? Give reasons for your opinions based on the fact sheet as a whole.

Remember to look at *what* it says and *how* it is said.

Now look at the article from the Daily Mail (Mother Nature Fights Back), written six months after the accident.

3 The Daily Mail article gives a different impression of the Shetland Oil Disaster. In what ways is it different?

Look closely at the detail of the two texts.

4 Look at the headlines, the pictures and captions, and the language of the Daily Mail article. How do they try to influence your thoughts and feelings about the Shetland Oil Disaster?

SECTION B: 1 hour

5 The World Wide Fund for Nature invited you to write to the Minister of Transport, expressing sympathy for the people of the Shetlands and urging Government action to prevent further accidents. You decide to do this.

You may use the resource material but you may also add any thoughts or ideas of your own.

Write your letter to The Minister of Transport, 2 Marsham Street, London, SW1 3EB.

This is a formal letter. Remember to set it out appropriately.

Article 1

A special WWF marine fact sheet

WWF

The Shetland Oil Disaster

On Tuesday January 5 1993 the MV Braer, a Liberian registered oil tanker, lost power and grounded on Garth Ness, Quendale Bay, on the southern end of the Shetland Islands. Over the following seven days the whole cargo of 84,500 tonnes of light crude oil, together with hundreds of tonnes of fuel oil, were released into the marine environment as the ship broke up in relentless storms.

Emergency procedures for salvage, clean-up and wildlife rescue were planned very rapidly but weather conditions meant that very little could be done for many days.

Being light crude, a significant amount of the oil evaporated – which made the air particularly unpleasant to breathe for many miles around. The sea spray carried oil onto the land and coated habitation, pasture, livestock and crops. The effects of the oil in the atmosphere and on land were of serious concern and plans were ready to evacuate the area around the wreck if it became necessary.

Complaints reported

Where possible livestock was moved. A lot of minor complaints were reported, including throat and eye irritations, headaches and nausea, so a scheme was set up to monitor the extent of the oil's effect.

Effects on wildlife

The more obvious effects of the oil were seen immediately on the birds and mammals. In the first two weeks after the spillage, large numbers of dead and heavily oiled birds were recovered. It is fortunate that in January many seabirds, for which the Shetland Islands are famous, were further south or offshore because of the stormy weather. It will be important to monitor the effects on birds returning to the area in search of breeding sites. Most important will be the effects on the food stocks – the fish – on which the birds are dependent.

WWF's work continues

The oil may have disappeared from the surface of the water but WWF's work on a number of Shetland Islands projects continues. Our interest in the marine environment is widely based, and we acknowledge its value as a source of livelihood to fishermen and fish-farmers and, through them, large sectors of the community.

They and other people who farm the coastal lands have been severely affected by this disaster, which need never have happened.

Questions must be asked

Questions must be asked about why a ship carrying such a hazardous substance was navigating a passage through this area in such dangerous weather conditions. It is wholly unacceptable that the shipping of hazardous materials around the world in busy, dangerous or environmentally sensitive waters can continue. WWF is committed to using its international influence to persuade governments throughout the world to strengthen controls on maritime navigation, ship design and seaworthiness, crew competence and ship-ping traffic control so that incidents like the Braer in Shetland, and others all over the world, will not be repeated. WWF welcomes the government's announcement of a public inquiry into ways of protecting the United Kingdom's coastline from pollution by merchant shipping and will be working hard to ensure that environmental considerations are fully recognised.

History revisited

In 1968, at the end of a report on the Torrey Canyon oil disaster off the Scilly Isles, scientists stated: "We are progressively making a slum of nature and may eventually find that we are enjoying the benefit of science and industry under conditions which no civilised society should tolerate."

In the aftermath of three major oil spills in two months, that sentiment is as relevant today as it was 25 years ago.

Please help prevent another marine disaster by writing to the Minister of Transport sympathising with the plight of the Shetlanders and making the point that the government must act urgently on these critical issues if further accidents are not to happen.

His address is: The Department of Transport, 2 Marsham Street, London SWIP 3EB.

Article 2

SIX MONTHS AFTER THE SHETLAND OIL DISASTER THE MAIL RETURNS TO THE ISLANDS AND FINDS NEW HOPE

Mother Nature fights back

REBIRTH OF BEAUTY

When the Braer (centre left) spilled its deadly cargo and coated wildlife, like this duck (centre right) in crude oil, many feared the worst. Yet just months afterwards common seals (left) gave birth to masses of healthy pups, and puffins (right) have no trouble finding sand eels for their young.

The tide turned ... the winds blew. It was a triumph over man's folly

FLOCKS of puffins are bustling about the clifftops answering the call of their hungry young with wriggling sand-eels fished from sparkling clean waters. On the rock ledges below are lines or young gannets, eyes bright with anticipation, watching their parents dive like torpedoes from the dizzying heights through a wheeling mass of screaming seabirds to the sea below.

In the waves are the bobbing heads of this season's seals swimming around the biggest fish ever to land in their home waters... the upturned bow or the ill-fated oil tanker Braer that brought the black death of oil pollution to the Shetlands when it was swept onto the rocks of Quendale Bay last January.

Where then, is the nightmare vision of dying seas and ruined islands choking in the 22million gallons of crude oil that spilled from the broken tanker? What of the predictions of the doom and disaster merchants whose voices were raised so loud and listened to by so many? When the Mail returned to these islands at the northernmost tip of Britain six months later all we found were signs of hope – a triumph of nature over the folly of man.

Twenty-one days or gale-force winds and awesome storm-driven tides were nature's reply to the indignity visited upon it. The winds reached 115mph and 40ft waves battered the coast, as the lament went up that it would break up the Braer and scatter more oil. The deep depression known as Low G was the lowest recorded of all time, worse than that experienced during the Great Hurricane of 1987.

The slick spread sickeningly around the southern tip of the main island and wintering seabirds were washed up dead on the blackened beaches and started filling the de-oiling units. Sheep on the shore and human rescuers were half-blinded by the oil-filled breezes.

And then the tide turned. When the veil of oil cleared from everyone's eyes it was obvious that nature had performed a miracle. The oil had been dispersed by its majestic force, broken up into units invisible to the eye.

The latest official statistics show that of the 800 otters that could have died, only four have been found dead – two killed in road accidents and the others by natural causes. Twelve seals and porpoises died, but the last oiled seals were returned to a 'clean' sea two months later. The latest official count of dead birds is 1,542 – shags and black guillemots suffered the most long-term damage – and not the tens of thousands feared to be at risk.

Shetlands naturalist Bobby Tulloch, sitting at his desk with its spectacular view over the islands, says: 'Even a month aiter what was supposed to be our worst-ever disaster it was as if it had never happened. We had 21 successive days of high winds and tides. When they dropped and we went to look at the damage, we wondered what the fuss had been about.

'The birds that died were long-tailed ducks and great northern divers from Iceland which spend the winter months here but the seabirds most likely to be affected by oil spills just hadn't arrived at that time.

'When they did come in late spring it seems they had a plentiful food supply. We never saw an oiled gannet, and they're all feeding their chicks on the rocks as usual. Guillemots and puffins are finding large numbers of sand-eels for their young. The common seals had masses of pups in June and they're all looking healthy. Above all, the sea looks clean and everything feels right.'

The authorities have already cleared whiting, haddock and herring as safe. Although the number of small cormorants in the immediate vicinity of the wreck seems to have been halved, other seabirds are having a record breeding season.

The Braer incident should never have happened but nature has fought back magnificently... and appears to be winning handsomely.

WORDS: JUNE SOUTHWORTH PICTURES: JIM HUTCHINSON

6 An American company has decided to locate a factory in your area. Most of the workers will be recruited locally but some senior staff will be transferred from New York. They need to know something about the area into which they will be moving.

You have been asked to write a report which will inform the Americans about your area, particularly such matters as schools, housing, transport, leisure and cultural facilities. You may also include other information which you think would be helpful and interesting. Remember that this is an important development for your area and you are keen to attract these people.

Write your report. Think about the way you set it out (e.g. using headlines such as Schools) to put your ideas across clearly.

WJEC (specimen)

8.4 Case study: a media project

Putting this into practice

The media project described below was undertaken by a group of twelve GCSE students. As you work through it, you will be given examples of the research they undertook, and you will be able to practise some of the tasks that they carried out.

You can then go on to put these skills to use on a local issue of your own, using your local paper as a source of ideas. Once you have found a topic, select from the strategies and activities described here to create a research project of your own.

A research project on nuclear waste

1 The original idea

The class was in the middle of an oral work topic about making persuasive speeches. They had already decided that a subject that provided plenty of arguments on each side was nuclear power. At the start, they were using an English text book for information, and the selection of materials had been done for them. Subsequently they gathered information from other sources.

2 Newspaper articles

On the 19th November, Hayley brought newspaper Article 1 to the lesson and said she had videotaped the Open Eye programme mentioned in the article. These highlighted the pollution said to be caused by the Springfields reprocessing plant. Many of the class had either read the paper or watched the programme, and were interested in using this information to help them write their speeches.

Bruce and Daniel brought in two more articles from the same paper on the two nights that followed the television broadcast. These were particularly interesting because Article 2 put forward the point of view of the BNFL managers, insisting that Springfields followed adequate safety procedures, whilst Article 3 (which was front page headline news) followed the shock tactics of the broadcast, revealing worrying 'facts' about the safety procedures at the Springfields plant.

By selecting information from different sources instead of just relying on the text book, these three GCSE students were showing promise of achieving at least an E grade. They were also able to show in their discussion of these articles the bias of the points of view put forward. Being able to explain how media texts use techniques of persuasion demonstrates at least D grade reading skills.

To reach the highest grades (A and A*) you would need to show that you were able to analyse alternative interpretations of the texts collected, to compare them carefully and to make cross-reference from one text to another. The greater the variety of texts, the more you would have to say, or write, about these things.

Article 1

A-plant 'puts children at risk' – report

By JOHN LAWRENCE

CHILDREN playing on the banks of the River Ribble could be risking radioactive contamination from a nearby nuclear plant.

A report by pressure group Friends of the Earth claims youngsters playing along the river in the Penwortham area near Preston could be receiving large doses of radiation from mudflats contaminated by discharged from the British Nuclear Fuels Springfields plant, it was revealed today.

Lancashire County Council leader Louise Ellman immediately called for an in-depth investigation from the independent radiation monitoring group Radmil.

Frightened residents living within yards of the River Ribble today said they feared for their health.

The worried locals called for a wide-ranging investigation into the damning report.

The shock survey coincides with a hard-hitting Granada TV investigation due to be screened tonight into radiation safety standards at the sprawling Salwick site, which features ex-worker Joe McMaster, 69, formerly of Greystock Avenue, Fulwood, Preston, and his wife Stella.

Mr McMaster, who worked for 31 years as an analytical chemist, claims that three of his daughters died between 1958 and 1987 from illnesses linked to fatal doses of radiation.

Levels

Friends of the Earth today said tests carried out on the stretch of the Ribble through Preston revealed pollution levels higher than those published by BNFL and the Ministry of Agriculture Fisheries and Food.

Researchers monitored radiation levels at four points upstream of the Springfields discharge pipe including the cadet hut at Penwortham bridge, Broadgate.

Other points were Lower Penwortham park and the mainline railway bridge.

Doses of radioactive thorium particles were found to be up to six times higher than normal.

Radiation campaigner Dr Patrick Green said the muddy river bed and bank were popular with children.

The report says a child would have to spend on average around 80 minutes a day over a year along the river bank to receive the maximum tolerable radiation dose of 100 units.

The man who helped spark today's controversy was Paul Brown, 52, of Welwyn Avenue, Southport.

Scrutiny

He has been carrying out independent testing on the Ribble using Geiger-counters for the last 18 months.

He said today: "My inquiries led to Friends of the Earth commissioning their own survey."

BNFL information officer Peter Osborne said the pressure group's finding did not stand up to close scrutiny and denied that youngsters were in danger.

Mr Osborne said: "Any doses that children would be receiving from playing in those areas would only be one per cent of any radiation that could be regarded as remotely dangerous. To be honest, the Ribble is a pretty inhospitable play area for other reasons and not many children play there anyway."

A MAFF spokesman said government scientists always carried out tests in areas that would provide the highest doses and published their results on a regular basis.

Local residents said if the alleged nuclear waste dumping was true it should be stopped immediately. Mrs Susan Hunter of Riverside Road said: "If it's true, it is absolutely outrageous and everyone round here will naturally be very concerned."

Graham Hunter of Stonefield, Penwortham, said BNFL had to "clean up its act" if the Friends of the Earth report was true.

Article 2

SAFE IN OUR HANDS

Nuclear boss hits back in water storm

Nuclear bosses said today the environmental impact of radioactive nuclear waste discharged from the Springfields plant into the River Ribble was trivial.

By JOHN LAWRENCE

BNFL health and safety manager Dr Tony Fishwick hit back at claims over contamination levels made by a Friends of the Earth investigation and the Granada TV Open Eye team. Friends of the Earth claimed that children could be at risk from radiation if they played along the bank of the river, particularly on its stretch through Penwortham, near Preston.

Dr Fishwick slammed the Friends of the Earth report as biased and claimed it used only test results taken when discharges from Springfields were higher than normal.

He said: "The group has taken a snapshot in time at the beginning of the summer when the plant was just starting up again after a six-month shutdown and discharges were higher than normal for a period of six weeks.

"Continuous monitoring by BNFL and independent groups over a period of years has shown radiation along the Ribble is either equal to or less than natural background radiation."

Dr Fishwick said it was scandalous for Friends of the Earth to suggest that BNFL was putting profits before safety when £1,250,000 had been spend on refurbishing the Springfields effluent drainage system and £1m on a new waste discharge station.

Three hundred million gallons of water are discharged into the Ribble every year from Springfields but most is rainwater and less than 10 per cent is radioactive.

Waste from uranium recovery work is sampled and monitored then treated with lime for acid neutralisation before being carried along enclosed drains, which pick up rainwater, and finally undergoing more monitoring at the discharge station before being pumped into the Ribble.

The only radioactive particles to be released from Springfields are soft non-penetrating beta particles, which Dr Fishwick described as "less intense" than other radiation.

Mr Tom Meredith, director of Preston's environmental health department, which carried out tests for the independent radiation monitoring group Radmil, said the risks along the Ribble were negligible.

Mr Meredith said: "According to our figures gathered monthly over two years, a person would have to spend 34 hours a week actually standing in the mud of the river bank – that's 1,785 hours a year – to receive any significant dose of radiation. As far as we know, no one does that."

Article 3

Exclusive: Scientist admits gap in monitoring

A-plant fails test

By DAVID CRAGG

NUCLEAR safety officials at the centre of an atom scare today admitted that for almost 45 years they have not carried out full radiation tests along the River Ribble.

Scientists at the BNFL Springfields plant at Salwick, near Preston, revealed they only began wide-ranging riverside searches for radiation hot spots this week.

The new comes just days after Friends of the Earth claimed children playing along the river at Penwortham, near Preston, could be receiving large doses of radiation from mudflats allegedly contaminated by discharges from Springfields.

The report coincided with a Granada TV investigation into the A-plant – which makes fuel for nuclear reactors – in which a former worker claimed three of his daughters died from illness linked to radiation.

Urgent

Today it was revealed that BNFL failed to carry out tests which specifically located the high beta radiation hot spots on the Ribble and a Springfields physicist admitted the tests have only been introduced in the last week.

Today Lancashire County Council leader Mrs Louise Ellman called for BNFL to stop discharges from the plant and said a special study by the council's own radiation watchdog, Radmil, was to be carried out. Local residents have also demanded urgent meetings with BNFL chiefs.

This week independent researcher Paul Brown, form Southport, revealed he found high levels of beta radioactive contamination – which can be harmful in high doses – in river mud.

Friends of the Earth has produced similar readings and claims BNFL has failed to meet a legal obligation to reduce radioactive discharge levels below newly-imposed limits.

BNFL has carried out riverside monitoring to find gamma radioactivity and taken random samples to monitor beta levels, but without testing for beta hot spots with Geiger counters.

Comprehensive Geiger monitoring sweeps over a wide area, of the kind carried out by Mr Brown, are considered essential.

Now, BNFL has been ordered by the Ministry of Agriculture, Fisheries and Food to begin regular Geiger counter checks.

Area Health Physicist (Environmental), for Springfields, Roger Wilson, said that previously radioactive pollution from the Sellafield nuclear plant was so high that pollution from Springfields was considered negligible.

He said: "We only began measuring beta radioactivity as part of the official programme last week.

"Previously, people's exposure to radiation levels was dictated by Sellafield, since their emissions were so much higher. As that plant has got a grip of discharges and the environment has adjusted, so the importance of Springfield's discharges has grown."

But he reassured the public that discharges were well below safety levels.

Mr Brown welcomed the move to monitor beta levels and said: "It is a vital part of assuring that strict safety levels of radioactivity are adhered to. The only way of locating where hot-spots might develop in the area is to take Geiger-counter readings of the mud."

Putting this into practice

Skim-read all three articles for the following information.

- What is said to be the problem?

- What is believed to be the cause of it?

- Name three areas said to be affected.

- Who has made the public aware of the problem?

- Find four reasons why the problem may be exaggerated. Who provided this information?

- Who are Paul Brown and Roger Wilson? What do they contribute to the debate?

- In conclusion, do you think local residents ought to feel worried, or reassured?

3 Television broadcast

After reading the newspaper articles, the group watched the television broadcast and discussed how it presented a particular point of view by means of selecting specific information: shocking facts about radiation readings and information about families who had experienced illness and death linked with radiation.

4 Collecting more information: letter-writing

The group decided they needed to know more facts about radioactive waste and more about the danger of radiation to make up their minds who was right.

They practised their formal letter-writing skills, contacting pressure groups like Friends of the Earth and Greenpeace, and British Nuclear Fuels to obtain further information about both sides of the argument.

They wrote to their MPs and received all sorts of information from them.

Philip also found information about radioactivity in a Physics text book.

5 Examining the information

Next came the stage of looking at all the information they had collected and sorting out what it had to say. They made a project grid and noted down facts from the various sources.

Putting this into practice

Skim through the additional information which the pupils collected (pp.129–134), and summarise the main points from all their sources on the grid on p.135.

British Nuclear Fuels pamphlet

PROTECTING THE PUBLIC

All of BNFL's waste management activities are strictly controlled. As well as being subject to government legislation, the disposal of radioactive wastes is overseen by various authorising departments which include the Department of the Environment, the Scottish and Welsh Offices and the Ministry of Agriculture, Fisheries and Food.

In the UK, no radioactive waste disposal is allowed unless the authorising bodies are satisfied that the principles recommended by the International Commission on Radiological Protection (ICRP) are adhered to. The basic principles are:

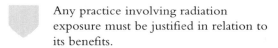

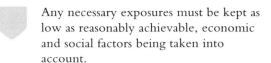

- Any practice involving radiation exposure must be justified in relation to its benefits.
- Any necessary exposures must be kept as low as reasonably achievable, economic and social factors being taken into account.
- Radiation doses must not exceed recommended dose levels.

Extensive monitoring around BNFL sites is carried out by the Company to ensure that radiation doses due to its activities remain a small fraction of recommended limits. For example, at Drigg, boreholes are used for the regular sampling of ground water, surface waters are monitored routinely and air samplers are situated around the Drigg site.

Regular monitoring of foodstuffs such as milk, fish and shellfish is also carried out around BNFL sites to ensure that they do not contain harmful amount of radioactivity as a result of BNFL's discharges to the environment. This monitoring process is also extended to other materials such as shoreline mud, vegetation and seaweed.

To put into perspective the effect of radioactive discharges from Sellafield into the Irish Sea, a person eating large quantities of Cumbrian seafood would only receive less than an additional one per cent of the radiation dose he would be exposed to if he lived in certain parts of Cornwall.

The Government departments involved in authorising radioactive discharges also have their own independent programmes of environmental monitoring. In addition, a number of independent researchers carry out measurements and publish results.

BNFL also publishes annual reports on health and safety matters covering radioactive discharges, monitoring of the environment and occupational safety.

BNFL welcomes the public debate about its waste management activities because it is vital that the public feels confident and safe in order to ensure that Britain can continue to reap the benefits of nuclear electricity generation.

National Radiation Protection Board poster

RADIATION PROTECTION PRINCIPLES

These are the recommendations of the International Commission on Radiological Protection (ICRP).
This scientific organisation has published recommendations for protection against ionising radiation for over half a century.

The three central principles of the ICRP recommendations are as follows.

JUSTIFICATION

1 No practice involving radiation shall be adopted unless its introduction produces a positive net benefit.

ALARA

2 All radiation exposures shall be kept as low as reasonably achievable, economic and social factors being taken into account.

DOSE LIMITS

3 The radiation dose to individuals shall not exceed the limits recommended for the appropriate circumstances by the Commission.

Justification

Obviously, the practice should be of overall value to society. Harmful effects and alternatives should be considered. This can raise profound questions often requiring resolution by governments, e.g. on nuclear power. Even some medical uses of x-rays, generally hugely beneficial, may require strong justification and careful techniques.

Some practices are clearly not justified.

Medical uses	✓
Nuclear power	✓
Smoke detectors	✓
Luminous devices	✓
Children's toys	✗
Jewellery	✗

Keeping doses as low as reasonably achievable

Since it is assumed that all radiation doses carry some risk, complying with the limit is not enough. Doses must be further reduced. However, dose reduction meets with diminishing returns.

Dose limits

Individuals must not be exposed to an unacceptable degree of risk. However, dose limits do not mark an abrupt change in biological risk but rather the level of risk that, if received over a lifetime, would verge on the intolerable.

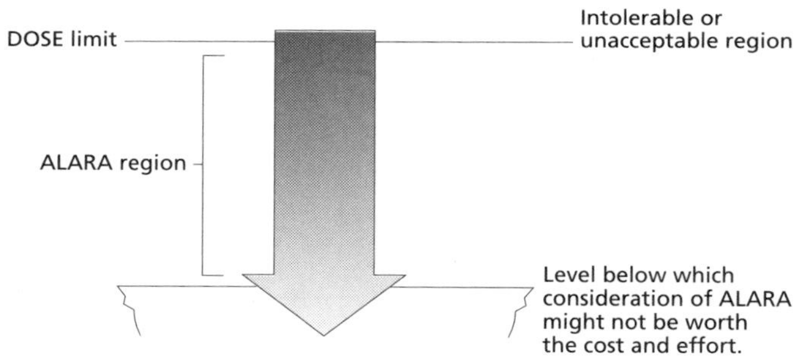

Dose limits have to be observed regardless of cost and represent a level that it is illegal to exceed. There is also a legal requirement for ALARA.

Governments put the ICRP recommendations into practice in a manner appropriate to their own countries.

National Radiation Protection Board poster (cont.)

RADIATION EFFECTS

There are two kinds, those that occur early and those that occur late.

Early	
Whole body, high radiation dose	Death in a matter of days or weeks
Limited area exposed briefly to high dose	Reddening of skin

Late	
Lower dose or same total dose over a long time	No early signs but presumed late effects – cancer and hereditary disease

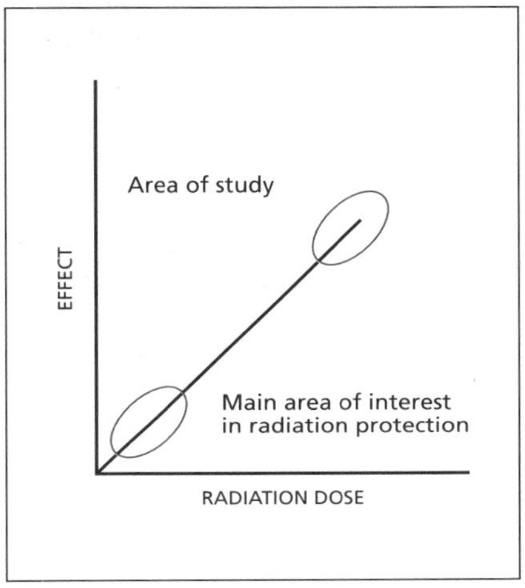

It is assumed that, however low the dose, there is some risk. This is derived from studies of people who were exposed to high doses of radiation, such as the survivors of the atomic bombing of Japan, patients exposed to radiation for treatment or diagnosis, and some groups of workers.

Information on the biological effects of radiation is reviewed periodically by the United Nations Scientific Committee on the Effects of Atomic Radiation (UNSCEAR) which was established in 1955. The Committee is made up of scientists from 21 countries round the world.

National Radiation Protection Board poster (cont.)

HARM AND SENSITIVITY

QUALITY FACTORS		
Alpha	(α)	× **20**
Beta	(β)	× **1**
Gamma	(γ)	× **1**
	x	× **1**

Different types of radiation vary in the effectiveness with which they cause harm in tissue. To allow for this, absorbed doses are multiplied by quality factors, to produce the 'dose equivalent'. However, we still have the problem that some organs are more sensitive to radiation than others.

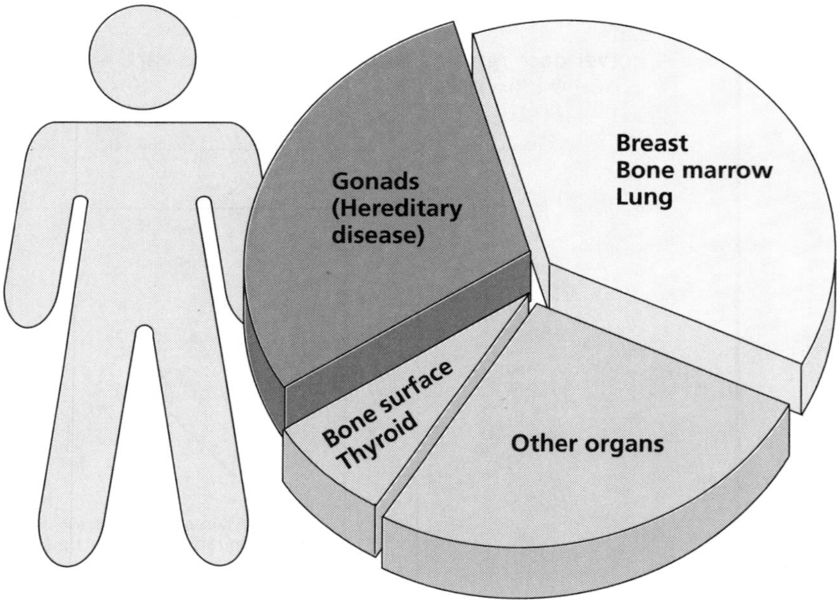

Relative sensitivity of different parts of the body.

So, the dose equivalent to each organ is multiplied by a weighting factor. This gives the 'effective dose equivalent', which measures the overall risk from any combination of radiation affecting any organs of the body.

Generally, effective dose equivalent is what is meant when the term 'dose' is used; its units are 'millisieverts'.

HIERARCHY OF DOSE QUANTITIES

Absorbed dose
energy imparted by radiation to unit mass of tissue

▼

Dose equivalent
absorbed dose weighted for harmfulness of different radiations (quality factors)

▼

Effective dose equivalent ('Dose')
dose equivalent weighted for susceptibility to harm of different tissues (risk weighting factors)

▼

Collective effective dose equivalent ('Collective Dose')
effective dose equivalent to all the people exposed to a source of radiation

Extract from Physics text book

7 The Hazards of Radiation

Measuring radiation

When scientists try to work out the effect on our bodies of a dose of radiation, they need to know how much energy each part of the body has absorbed. After al the damage done to us will depend on the amount of energy that each kilogram o body tissue absorbs. The unit used to measure a **radiation dose** is the **gray**, (symbol Gy). A dose of 1 Gy means that each kilogram of flesh absorbs 1 joule of energy.

$$1\ \text{Gy} = 1\ \text{J/kg}$$

Some radiations are more damaging than others, so scientists prefer to talk in terms of a **dose equivalent**, which is measured in **sieverts** (symbol Sv).

$$\text{dose equivalent (Sv)} = Q \times \text{dose (Gy)}$$

Q	Type of radiation
1	beta particles/gamma rays
10	protons and neutrons
20	alpha particles

Table 1

Q is a number that depends on the radiation, as shown in Table 1. Alpha particle are very strongly ionizing and cause far more damage than a dose of beta or gamma radiation that carries the same energy. Usually the amounts of radiation that we are exposed to are very small. Most people receive about 1/1000 sievert each year, this is a **millisievert** (symbol 1 mSv).

The Chernobyl nuclear reactor near Kiev in Russia. During an unauthorised experiment in 1986, the core of the number 4 reactor unit melted, causing an explosion which released a large amount of radioactive material. This will be a very serious health hazard for many years to those living close to the reactor. Winds carried some of the radioactive material to many countries in Europe

Risk estimates

On 26 April 1986 there was an explosion in the Russian nuclear reactor at Chernobyl, causing a large leakage of radiation. During May the **background count** in Britain increased causing us all to be exposed (on average) to an extra dose equivalent to 0.1 mSv. This is a small dose and no worse than going on holiday in Cornwall, where granite rock areas produce low amounts of radiation. However, estimates have been made to suggest that over the next 30 years, extra people will get cancer as a result of the Chernobyl disaster.

Research suggests that for a population of 1000, about 12 fatal cancers will be caused by a dose equivalent of 1 Sv. In Britain, the population is about 50 millior so the number of deaths expected by a dose for all of us of 1 Sv would be:

$$\frac{12}{1000} \times 50\,000\,000 = 600\,000$$

However, the dose from Chernobyl was only 0.0001 Sv, so the estimated number of deaths from the Chernobyl disaster, in Britain over the next 30 years, is about 600 000 × 0.0001 = 60.

How dangerous is radiation?

Radiation affects materials by ionizing atoms and molecules. When an atom is ionized, electrons are removed or added to it. This means a chemical change has occurred. In our bodies such a chemical change could cause the production of a strong acid which will attack and destroy cells.

- **High doses** of radiation will kill you. There is only a 50 per cent chance of surviving a dose equivalent to 4 Sv. A 10 Sv dose equivalent would give you no chance of survival. Such high doses kill too many cells in the gut and bone marrow for your body to be able to work normally. You could be exposed to such doses in a nuclear war, and people certainly died in Hiroshima and Nagasaki as a result of such doses.
- **Moderate doses** of radiation below 1 Sv will not kill you. Damage will be done to cells in your body, but not enough to be fatal. The body will be able to replace the dead cells and the chances are that you would then recover totally. However, a study of the survivors from Hiroshima and Nagasaki shows that there is an increased chance of dying from cancer some years after the radiation dose. Even so, you would only have a chance of about 1 in 100 of getting cancer from such levels of radiation.
- **Low doses** of radiation, below 10 mSv, are thought to have little effect on us. However, some people think that any exposure to radiation will increase your chances of getting cancer.

There can be no doubt that radiation doses can cause cancer or leukaemia (see Table 2). Uranium miners are exposed to radon gas, and girls who painted luminous watch dials were exposed to radium.

Workers in the nuclear power industry are exposed to more radiation than the rest of the population. Special monitoring and remote control are used to keep this extra radiation exposure as small as possible.

Source of radiation	Type of radiation	Number of people studied	Extra number of cancer deaths caused by radiation
uranium miners	alpha	3400	60
radium luminisers	alpha	800	50
medical treatment	alpha	4500	60
medical treatment	X-rays	14 000	25
Hiroshima bomb	gamma rays and neutrons	15 000	100
Nagasaki	gamma rays	7000	20

Table 2. This table illustrates the connection between radiation and the increased chance of cancer.

Questions

1 In Table 1, the value of Q for alpha radiation is 20. Why is it so high?
2 What does a sievert measure?
3 Summarise the effects of high, moderate and low doses of radiation on us.
4 Many modern watches do not have luminous dials. Instead they have small lights that turn on at the press of a switch. Explain why lights are safer.
5 Use the data in Table 2 to show that exposure to alpha radiation is more likely to cause cancer than exposure to gamma radiation or X-rays.
6 In a nuclear reactor disaster about 200 workers are exposed to a radiation dose equivalent to 2 Sv. Use the data in the text to estimate the number of them likely to die from cancer some time after the accident.

Topics / Texts	Newpaper article 1	Newspaper article 2	Newspaper article 3	BNFL pamphlet	NRPB poster	Extract from Physics text book	Friends of the Earth, etc
Natural sources of radiation						p. 265 – rocks, the sun	
Diseases caused by radiation							Leukaemia? Cancer?
'Safe' levels of radiation					50 millisieverts per year		
Environmental damage	Rivers and mudflats			milk, fish, shellfish, p.19			
'Half-life' of radiation							
Disposal of radioactive waste							
Types of radioactive waste							

6 Role-play: writing a persuasive speech

Next, they made use of what they had learnt by role-playing a public enquiry meeting. They split into four small groups:

- One group represented the views of the managers of BNFL;
- One group represented the views of local parents;
- One group represented the views of employees at Springfields;
- One group represented the views of Friends of the Earth.

Each of them wrote a persuasive speech, using information they had selected from what they had read to put forward the personal worries, concerns or reassurances.

7 Role-play: acting out a public debate

Finally, they acted out the meeting, using the best of the prepared speeches, and the whole class took part in a debate. The role-play was videoed so they could watch their own performances afterwards and assess their performances.

Putting this into practice

Which group would you have chosen to be in? Use the information you have learnt and the advice about making a speech on p.42 to prepare notes for the points you would make.

Analysis and evaluation

Media coursework must show that you can analyse and evaluate texts you have chosen. Ideas for writing about these nuclear waste texts could include:

- a comparison of the attitudes and bias you found in two different pamphlets;
- a comparison of the way newspapers and television documentaries presented the issue;
- an in-depth analysis of bias in a newspaper article, including use of typefaces, photographs and diagrams;
- an analysis of a radio programme/video/newspaper article you have produced yourself, explaining decisions you made about how to present your particular point of view.

If your final examination includes media texts amongst its pre-released materials, your ability to extract factual information and to recognise biased opinion will be of great use. When you are annotating your texts in preparation for the writing tasks in your exam, remember to make use of these skills.

Examiner's tip

10% of your English marks come from coursework based on reading.

Make sure your folder has evidence of:

- a range of reading, including a Shakespeare play, a novel, some poetry;
- reading of texts written before and after 1900;
- reading of at least one text by an author listed in the National Curriculum;
- reading of texts not covered on your examination paper (e.g. media texts, texts from other cultures – check your syllabus requirements with your teacher);
- records of any spoken assignment based on reading in which you have taken part.

Examiner's tip

30% of your English marks come from reading the final examination.

Make sure you go into the exam well prepared, with all the texts you will need to use:

- pre-released materials and anthologies;
- books you have studied.

Check the information on p.89 to remind yourself of the importance of annotating texts.

Learn the names of the literary techniques listed on p.88 and practise explaining how and why writers use them.

Make sure you have read (and re-read) your texts sufficiently often to be able to make use of them in the exam without wasting time.

Make sure you choose questions which allow you to demonstrate your detailed understanding of your prepared texts.

Chapter 9
Your own writing

9.1 Building on what you know

Writing is the most important skill you have to show evidence of in your English coursework and examination. You are assessed on your ability to write in different ways for different purposes and to use writing to comment on your reading. Your writing is also assessed to see that it is correctly punctuated and spelled, re-drafted with care and legibly presented. That is a lot of work to cover.

You will realise from your reading of Section Two that learning about language and the dialect of English called standard English is a major part of your English course. But it is part of writing as much a speaking and listening. When the spelling mistakes you make in a piece of writing are corrected by your teacher, he or she may well be telling you that your spelling of that word is wrong in the sense that it is not written in correct standard English. When people first started to use writing, and even in the early days of printing, words were spelled in all sorts of different ways. The words themselves were often different, or used in a different order, or the same word had different meanings to different people, depending on where they lived.

However, as the printed word has became commonplace – in the last two hundred years or so – standard English has increased in importance. It has become the accepted, correct form for writing of all kinds so it is important that you are able to write it confidently and to express yourself clearly through it. It does not matter at all if you speak with an accent – in fact, we all do – or if you use dialect in your speech – nearly all of us do – but you do need to be a competent writer and that means using standard English correctly. In this book a lot of emphasis is placed on careful re-reading and re-drafting of everything you write. One of the reasons for this is that writing in standard English does not come as naturally as talking. It takes practice, thoughtful reflection and continual correction to do it as well as you can.

The written work that you do says a lot about you. It is the written record of something which is going on inside your head! A stimulus, such as reading a story or listening to a poem, is processed inside your brain into a piece of writing. Speaking and listening help to sort out the process before you write.

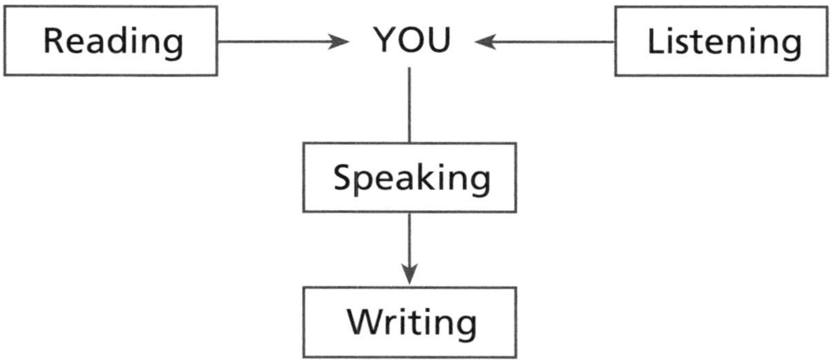

One of the consequences of this is that the only record of your achievements in reading, listening and speaking may be in the form of writing. In one sense, although Reading is a separate Attainment Target in the National Curriculum, your achievements in reading have to be assessed through writing. Even if you talk about a book you have read, there still has to be a written record of the event before it can be assessed!

9.2 Areas of assessment

The GCSE syllabuses ask a lot from you as a writer. There are five areas where you have to show evidence of what you can achieve. In practice, they tend to overlap so that one written task is likely to cover nearly all of them, but for assessment purposes they are likely to be separated. The areas are:

❶ **Writing for a range of audiences and purposes**
All the writing you do has an audience, even if it is only your teacher! Other pieces of writing may have very specific audiences, like a secret note to your best friend or a story written for young children. You need to start thinking about **who** you are writing for and why you are writing, whenever you start a new piece of work.

2 Structuring and organising writing in different forms and genres
All good writing is structured and organised. In a story, the sequence of events provides structure, but other kinds of writing may have to be structured and organised in different ways. You have to develop an awareness of how to plan your writing, so that the structure is clear to a reader. Punctuation and paragraphing are important here. You have to organise exactly what you want to say in your writing.

3 Using standard English
This is concerned with your ability to use different styles in your writing and to know when you are being literary, formal or informal. It is also concerned with grammar and your choice of vocabulary.

4 Spelling correctly
Your spelling is assessed here. You are expected to know how to spell common words and to know how longer words are often made up from or based on combinations of shorter words.

5 Using legible handwriting and presenting work neatly
Presentation is assessed as part of English. It means that you must write legibly. Ideas about improving the presentation of your work will also earn your credit: for example, the way you set out a poster with bold headlines, capitals and underlining.

9.3 What do I have to write?

As with Speaking and Listening, for Writing you need to produce different kinds of writing, either as part of your coursework, or in the examination. These different purposes for writing are arranged in clusters:

1 Writing to explore, imagine or entertain
This means imaginative writing, like fictional stories, playscripts and poems.

2 Writing to inform, explain or describe
This means non-fiction, which could vary from being a leaflet giving details about road safety to a piece of autobiographical writing – anything that gives factual information, but does not explicitly set out to influence the opinions or actions of the reader – which is the function of the next cluster.

3 Writing to argue, persuade or instruct
This could vary from a set of instructions about how to fix a puncture to a written version of a persuasive debate speech about an issue. This kind of writing is intended to change the way a reader behaves or thinks.

4 Writing to analyse, review or comment
This kind of writing communicates not just your thoughts and opinions, but also your reasons for reaching these conclusions. You could be writing about how a television advertisement uses certain techniques to create a particular image for a product, or reviewing a film, or writing an essay about one of your literature texts.

Different syllabuses have different ways of assessing your skills as a writer. For example, non-fiction writing may be a compulsory piece of coursework, or it may be tested in one of your examination papers. Your handwriting may only be assessed from your coursework. Written work on your reading may be expected to demonstrate some types of writing, too.

In this section, the focus is on how to improve your skills in the different areas of writing summarised here.

Chapter 10
Audience, structure and purpose

Writing does not take place in a vacuum. It is impossible to imagine writing that does not have some communicative purpose – i.e. writing that does not say something. At the same time, the purposes and audiences for your writing are enormously varied. In your coursework alone you could be showing some of these things about yourself:

- that you appreciate literature and understand and enjoy the books, plays and poems you read;
- that you can read and enjoy a long and quite difficult book or play;
- that you can be moved or affected by someone else's personal, imaginative or descriptive writing;
- that you can understand informative and argumentative language, whether you read it or hear it.

And to show this, you might be expected to produce any of these kinds of writing clearly and accurately:

- personal writing about yourself;
- argumentative writing which gives your opinions;
- descriptive writing;
- imaginative narratives or stories of your own;
- writing which sets out instructions for others;
- writing which gives information;
- writing where you imagine that you are a character in a book or play;
- writing which describes a character in a book or play;
- comments about or analysis of what you have read.

10.1 Audience

What is important is that, when you start to write, you have an idea of who your audience is going to be. That knowledge will affect the style you use. You may do this without realising it. Asked to write a simple story for young children you would – almost without thinking – use short sentences and simple words.

But sometimes your audience is more complicated, and you need to think before you write.

Even with a simple subject, you might be surprised to realise how much you modify your language to suit different audiences.

Who you are talking to	What you say
Your Audience	***How you modify your language***
Young people	You just wait until September. You'll hate it when you see what the older kids do to the new ones!
Your friends	I'm sick of this place. I just can't wait to get out. The theatre trip will be a laugh, though.
Your class	School is a place where – although we become young adults – we continue to be treated as children.
Your English teacher	I hate school... but your lessons are OK, suppose.
Your headteacher	Dear Miss Whiplash, We the undersigned members of 11PJ would like to be excused from Upper School Assembly on Thursdays because...
Your parents	I need £8.50 for a theatre trip, by yesterday. We've got to go, as it is part of the course.
Old people	Yes, Gran, I know it was harder in your day but you didn't have ten GCSEs and a National Curriculum.
Experts	In the last days of Kevin Keegan, a series of errors in the transfer market rocked the confidence of the team which had dominated English football for twenty years.
Non-experts	Liverpool FC was formed over a hundred years ago and their ground, Anfield Stadium, has become a Mecca for fans of the game.

Putting this into practice

Writing for different audiences

Try writing some of the following to get into the habit of thinking about your audience. Each piece of writing is started for you. Do not try to complete the task, but write enough of it to feel confident with the style required. Write:

❶ The start of a story for five-year-old children about a cat called Celestine and the little girl, Jessica, who owns him.

Hints:

- Write short sentences, use simple words.
- Repeat words from sentence to sentence, rather than referring back with words such as 'he'.
- Use only simple connecting words, like 'and' and 'then'.

> *This is Celestine the cat. Celestine is a big, black cat. This is Jessica. One day Jessica and Celestine went out to play in the park.*

❷ The ending of a speech opposing deer hunting, to be given at a school debate.

Hints:

- Address the audience.
- Use emotive and persuasive language: 'bloody', 'torn apart', 'wicked'.
- Ask questions.

> *Ladies and gentlemen. Imagine the exhausted and cornered deer. Imagine its suffering as the dogs begin to tear it apart. How would you like to watch this sickening and bloody spectacle? How would you feel if your own father or mother enjoyed doing this for pleasure?*

❸ The climax of a ghost story in a teenage novel.

Hints:

- Build up the suspense with short sentences.
- Use descriptive adjectives.
- Hold back surprises.

> *The wardrobe door was open. He knew he had left it shut. There was an unfamiliar odour in the air. It might have been damp earth with a hint of rotting cheese. He could feel the hairs on his neck rising with fear. If only Wayne were here. He would know what to do. Suddenly...*

❹ A letter to the paper about increases in bus fares.

Hints:

- Make it clear what you are concerned about by using simple language and separating points.
- Say exactly what you would like to happen.

> *Our opposition to these fare rises is based on three points: the steepness of the increase, the lack of notice given and the withdrawal of travel cards for school pupils. In our view, the council should...*

10.2 Structure and purpose

There are many purposes for writing. You could be writing to achieve all kinds of results. You may be asked to write in a particular form as well. The purpose for writing is concerned with what you want the writing to achieve and its form is the structure and style which you adopt to make it do that, In practice, that is not as complicated as it sounds. What usually happens is that you select a style of writing once you decide on the purpose or select the purpose once you are given a style. In examinations, it is likely that you will be told which form to use.

Form of writing	Purpose for writing
Form	***Intention***
Autobiography	informing
Letter	persuading
Article	describing
Summary	narrating
Diary	explaining
Poem	instructing
Leaflet	analysing
Poster	comparing
Script	narrating
Notes	exploring
Story	etc
Essay	
etc	

In your coursework, it is important to show some variety of style and purpose, but this will inevitably be limited by the kinds of writing required by your examining group's syllabus.

The purpose of your writing is an important consideration. In the last 'Putting this into practice' task, your purposes were to entertain, to persuade, to frighten and to inform and those purposes dictated the style of your writing.

Here are some examples of how some different writing purposes can affect the style and content of writing.

1 Explore, image, entertain

Writing purposes	Writing features
Imagining and entertaining	• A story structure. • A chronological account (events in their order of occurrence). • An introduction. • Use of adverbs and phrases to describe how things happened. • Variations in pace and sentence length to lead to a climax. • Use of direct speech (the words people say enclosed within speech marks). • Use of familiar description. • The development of characters by description.

Now it began to fit together in the detective's mind. The declining relationship, the boat trip, the sudden push, water and then darkness. "Miss Marple," he said, "I know what you did with the body. Unless I am very much mistaken, the body of your husband Eric rests at the bottom of the Kenilworth Canal!"

2 Inform, explain, describe

Informing	• Clear introduction. • Straightforward sentences and paragraph structure. • Use of subheadings. • Use of facts and figures. • Factual details.

The Kenilworth Canal is eight miles long and runs from Kenilworth Castle to Baginton, on the outskirts of Coventry. A culvert carries the canal under the A46 Warwick by-pass and there is an aqueduct where it crosses the old GMR railway line.

History: Work started on the canal in 1843 when a local employer...

Explaining

- Careful structure in which each piece of information can be understood by reference back to what came before.
- Definition of technical terms and the use of technical language.
- Factual description.
- A strict and formal structure – possibly numbered in some way.

The canal locks operate in this way. Gates hold back a head of water which is released by the operation of what is known as a paddle. When rotated, this opens a sluice, allowing the level of water in the lock to rise or fall. The canal boat rises or falls with the water level and can thus ascend or descend the lock.

Describing

- Longer sentences.
- Use of adjectives and comparisons – similes and metaphors.
- An organisational move from overall description to the specific.

Deep in the heart of leafy Warwickshire lies the tranquil Kenilworth Canal. In the eight miles of countryside through which it slowly wanders, expect to see herons and water fowl in abundance, open fields — golden with corn in the late summer — and to hear only the sounds of nature in full flow. Sometimes the silence is disturbed by the gentle chug of a pleasure boat, brightly decked out in transfers and awash with colour...

❸ Argue, persuade, instruct

Arguing

- A staged series of points.
- Invitations to the reader to agree.
- Factual language.
- An objective style suggesting that 'we' all agree.

There are three clear reasons for restoring the canal. The first is the need to care for a declining environment and all of the bodies involved agree on this because of the danger it currently poses to children and pets. The second is tourism and, in this connection, Kenilworth Council has recently stated that the encouragement of more visitors to the region is its main ambition for the Millennium.

Persuading

- Use of rhetorical language and questions: "Surely you would like to help... would you leave an innocent man in prison?"
- Colourful and descriptive language.
- A personal style, 'you', to create the reader's involvement.

The Kenilworth Canal Preservation Trust needs your help. Please give just a few hours of your time, or a small donation, to help restore this beautiful, old waterway. Don't let more of our local history be lost forever...

Instructing

- A stepped structure with a series of mini-tasks to complete on the way to a specific intention.
- Use of imperatives: "Do this...", to tell the reader what to do.
- Short, clear sentences.
- Factual description to identify information, rather than describe it.

On your arrival at a lock, you should first inform the lock-master of your presence. Do this by ringing a bell or sounding your hooter. In busy periods, moor your boat first. When invited to proceed, enter the lock very slowly and stop your boat within two metres of any other craft in the lock. Then wait for further instructions.

4 Analyse, comment, review

Analysing

- A paragraphed structure in which each paragraph deals with a particular aspect.
- References to what is being analysed, either through summary (a shortened version), quotation (the words of an original) or anecdote (your version of something in the original).
- An introduction setting out the extent of the analysis, and a conclusion which sums up its findings.
- Longer sentences to cope with the complexity of the analysis and to make points supported by reference.

While a worthy ambition, the reopening of the Kenilworth Canal poses some serious engineering problems. The culvert (see fig. 14) is in a poor state of repair and has been losing water into the surrounding ground for some time. The consultant's report suggests that it will cost £70,000 to renovate this stretch, and additional funding will be required to bring the railway crossing up to standard.

Reviewing and commenting

- A structure where ideas or facts are weighed or evaluated.
- Complex sentences, using a wide range of connectives and connecting phrases: 'nevertheless', 'on the other hand', 'but', 'in contrast'.
- Reference to support a point of view, often given as quotation or anecdote.
- An introduction, stating the scope of the review, and an evaluative conclusion to list its findings.

While the renovation of the Kenilworth Canal is attractive, the large sum of money involved might be better spent elsewhere on the Kenilworth Steam Railway. While the canal may be used by boats and hikers, in the future it should be noted that the canal project is starting from scratch. Its success is by no means guaranteed.

10.3 Structuring and organising writing

You will have noticed how the choice of an appropriate audience and purpose actually has much to say about the way that it should be structured and organised. In fact, it is those factors which should determine the structure of a piece of writing. The punctuation is a different matter.

Any piece of writing is certain to have some structure. For all grades at GCSE you have to set work out clearly, so as to make sense to the reader. For the higher grades you are expected to start to make some conscious decisions about structuring as you work.

Putting this into practice

Developing a structure

Study the map on p.147 and the accompanying information about popular places for tourists to visit in the British Isles. Then complete the task on p.148.

Notice how the task expects you to be able to:

- sort out what information should go in each section;
- write in the form of a leaflet and to a specific number of words;
- write for a specified audience – tourists;
- write with a specific purpose – to inform them of what is available in a descriptive way.

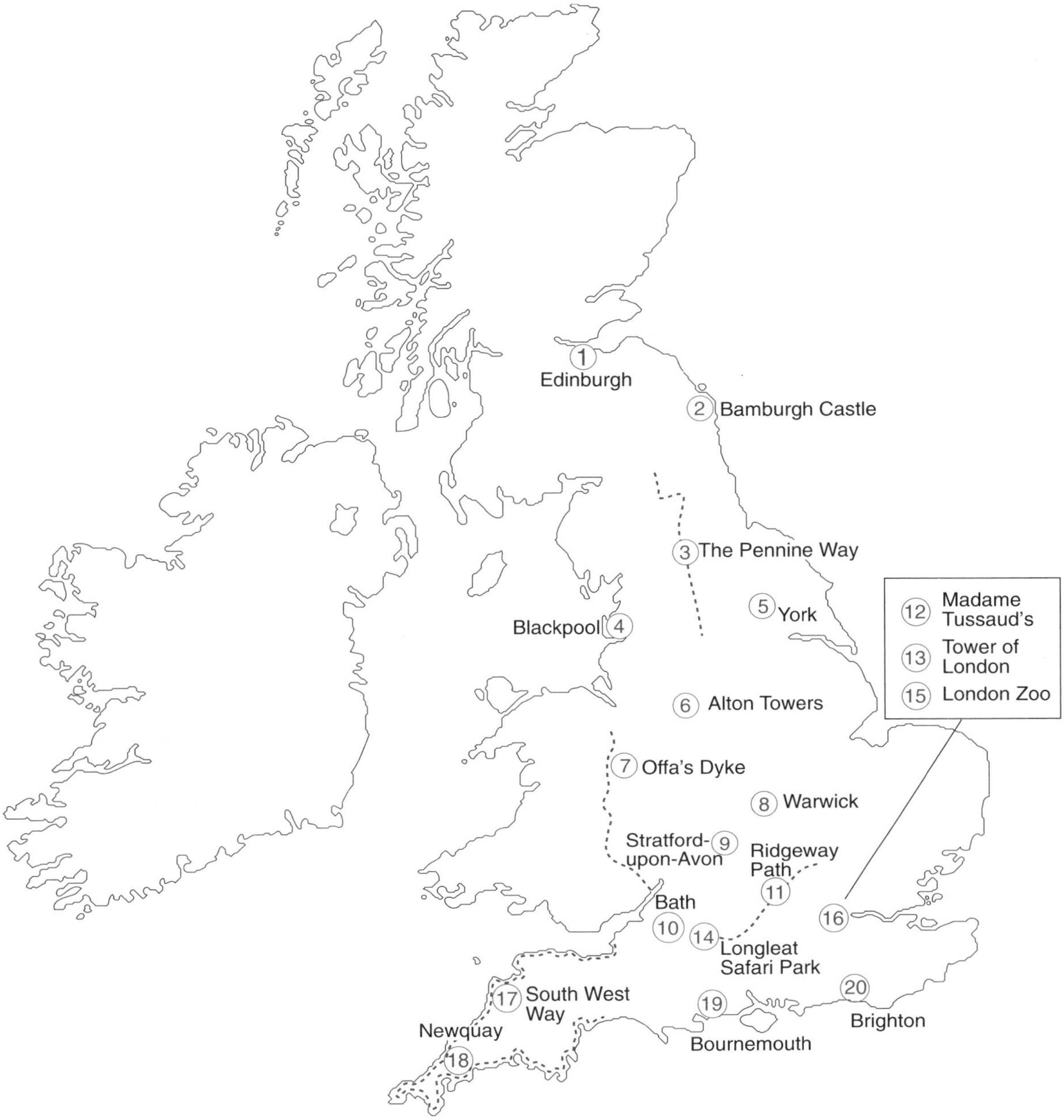

What is important in completing a task like this is that you are shown to be thinking about the structure you are going to employ. Leaflets, posters and reports are all good examples of tasks where thinking about structure is vital.

① **Edinburgh** was built in an area of deep canyons. Steep winding streets look down over rooftops and up to the Edinburgh Castle battlements. Parts of the castle date from 1100. In one room Mary Queen of Scots gave birth to James I of England in 1566. Throughout the city, traces remain of such famous citizens as writers Sir Walter Scott and Robert Louis Stevenson. Exploring Edinburgh's streets, especially during the busy August festival period, is a rich experience.

② **Bamburgh Castle, Northumberland** — a scenic castle with splendid views of the coastline.

③ **The Pennine Way** — the most famous path along the backbone of England.

④ **Blackpool**, the entertainment centre of the North, is home to Pleasure Beach – a 40-acre site that's famous for its 360 degrees roller coaster, the first in Europe. Blackpool is convenient for touring the lovely Lake District and the ancient walled city of Chester.

⑤ **Jorvik Viking Centre, York** — A celebration of Viking England and a trip through a re-creation of Viking life.

⑥ **Alton Towers, Staffordshire** — Leisure park.

⑦ **Offa's Dyke Path** — runs through the Welsh border country.

⑧ **Warwick Castle** — Superb grounds. Claims to be the best preserved castle in England.

⑨ **Stratford-upon-Avon** — Shakespeare's birthplace. Home of Royal Shakespeare Theatre. (Performances at 1.30 and 7.30)

⑩ **Bath** is the site of an ancient Roman spa built round warm mineral springs and dating from AD44. The city is an elegant showcase for Georgian architecture with magnificent examples of crescents and terraces, and some beautiful gardens.

⑪ **Ridgeway Path** — runs through the Chiltern Hills.

⑫ **Madame Tussaud's, London** — world-famous waxworks.

⑬ **The Tower of London** — London's historic castle.

⑭ **Longleat Safari Park, Wiltshire** — the first safari park in England, famous for lions.

⑮ **London Zoo** — One of the biggest animal collections in the world.

⑯ **London** is filled with history, pageantry and entertainment. Discover its rich and glorious past, visit Westminster Abbey, Buckingham Palace and the Tower of London. Take a river cruise up the Thames to Hampton Court or down the Thames to Greenwich where 'The Cutty Sark' is moored. Check out museums and galleries. Wander round Covent Garden's piazza and stroll through the City with its fine skyscrapers. Find London on foot with the 'Wimpy Walks Guide' to local sites which is available free from the British Tourist Board.

⑰ **South West Way** — 515 miles of coastal paths around Devon and Cornwall.

⑱ **Newquay** in Cornwall is Britain's main surfing centre. Its scenery features headlands and sandy beaches with plenty of nightlife for the young and young at heart.

⑲ **Bournemouth** on the south coast is a year-round resort with the best sunshine record in Britain. "Bournanzas" are short breaks with full board.

⑳ **Brighton** is ideal for seaside weekends. If the ocean is too cold try the King Alfred Leisure Centre with tropical pools, badminton and sauna.

Your task:

A leaflet using this map and entitled 'British Holidays' is to be made for the British Tourist Board. It will have separate sections on these subjects:

Historic Britain
Sea, Sand and Surf
Out and About

Your task is to write the copy (the writing) to go in this leaflet. The purpose of the leaflet is to give the tourist an attractive impression of the range of holiday activities that Britain has to offer. Do not write a set of lists or copy out the information. Keep each section separate and write about 150 words for each.

Chapter 11
Using standard English

There is a definition of standard English in Section Two. Standard English is the accepted form for writing in English. Using standard English means that people share word meanings, construct sentences in the same way, and use the same spellings. This has not always happened. Shakespeare, for example, wrote his plays out in longhand (his own handwriting) and they were then copied by other people. His spellings vary from one copy of his plays to the next and he often spelled the same word differently. So did the people who made copies of his work. In modern terms, Shakespeare would not be classed as an excellent speller but, in those days, there was less agreement about how words should be spelled. In fact, it was not until the invention of the dictionary – about a hundred years after Shakespeare died – that anyone thought anything of correct spelling and it is only with the widespread use of printing that spelling has become a cause for concern.

However, as far as your writing is concerned, standard English is what most people would call 'correct' English. That means the choice of words is appropriate, the way they are linked together into sentences makes sense and the punctuation and spelling is accurate. Remember that 'correct' English is not the same as 'good' English. Writing which is poorly organised or lacks any focus on the audience or the purpose for writing will not communicate anything to the reader – whether or not it is written correctly.

For example, if you were writing your leaflet for tourists and you used a lot of long words which they were unlikely to understand and used very long, complex sentences which were difficult to follow, you could well fail to communicate with your readers, even though you were writing correctly.

11.1 Improving your use of standard English

How can you improve the way in which you write standard English? This is a difficult question to answer. All the English teaching you have ever experienced has been directed towards doing exactly that. Speaking, listening, reading and writing standard English over a lifetime of education will all help you to become more familiar with this kind of language and more accustomed to using it. But what can you do to improve your use of standard English in a short time, when you have an examination to face in a few months or weeks? Below is one way to approach the problem. Look on it as a 'crash course' in standard English.

Read standard English

The best way to take in new ways of speaking and writing is to read good examples. Start off by reading a quality newspaper each day or read some highbrow magazines. This does not mean you have to read about difficult subjects. Look for clear accounts and descriptions and study them as you read. Concentrate on how words and sentences are linked and pick out phrases which you find particularly effective and you could use in your own writing.

Speak to standard English users

Make the effort to talk to people who use standard English themselves. What you must try to do is to have conversations with people other than your good friends or those in the same group at school. Asking people their views is a good way to start. Joining a new club or society could turn out to be excellent examination preparation!

Review your own writing style

Look at how you write. You will probably find that you write standard English with mistakes in it. These are likely to be of four kinds – tense errors, agreement errors, punctuation confusion or omission, and misspellings.

❶ Tense errors

The use of a tense in writing tells the reader when something happened – in the past, the present or the future. A tense is a form of a verb – an action word. The word changes to show when the action takes place. The use of tenses is more complex in writing that in speech. Young children, when they start writing for the first time, often only use the present tense:

> *My name is Amy. I go to school. I am in Mrs Wilson's class. My friend is Polly. We paint. Sometimes we play in the sand.*

But if Amy looked back on her schooldays, she might write in a more complicated way:

> *I recall the time when I was in Mrs Wilson's class. She was a kind teacher and I look back on those days with pleasure. I had a friend called Polly and we used to play together. Sometimes we painted and at others we played in the sand pit. Looking back, how I wish that we had received structured lessons in standard English. Then I could have gone to university and I would no longer have to spend my days working behind the counter at Joe's Cafe. Taking my examinations would have helped me to achieve something in my life.*

What you should notice here is that what Amy has to say has placed a greater demand on the tenses she is using.

Putting this into practice

Using tenses

- Read the letter on p.151 sent to a magazine by Wayne. Write a reply to it answering Wayne's questions and giving some helpful advice. You will need to use a range of tenses.
- Think about a place you have visited on holiday. Imagine that it has been hit by a natural disaster – an earthquake or flooding, for example. Then think about how it might be restored, rebuilt or changed in the future. Write an article for a magazine about how the place was, what happened to it and what will have to be done in the future.
- Write about what happened in a situation where you ended up feeling rather embarrassed. Make it up if you like! Then write about what you wish you had done as the situation developed. Lastly, write about what you will do if it happens again!

Dear Jackie

Two weeks ago I went on holiday to Majorca and met this gorgeous girl called Mandy. We spent a wonderful week together going to discos and partying the night away and I thought that our relationship would last forever. Then, I found her at the disco with a man called Pedro who worked in the hotel. She said he was her brother but they were not behaving in a very brotherly way! The next day she apologised and said I was silly for being so jealous. I forgave her at once.

When we left, she promised to write to me but has not done so. I wrote to the address she gave me but I have had no letter from her. I am also a bit worried because I seem to have mislaid my bank card and today I had a letter from the manager saying I am £200 overdrawn although I thought I was £100 in credit. Do you think I have been taken for a ride? What should I do?

Confused of
Shepherds Bush, London W12

Doing exercises like these and practising writing will not on their own help you to use tenses more effectively. You need to think about *how* you are using them and watch out for tense use in your writing as well. This is especially important when you revise your work.

2 Concord errors

One of the most common forms of mistake in the use of standard English concerns concord or agreement errors where the use of a singular or plural word is not followed up later in the writing. Correct this piece of writing yourself. There are many mistakes including concord and tense errors.

> *Trevor and me was going to the park when we come across a gang of bikers. They was obviously looking for trouble. The leader were a huge bloke about seven feet high and all of the gang were nearly as tall. I were ready to run but Trevor stays put. The gang got off their bike and the leader walks towards me. "Is there a McDonalds near here, please?" he asked us.*

Of course, these are obvious errors and you will easily have spotted them. But watch out for other examples, where a singular word describes a number of people or things, as in the words 'range' or 'variety'.
e.g. The **range** of portable CD players available **is** quite limited.

3 Punctuation errors

The best way to improve the punctuation of your written work is to revise it carefully. One way to do this is to read it aloud in your head because most punctuation marks are just ways of showing in writing the pauses and emphases we make in speech. These are common errors to watch out for. Make sure you don't make these mistakes!

- Using commas where you should use full stops:
  I got up late, I had a shower and then went down for breakfast, my uncle was there and asked if I wanted to go fishing.
- Forgetting to use capital letters:
  We went to the river in his car. it was a long way, he told me about the biggest fish he ever caught.

- Forgetting to use commas, speech marks and apostrophes:
  I was on holiday he said and I thought it would be good to spend some time fishing as there had been quite a lot of rain and it wasnt very warm.
- Forgetting that for each new speaker you start a new line; omitting question marks:
  "What did you catch" I asked. "Was it a salmon" "No," he answered, "but it was nearly as big."

④ Spelling errors

If you have problems spelling, remember these basic tips to help you.

- When you revise, if you are not sure about a spelling, look it up in a dictionary. If your teacher advises you to check work, make sure that you do. *Always check as you re-draft coursework.* Get used to knowing when a word 'looks' right.
- In an examination, it is worth avoiding words which you know you always get wrong! If you always write 'recieve' when you mean 'receive', get used to writing another word or phrase instead. If you know that you have problems with spelling words like these, look out for them when you revise and check your writing.
- Keep a spelling book containing words you find difficult and new words. Look at it regularly when you write. This will help you with your vocabulary-building as well.
- Learn spelling rhymes and memory tips. Remember 'I before E except after C' and that the difference between 'practice' and 'practise' isthe same as between 'advice' and 'advise' (the first is a noun and the second a verb in each case).
- Learn about word-roots and words from other languages to help improve your word-building skills.
- Never misspell words you have been given as part of an examination paper or the names of characters in books you have in front of you.
- Don't scrawl over words in an examination and hope that the examiner will think you had the answer. An illegible spelling is a wrong spelling and you could lose marks for untidy presentation.

Putting this into practice

Using punctuation

Write out this story in standard English with the correct punctuation and then continue it for about a page of writing. Make sure there is plenty of conversation.

> *Mandy and me was at the shops on a Saturday evening to get a lottery ticket for her mum and her aunt when we seen a fire engine with his siren going heading down her street. Then it stops outside her house and all these firemen rush out. We run back and seen flames shooting out of the kitchen window. "Oh no, not my chips!" shouted Mandy.*

If, after completing this exercise, you are confused about the rules which govern punctuation ask your teacher for help. In an examination, don't be afraid to put in more punctuation – rather than less – especially where the breaks between sentences are concerned.

You can find more advice about slips you might make in your use of standard English on p.46. There is further comment about punctuation and vocabulary on pp.193–4.

Chapter 12

Revising your writing

There is extra advice on drafting and re-drafting, or revising, your work in Sections Five and Six. In fact, in all your English work you should always take the time to stand back and review what you have done. Starting with notes or a plan and then re-drafting allows you to change and improve what you write as you go along. In this sense, re-drafting means more than correcting your mistakes. In your writing, you will probably be expected to show that you can re-draft work.

12.1 The re-drafting process

Imagine that you have been asked to write about your favourite television programme, saying what it is and explaining what you like about it.

❶ **Your plan** Decide what the programme will be and make some brief notes about it. Notice how the notes should be structured to allow you to group information as you think.

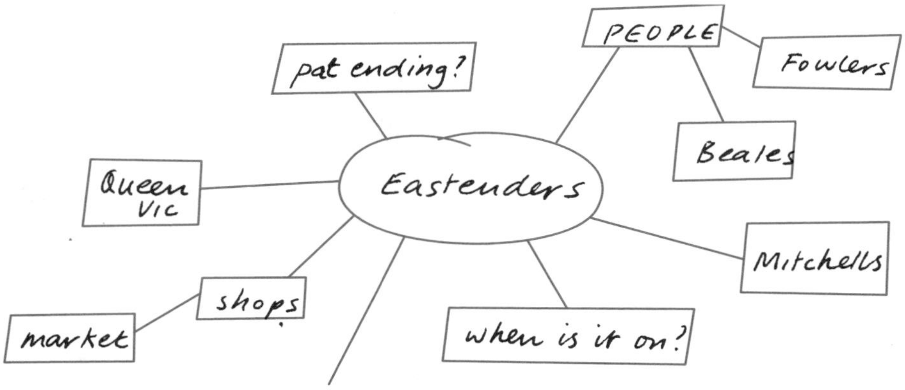

❷ **Reviewing your plan** Are you answering the question you have been asked? Are you saying too much about the the programme and not enough about what you like about it? You can easily modify the plan. It would be much harder if this were a piece of finished writing.

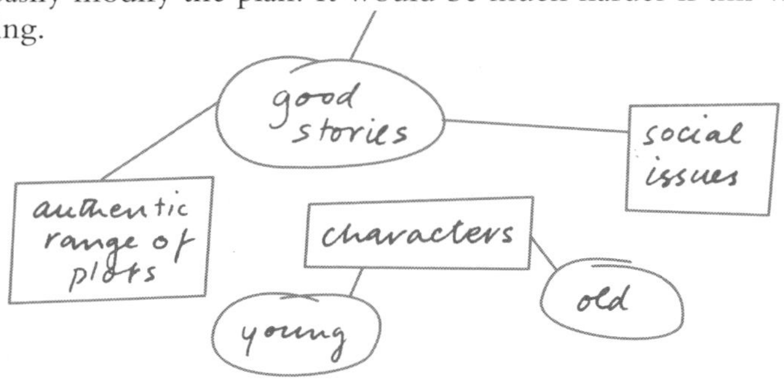

❸ **Writing the first draft** Don't worry too much about the introduction at this stage, but try to get involved in the writing. Don't worry about minor errors either – focus on what you want to say.

The most important family used to be the Fowlers. Arthur and his wife ----- and their son ---- and their daughter Michelle. They lived in a small house on the square. But Arthur has now died and Michelle has left the series. Their son is H.I.V. positive and has also recently left. They will be hard to replace.

❹ **Revising the first draft** Look for areas of your plan which you have neglected. See if there are obvious omissions in what you have written so far. Is the balance of the writing all right? Add new sections or paragraphs and write them out on fresh paper or at the end of the draft. Work hard on your introduction and the conclusion to your writing. Ask a friend or a teacher to read your work so far and comment on it for you.

If you have made a lot of changes or the writing is beginning to look messy, you may want to make a second draft before you start revising the writing in detail.

I like the way that the programme tackles ^social issues like unemployment ^and AIDS. It does not take sides over things but shows them as they really are. One character's business has just gone ~~bust~~ bankrupt but he is planning to start again.

Another character has just got pregnant by ^her boyfriend who was a homosexual. It asks the question about whether he should ~~of~~ have told her.

❺ **Looking closely at your writing** Do **two** specific things:

- **Add** extra linking words, new paragraph beginnings, descriptions or phrases to sum up where you have got to. All of these will make your writing more interesting and readable.
- **Check** your use of standard English, your punctuation and your spelling. Look closely at the names of people you have mentioned.

'Eastenders' is probably the most successful 'soap opera' ever to appear on British television. Screened three times a week, it has overtaken 'Coronation Street' as the preferred viewing for millions of teenagers. In this essay, I intend to explore its popularity and its continuing success.

6 **Writing the final draft** Head the writing correctly with the title you have been set. Take your time and think as you write. This is not just a fair copy. While you are writing, think about the effect you want to have on the reader.

Practise redrafting in all of your coursework and don't be afraid to go to two or even three drafts if the work is unusually complex. Remember that almost all of the printed material you see around you – articles, reports, advertisements and so forth – is the product of many drafting sessions and long discussions between the writers, editors and clients.

12.2 Handwriting and presentation

One of the requirements of the National Curriculum is that you show that you can write neatly and legibly. All syllabuses ask you to show this in at least one piece of coursework. The marks involved are unlikely to make a significant difference to your final grade but there are plenty of other good reasons for writing neatly, so practise neat handwriting as a habit.

If your handwriting is generally untidy and hard to read, think about modifying your style. Look at other people's handwriting and copy styles you like. If it is really bad, get a book to help you form letters from scratch, but only do that in a crisis situation! You will be surprised what a few weeks of concentration can achieve, especially if you are prepared to buy a new pen and to write a little more slowly. And, if your handwriting gives you real problems, use a word processor for as many assignments as you are allowed – usually all the pieces but one.

Your folder can also be given credit for its presentation. Try to include one piece of work where presentation is a feature. If you write a report, use subheadings and diagrams. If you write a children's story, a poster, a leaflet or a playscript set it out like one with different sizes of writing and make sure that it is appropriately spaced on the page.

Examiner's tip

This section should have raised your awareness about some very important, and widely misunderstood points about written English language:

- There is no 'bad' English, there is not 'right' and 'wrong' English. But there is English which is appropriate or inappropriate for different circumstances.
- Being good at English means being flexible: being able to choose from a variety of styles to suit particular circumstances. Your work should reflect this.
- Some purposes, forms and styles are more difficult to sustain than others. Your final grade will reflect how well you handle the 'difficult' styles. Make sure you do this well.
- Being able to recognise and discuss the styles of your own and other people's writing in a conscious way will improve your final grade.

Preparing your coursework

So far, this book has concentrated on the content of your English course and the kinds of skills you must acquire to be successful. In this section and the next, the focus is different and looks at the ways in which you will be assessed through a mixture of coursework and terminal examination papers. You should remember from Section One that the coursework assessment is less important than the examination in determining your final result. Nonetheless, a good coursework performance could certainly raise your grade for the subject as a whole.

xaminer's tip

ing well at coursework is best examination paration you can make.

The good news about coursework is that you will have the time to ensure that the work you do for English reflects your best efforts. You will be able to rewrite pieces of work which were not too good in the first place and you will only have to submit the best of your work to the examining group at the end of the course. In other words, the ball is in your court!

The bad news is that you will have to work consistently throughout your course. You will not be able to leave it to the last minute and then redeem yourself by working hard for the examination. If you do not mind doing examinations and are not generally a well-organised person, you may see grave disadvantages in coursework!

It is important as you do your coursework to bear in mind what you are trying to show your assessor. Much of the help this section will give you is concerned with making certain that the coursework you do reflects your abilities and capacities to the full so that you do not sell yourself short in any way. Remember that your coursework says things about your intelligence, your sensitivity to what goes on around you, your ability to communicate with other people and your willingness to learn new skills.

Also, coursework should show you at your best. If you did badly in an examination, you could say you were nervous or that you answered the wrong questions. But coursework allows you the time to make the right choices and to show your best abilities. If you are prepared to work through this section and follow its advice, then you can improve your coursework performance and learn about being a better reader, writer, listener and speaker as well. This section sets out some general steps you might take to do any piece of written coursework well.

Getting organised

Being well organised is the starting point for any piece of coursework. Good organisation involves careful planning of three things: your time, your equipment and the space where you work, as well as a distinctive attitude towards your writing. Do not ignore the first three of these. Many excellent students fail to get the grades they deserve because, although their writing is basically very good, the preparation of their work is hurried and its presentation is scrappy.

Managing time

A problem you are likely to encounter as soon as you start doing coursework is that you will be taking a number of other subjects at GCSE as well as English. These will make demands on your time, with even more coursework. You need to organise your time and you will need a lot of self-discipline to make sure work is not left to the last minute.

You will have to get used to working to deadlines. This is the most important change your GCSE coursework will make to the way you approach classwork and homework. Before you started your GCSE course, if you did not complete your homework you might have ended up in detention, but it probably would not have caused major problems with your school work. English coursework is different! Some deadlines for the handing in of assignments will be set by your teacher. These are not intended to ensure that you die of overwork: they are set to help you to progress through your coursework at a steady rate.

E

Don't miss coursework deadlines. There are no second chances.

If you fail to stick to deadlines, you will find yourself frantically trying to complete work at the end of the course. If you do not manage to complete enough, then you will not gain a grade for the subject. It really is worth sticking to the deadlines your teacher sets, or, better still, planning ahead and getting a piece of work in early if you can see another subject about to demand other coursework from you.

Some more important deadlines are set by the examination group. Sometimes, certain pieces of work have to be completed by certain dates during the course. All GCSE courses give a final date for coursework to be with your teacher for assessment at the end of the course. If you miss that deadline, there are no second chances.

Managing equipment

It is vitally important to make sure that your work is well presented. Not only is good presentation now part of the formal requirement for assessment, but there is little doubt that assessors look more kindly upon work which is neatly written. There is some educational research which shows that teachers and assessors, in all subjects, give higher grades to written work which is neat and legible. Exactly the same work, when untidy and hard to read, was found by the researchers to receive lower grades. That is why this guide encourages you to be tidy and organised in the presentation of your writing – it really is a simple way to improve your marks. It is worth investing in a few basic pieces of equipment to help you look after your coursework properly before you start the course. Even if you have picked up this guide in the middle of the course, now could be the time to get rid of that dog-eared, coffee-stained old folder which lets the edges of your pages get grubby and torn. One of the biggest differences between English and coursework in other subjects is that in English you will do a larger number of short pieces of work. These take more looking after than a couple of long projects.

If you have just moved up from Year 9 into Year 10, you may be used to doing your English work in an exercise book. Working on loose-leaf, A4-sized paper can cause problems, particularly if you are not the world's neatest person, or you are the type who loses things! One of the things to learn about coursework is that you can make your task, and your teacher's job, a lot easier if you are organised and methodical. Being organised and methodical when you are scatty and untidy by nature may not be easy but it will pay dividends.

However, looking after coursework while you are writing it is not as simple as it might seem. Pieces of paper can easily be lost, screwed up, or even destroyed if they are not looked after. You will need the following items. Your school may provide some of them, others you may already have at home.

- **A notebook** for rough notes and early attempts at written work. This is easier to handle than file paper and also gives you a record of your work in case the worst happens and you lose an assignment.
- **A4 punched file paper.** Don't use very thin paper, or notebooks where the top of every sheet in your folder is an ugly tear. Don't use narrow feint (the distance between each line which dictates the number of lines on the page) because, even if your writing is small, there will not be space for teacher comments and corrections. If you can find paper with a printed margin (the line which runs down the left-hand side), so much the better.
- **A strong waterproof file** for carrying assignments to and from school or college is vital. It protects work from rain as well as leakages! It does not have to be fancy – a strong polythene bag and a piece of cardboard to stop your work getting crushed is perfectly adequate. Don't buy the biggest file in the shop, either. Remember you have to carry it around with you.
- **Your own file for storing finished assignments.** Make sure that it has plenty of space in it and that is a true A4 size with overlapping edges to protect your work.
- **A small stapler and a hole punch.** Most of the paper you use will already be punched, but you may want to include working notes or materials which you collected for an assignment – like work on leaflets, for example.
- **An efficient pen with blue or black ink.** The best pens for writing lengthy pieces of work are ink pens with either roller balls or nibs. Fibre-tips are all right but, as soon as they start to age, the ink begins to dry up and they become harder to write with and scratch the surface of the paper. Do not use very cheap ballpoints, felt-tip pens or coloured ink for written work. It may look snazzy at the time, but you will probably feel different about it twelve months later when you are submitting your finished folder.

You may be lucky and find that, once your work is finished and marked, your teacher will keep it safe until the end of the course. This may be disappointing if you want to take a good piece of work home to show around but, in the long run, it does stop work getting lost. A whole set of folders locked up in a school is less likely to disappear than an individual assignment in your bedroom! On the other hand, if the folders are left in an insecure cupboard in a classroom where anyone can rummage through them, you may feel that your work will be safer at home. It is up to you to negotiate this with your English teacher and, once you have agreed on a system, stick to it. So do not say you will keep your work at home and then start leaving it in the classroom cupboard – that is where things can go seriously wrong!

Remember that if you do not have the correct number of pieces of coursework, or include the right types of writing, you will run the risk of not being entered for the examination at the end of the course. If you *are* entered, and then do not have the right work, you may end up having to pay the exam entry fee if it is your fault that work has gone astray – so be careful.

All examining groups now allow the majority of coursework to be completed using a word processor, although they require evidence of your abilities to write using script to be included somewhere in the folder. If you use a word processor, remember to save each draft. Choose a clear font and leave a double space between paragraphs. Leave good-sized margins on the left and right of your writing, and use no more than 80 characters to each line.

Managing space

One other piece of equipment is space. Try to find a reasonable space in which to work at home, so that your coursework is not buried under books and other writing. If you are to do your best you need to give some thought to where and when you will work. For a start, you will need a place at home where you can read. Most of the time, the only requirements for this are a comfortable chair (or a piece of floor, or a bed) and peace and quiet to get on with it. The furniture should not cause too many problems.

Getting the right kind of atmosphere for concentration might be more difficult in some households, though. Wearing headphones to a personal stereo (without music!) is a good way of blocking out unwanted interference and noise.

When it comes to written assignments, or even making notes on your reading, you may have more difficulty finding a good place to work. You will certainly need a desk or table where you can spread out your books and papers. Working on the floor, or with your book on your knee in front of the television, will not help you to do your best work. On the other hand, if you do find a good place to work you should find that your best work is written in your own time, when you are in the right mood, away from the distractions of the classroom.

If you are looking after your own coursework, you will need a drawer or cupboard to keep it in, where you are sure nobody and nothing will be able to interfere with or damage it.

Finally, if you can already see that any of this will cause you problems, do discuss possible solutions with your teacher. Most schools are open long after you leave at night: it may be possible for you to stay behind to work, and arrange somewhere to keep your work there, too, if you feel that it may not be safe at home. The public library is also a good place to find some peace and a big table.

If you are lucky, you will have a room of your own at home where you can organise and keep your work, but do not despair if you have not: plenty of people get good GCSE grades by using their ingenuity to create the right working conditions. You can, too, if you are determined enough.

Approaching a coursework task

You have been in an English lesson. Your group has read a story and done some discussion about it in small groups. Towards the end of the lesson, the teacher tells you you are to do a piece of writing, using some of the ideas from the story. There is a choice between writing another story, a diary entry or a piece about the characters in the story. You are given a sheet of written guidelines and your teacher leads a brief discussion about good ways to start, warns you of problems you might encounter in the work and discusses ways to deal with them.

Then you are told you have tonight's homework, the next English lesson in school and another homework to complete the task. It is to be handed in a week on Friday.

Now you have sorted out your equipment and divided up the time you have been allowed, it is time to think about the subject of your writing. This is the kind of approach you should adopt.

The first homework

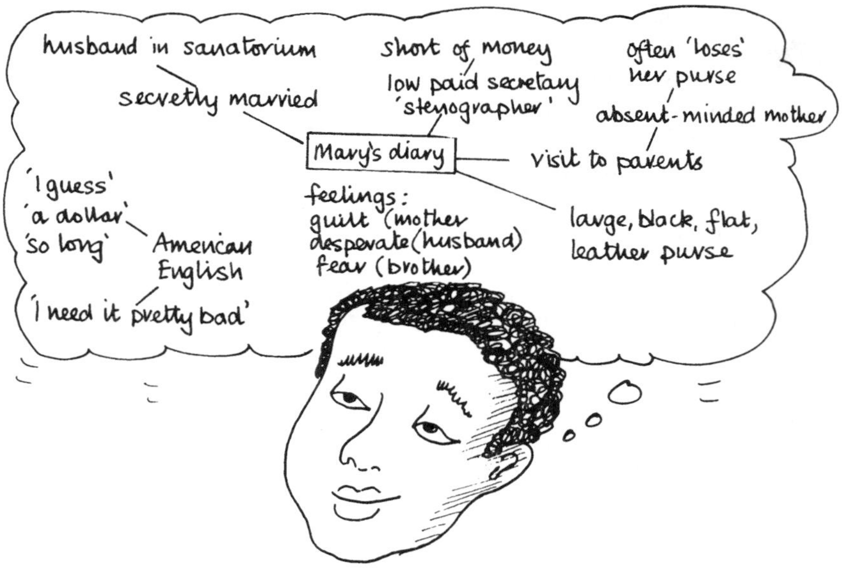

If you are the type of person who can think better at home (or in the place you have chosen for out-of-school work), use this homework time to get some rough ideas for the assignment down on paper. The last thing you should be worrying about at this stage is how long it is meant to be. Concentrate on what needs to be included: this is much more important.

There are a number of ways of approaching a piece of written work, depending partly on the kind of writing it is, but also depending on how your mind works, too.

Some people like to begin with a preparatory activity like brainstorming, where you write down any and every idea that occurs to you, or collect linked ideas together on a spider-plan.

If your mind works better in straight lines, then you might start off by making a list of a sequence of connected ideas.

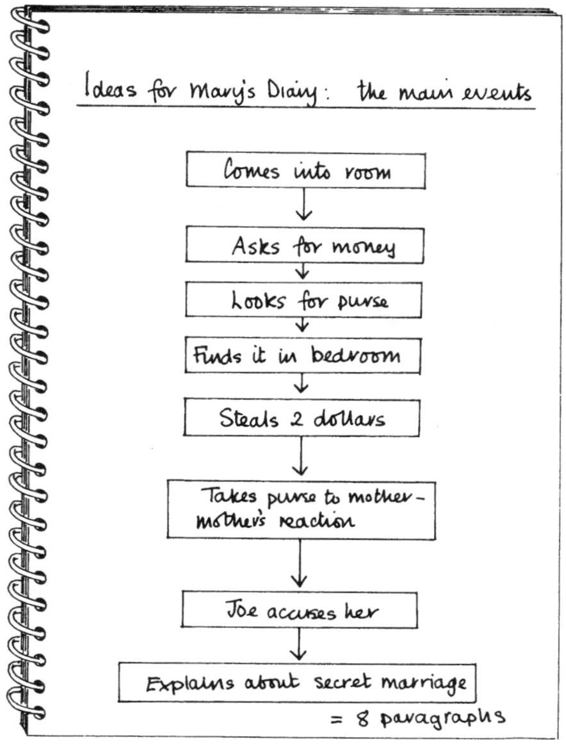

You could re-read the original story quite quickly and jot down ideas as they come to you.

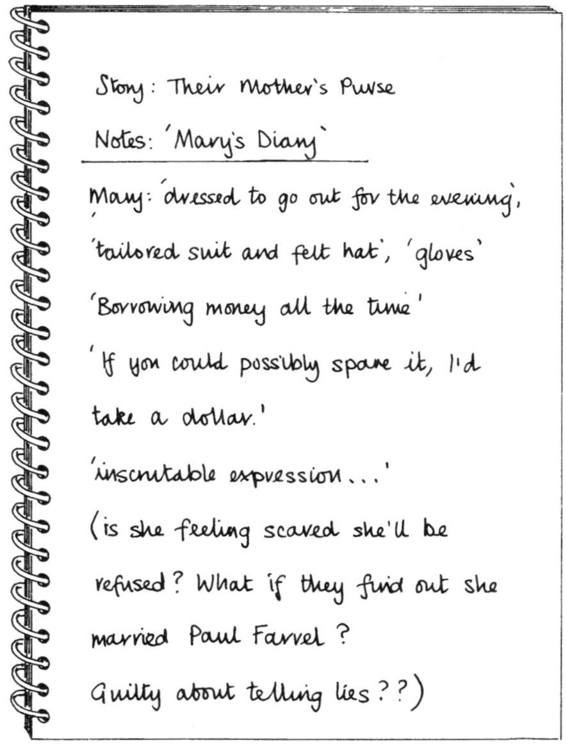

Some tasks lend themselves to one of these approaches in particular, but you should try them out and decide which one suits you best. You will notice that in all these alternatives you have been asked to write something and not just to think. That is because, as you write, you are taking the first steps towards organising your thoughts on paper. Next, you could:

Go on to decide what will go into each paragraph. You could number the random ideas from your spider-plan into a sensible order for writing.

'Scan' read the story (this is where you read quickly in order to find particular information, like looking for a character's name) and write down brief passages which you might be able to incorporate in your work.

You could have several attempts at good opening and closing paragraphs. These will not necessarily be the ones at the beginning or the end of your notes! Starting a piece of writing is often the hardest part of the whole process. Doing it this way, you have not wasted a whole hour trying, and failing, to get started!

Remember that even this work is best done on A4 paper. Scraps of paper are too easily lost: you may even screw up and throw away the beginnings of a good idea if you do preparatory work on smaller sheets. Also, all of this work is valuable. You do not know yet which parts of it you will be able to use or improve later, so keep it all.

Examiner's tip

Making notes

- Notes are NOT the same as scribble and they should never be done in an untidy scrawl. They need to be easy to read, so write them neatly.
- Space your notes clearly. DON'T cramp your notes on the page, because you will have to add to them as you go on. You will need space for this.
- DON'T copy out large chunks of writing. When you write notes about something, use your own words where possible to show that you are making sense of what you read.
- By the end of the time allocated to your homework, you will have something concrete down on paper and your mind will be applying itself to the assignment. Notice that there is a big difference between worrying and planning! If a good idea strikes you before the next lesson, make sure that it is added to your notes.

The lesson

Here is a chance to start writing your first draft when you will have help available if you need it.

First, turn your notes into a first draft of your assignment. Do a bit of thinking first. Have you got your ideas into the right order to commit them to paper?

Think about the type of writing you are about to undertake and decide what would be an appropriate style to suit the task and your intended reader. Is this a story which, like an essay or composition, needs to be written in a very formal style? Or is it something more like a diary entry, where a more colloquial (conversational) style would be appropriate?

- Begin with a suitable and interesting introduction. Try to get your reader's attention by being slightly unusual.
- Organise your ideas into well-formed paragraphs, each of which links logically and smoothly with the next one.
- Try to end with a suitable conclusion. Be careful not to let your writing fade out into a weak ending.

At this stage, do not worry if you need to cross out and correct details, or even begin a short section again if you are unhappy with the first attempt. However, do make sure that this version could be read and made sense of by someone else. It goes without saying that you need to take care with spelling and punctuation. No matter how brilliant the quality of your ideas, you will lower your final grade if your writing skills are weak technically.

Read through what you have written at the end of the lesson, correct spelling and punctuation errors and rephrase ideas which are clumsily expressed. Identify words which do not feel quite right for the style you have adopted, or places where your sentence structures seem awkward. Mark any words that you ought to check in a dictionary. If you cannot think of ways to improve the writing yourself, make a pencil note in the margin that it needs further thought and perhaps discussion with your teacher.

Examiner's tip

Keep your drafts tidy. Write as legibly as normal and leave space for revisions.

Getting help from your teacher

Examiner's tip

Don't be tempted to use anyone else's work in your coursework. Experienced moderators will catch you out and the penalties are severe.

Towards the end of the lesson – not when the bell has gone – is a good time to ask your teacher to read the draft through and give you some guidance about the things you need to improve. However, the examination groups have strict rules about the amount of help you may be given with some coursework, by teachers or by anyone else. This is necessary in order to be fair to everyone and to ensure that the work you are assessed on really reflects your ability.

Your teacher is not supposed to:
- correct spelling;
- correct punctuation;
- rephrase sentences for you;
- tell you what to include when you rewrite.

But your teacher is allowed to:
- discuss your work with you;
- give you guidance;
- suggest briefly other ideas you might include in the final draft;
- point out repeated errors and factual slips;
- give you an idea of the grade the work is worth in its present draft and how much you could realistically hope to improve it by a re-draft.

So, for example, your teacher could say, 'The style of your introduction is too colloquial and the spelling is shaky in the final paragraph' but not, 'deceive has the "e" before the "i" ' or, 'say that the book is "entertaining", not "loadsa fun".'

Essentially, your teacher must not add to the quality of the work, but he or she can tell you where, and generally how, you might improve it. Examination groups allow general comments of this sort to be written on pupils' rough drafts. Now that drafting is a highlighted aspect of the writing course, it is essential that your teacher sees your work and comments on it – however briefly – before you continue.

Examiner's tip

Writing the final draft
- Like this guide, most examination groups recommend the use of A4 paper. Use it unless you have a particular reason for using another size to suit a particular type of writing.
- Unless you have a really good reason not to, write on both sides of the paper. Don't be wasteful: you will use a lot of paper on this course.
- Remember that several people will have to read the assignment, not just your own teacher, who is used to your usual scrawl! So keep your handwriting neat. It can affect your results!
- Use black or blue ink, unless you have a particular reason for working in pencil or some other colour.
- Remember that bad word processing – big gaps, poor punctuation, faint print – is as hard to read as poor handwriting and that the word processor shows up spelling mistakes and an absence of punctuation very clearly. Typographical slips may count as much against you as spelling mistakes.
- Avoid the use of correcting fluid: it can look as if you have altered work after marking, and writing on top of it often fades over a period of time.

The second homework

By now, you should see where you are going. Your first draft has been looked at by your teacher. Only if you, or your teacher, feel that the first draft was absolutely disastrous should you need to do a second draft. At this point, your writing 'goes public', so you need to bear a few more points in mind as you begin the final draft.

To begin with, always head assignment pages carefully. This should become a habit and be the first thing you do when you begin a final draft. If you do not do it properly each time you write, it will take you hours to sort all your work out at the end of the course.

The front page should have your **name**, the **date** (including the year because this is a two-year course) and the **full title** plus an assignment number, if required. You must include details of any titles and authors' names if your assignment is based on literature you have read. Writing out the title might seem a waste of time but it will help you to

► 20/11/96 ► 9a

► Mary Farrel's Secret Diary
(based on the short story "Their Mother's Purse")

► Sharon Wright

ENGLISH COURSEWORK FOLDER

► Diary writing, based on
a literary text.

► Story read and discussed in class.
2 homeworks and one double
lesson in school for writing.

fix your mind on the exact task you are to undertake, as well as making your work easier for other people to assess. It makes sense to put your tutor group and the name of your school, too.

Because you have to show coverage of varied aspects of writing for the GCSE, it is important to make sure that the nature of the task you have been set is clearly noted. Writing down 'Work based on *Lord of the Flies*' is not enough. You must say whether you are writing a character study, a story, an empathic account, or whatever.

Each page should have at the top the date (including the year, as this is a two-year course) your name and the assignment number. Not all the examination groups ask for these, and if your syllabus wants anything more, your teacher will tell you. Of course, it also makes sense to number your pages.

Some schools develop their own cover sheets for assignments. These are duplicated forms which are used as the top page for an assignment and include spaces for all the details mentioned above. An example of one is shown above. You could adapt and use this to make sure that you include all these details on the front sheet every time.

Examiner's tip

As you write, check the following:

- Your opening paragraph should have clear links with the title and should set the tone and style for what follows.
- Ensure that the paragraphing you checked in your first draft is maintained, or improved.
- If you were dissatisfied with any parts of your work, uncertain about the style or you need to add sections to make the final draft more complete, you should experiment with these sentences or paragraphs in a notebook before committing them to paper.
- Make sure your conclusion still has a connection with the title. Do not let your work wander off the point.
- When you think that you have finished, have a last read-through to check for careless errors. Remember the warning about correcting fluid. A tidy crossing-out and correction may well be better.
- Number your pages, staple them together and take your completed assignment to your teacher, clean and tidy in your waterproof folder.

Your coursework folder

Organising your folder

Whether your work is stored at school or kept at home, it will help you to ensure you are working towards the grade you want if you keep an index of the assignments you have completed and the marks you get for each piece of work your teacher assesses.

After reading Section One carefully, you will know that the examining groups are quite precise in stating not only **how many** but also **what kind** of coursework assignments you need to do to gain a grade.

It is true that only your best work is assessed at the end of the course, but it is also true that your folder must contain examples of a wide variety of types of written work to meet these syllabus demands. So, you may be a brilliant writer of imaginative stories, Grade A or B every time, but if you find close-reading assignments or media work difficult, your hopes of a high grade may be dashed if your syllabus states that you must include one or two pieces of work done in this way.

It is the same with work on literature: you may gain high marks for your work on Shakespeare's plays, but find that the marks are lower for reading assignments which include books you have chosen and read for yourself. If your syllabus says you have to include one of each, then you will have to work hard to raise your grades in the weaker areas of your work.

The lesson to learn is that you certainly cannot avoid having to do work you find difficult: if you do, you run the risk of not being entered for the examination at all. Careful indexing and organisation will help you to see the gaps and identify which aspects of your coursework will repay extra effort.

Your index should be divided into sections which reflect the kinds of writing on which your syllabus requires you to be assessed. A good index does three things:

❶ It highlights those sections where you are very short of work.

2. It highlights those sections where your grades are low, so you will know where improvement is needed.
3. At the end of your course it will help you to sort out which piece, or pieces, of work from each section will be the best to submit for your final assessment to ensure the highest grade possible.

When you are looking after your own folder, you may find it useful to separate different types of writing, using cardboard dividing pages. You may well have difficulty telling which kind of writing is which. Don't worry that you find this difficult. It is complicated, and some pieces could go in more than one section. Ask your teacher for help if you are not sure because, if you don't know this, you will have no way of telling where you are going wrong or which areas of your English work are weak and need some extra effort. Once you have identified your weak points, then you can pay special attention to those particular types of assignment.

Preparing for the examination

Before the introduction of National Curriculum assessment, it was possible to get a GCSE in English or in English Literature without taking an examination paper. Now, not only must you take examination papers, but how well you do will have a considerable effect on your final result. However good your teacher's assessment of Speaking and Listening is, and however well you have done on your coursework, the examination is a hurdle you have to cross.

Even if you dislike examinations, it is important to remember that, if you are well-prepared, they should contain few unexpected and unpleasant surprises. The purpose of this section is to help you to take the examinations in your stride.

There are three things to concentrate on if you want to do well in examinations:

- preparation;
- organisation;
- practice.

Preparation

You should be preparing for your examination almost from the first day of your course. As you learn something, it is important to store that information in a form which you can draw on later, when you are revising for the final examination. As you work, you need to get used to answering the types of questions at the kind of speed that will be required in the final examination. There are also some basic things which you need to find out about early in the course.

What does the terminal examination consist of? How many papers are there? How long are they? Do they ask many short-answer questions, or fewer questions which require longer answers? Do they give stimulus material for you to work from on the paper, or in an anthology which is sent to schools in advance of the examination date? Examination papers are usually given titles and these give you an indication of what they test as well as which attainment targets they cover. All of this information is in your examination syllabus, but it is something you need to be familiar with from the start.

What special requirements are there? Some examination papers are now based on an anthology of material. This is issued to schools before the date of the examination and some of the questions asked in the examination are based on it. Others use less material but it is still **pre-released** – given out in advance of the examination.

Organisation

Examiner's tip

Start planning early. Obtain past, or sample, question papers well in advance.

As you go through your course, it is vital to make sure that you know what you have done and what remains to be done. This is as important for the examination as it is for your coursework, because you must make sure that you have rehearsed all the skills that you are likely to be asked to show in the examination. Collect sets of sample papers and start to plan your revision timetable early. Aim to get your coursework out of the way by the spring half-term (the end of February) in the year you are taking the examination. That will allow you enough time to revise and prepare for the examination papers.

Practice

There is a real difference between the techniques you have to use in writing coursework answers and those used in sitting examination papers. Most people would agree that it is easier to do your best in coursework than in the examination. Some advantages of coursework over examinations are listed below:

Coursework	Examination papers
Time to think and plan	Exact time limits make you feel hurried
A chance to revise your writing	Time for only one draft plus corrections
Familiar material	Unseen material
The opportunity to revise spellings and word meanings	No dictionaries are allowed
A chance to consult your teacher	You are on your own
You don't have to submit a weak piece for assessment	You only have one chance

What matters is to make sure that you feel relaxed when you have to work within the constraints of the examination. The way to make sure of this is to practise reading and writing under the kind of pressure you will have to face in the examination room. In class, that may be difficult to achieve. Even if you try to treat a writing task as a test, other people will be asking questions, looking for reference materials or consulting the teacher. So it is important to take every chance you get to work under what are called examination conditions.

Sometimes in the classroom you will be asked to complete an assignment under controlled conditions. This kind of work is a half-way stage between classwork and examination conditions. Unlike an examination set externally, controlled tasks are set by your teacher. He or she chooses the time, the place and the work you are to do. Sometimes all the teachers in an English department may decide to give the whole year group the same task to do at the same time, but they still decide what it should be and also mark the work themselves, so they will be able to give you advice about how to do better next time, which is useful.

You can do controlled work in a manner very like a traditional examination: a time limit on the session and all work to be finished by the end of that time. Some people respond well to that pressure and produce better work under those circumstances. Others, of course, do not. The important thing, however, is that you are not allowed any help from or discussion with the teacher or class before or during the work: the work must be completed while the teacher is supervising you, to ensure there is no discussion or copying. That is why your teacher will have to collect and keep all your work and any stimulus material at the end of each session of work.

You may be allowed to use reference works: a dictionary, a thesaurus, and even notes you have prepared out of school. The assignment you are set will frequently be a piece of work which provides a test of your close-reading skills (like questions designed to test your understanding) and a test of your extended-writing skills (like writing a story or giving an opinion).

Very often, you will be given a fairly lengthy piece of factual writing to read before you begin to write. This could be anything, from a letter to the press, to a newspaper or magazine article (possibly including diagrams or charts adding further information to that in the written part of the article) about a topical issue. You may even be asked to read something persuasive, like the copy of an advertisement or the descriptions of seaside resorts from a holiday brochure.

The tasks will vary a great deal, too, because of the variety of possible things you could be asked to read but there may be a set of questions, either to test that you understood the details of the writing or to focus your attention on some details which you will need to concentrate on in the longer piece of writing you will be asked to do later on. They will tend to be similar to the kinds of tasks you will be set in your final examination.

The tasks you are set can be of several types. Those which ask a set of questions or expect you to write a formal letter are known as **closed assignments**, because you have little choice about what or how you write. In answering them, you will be writing about a certain subject, using a particular type of writing for a specified audience. An **open assignment** asks you to extend the situation or to add to information you have been given. For example, if you had read some holiday brochures you might be asked how you would write something similar to promote the good points about the place where you live.

To test your reading achievement, you may well be set a **literary closed assignment**. For this, the stimulus material will be a passage from a novel, or a whole short story, or maybe an extract from a play, or a poem. The task may be a comparison of any two of these, where a similar subject is discussed from different viewpoints. It may be what is called an 'unseen' passage. That is something you have never seen before: you may not even be told the title or who wrote it, so all you have to go on are the words on the page. On the other hand, it could be a passage from a book you are studying in class, provided your teacher has not told you exactly which passage it is in advance and you have not at any time discussed the task you are set.

xaminer's tip

tice writing against the
: using genuine exam
ers.

For the task itself, you may be asked a number of questions on the passage, either in the way of a traditional comprehension to test your in-depth understanding of the passage, or as preparation for a longer piece of writing to follow. You may be asked to write **empathically**.

As you become familiar with writing under controlled conditions, you will be getting ready to face the problems set by an examination paper, where the limitations on time and the unfamiliarity of the material will make your work that much harder.

The next stage is **examination practice** or **rehearsal**. It is absolutely essential that, towards the end of your course, you take advantage of every opportunity to write under examination conditions. That means working on a number of problems against the clock, in silence and without the help of reference books or your teacher.

Some people believe the old story that you cannot revise for English. It may be true that there are no actual facts to learn, but there are ways of preparing, and things to check up on, which might help to raise your grade.

Doing yourself justice

There are plenty of things which you can do to make sure that an examination shows you at your best. Look on the examination papers as a message to the examiner, saying 'In these few pages I am going to show you all the things in the syllabus which I can do well.' Don't make any of the silly mistakes that your teacher will have warned you about!

DO make sure you have the right pre-released material or anthology with you

DO arrive fresh and relaxed

DO sit back and read the paper through

DO make sure that your pens work

DON'T try to revise all of the night before

DON'T leave too little time to get to the examination – especially when its starting time is different from the time you normally arrive at school

DON'T forget your equipment

DON'T start writing as soon as you turn over the paper

Countdown to the examination

The final countdown to the examination should begin as soon as you have completed your coursework folder. Then is the time to work out a clear timetable for yourself.

❶ When you complete your coursework folder

Photocopy any work which it will be useful for you to have to re-read before the examination. For example, you may well have writing in your folder on the texts which you are studying for the examination.

Get hold of as many sample examination papers and tasks as you can. Your teacher may have these, but they can also be obtained direct from the examining groups for a small charge.

❷ In the next few weeks

Make sure you have detailed revision notes and keep these together.

Take every opportunity you can get for examination practice. Do homework under examination conditions, for example. Set yourself some work from your sample papers.

Assess how well you are doing by looking at the marking criteria (pages 6–8) comparing your performance with what they ask for. Ask your teacher to look through your work.

❸ In the weeks before the examination

Start to learn your notes. If your examination is open-text and you can take copies of the book in with you, then make sure that the permitted annotations are clear to you. Ask your teacher to set you additional work.

Make sure that you understand how the papers are structured and, if necessary, which sections you should answer questions from.

Practise writing examination answers in – at least – one hour blocks.

❹ On the night before

Do a quick last-minute check on any notes you have made.

Check your equipment: take two pens. Don't forget any books that you are allowed to use in the exam.

When you have done your preparation, go out and enjoy yourself, get to bed at a decent time and have a good night's sleep.

❺ On the day

Read through all of the paper, identifying what you have to do. If something about the rubric (the instructions) is unclear, ask the invigilator for help.

Re-read the details of the tasks first, even if they are printed after the written stimulus, so you can think about the tasks as you read the stimulus material. As you read, jot down notes as you read of ideas which you might use when you write. If you are allowed to write on the stimulus materials, underline useful parts.

Don't rush: read the whole thing through, twice if you need to, before you start work on the task. Decide roughly how long to spend on each task or part of a task. Leave time to amend and correct your work. Make sure you stick to this schedule during the examination. An incomplete paper where questions have not been attempted is much more likely to lower your grade than the odd piece of unfinished work.

Start your answer with a very rough draft or a plan. Think hard about the task at this point. Check that you are producing the sort of writing it asks for. Make sure that your plan can be read by the assessor, if necessary.

Allow ten minutes or so at the end to check your work. Marks for examination work are usually lower than for normal classwork, simply because of bad organisation, lack of time and carelessness. Make clear, neat corrections. If you want to insert extra material, use an asterisk at the point in the writing where you want the insert to begin and write it neatly at the end of your answers.

Examination practice

By now it should be clear that there is no substitute for examination practice, especially in the last few weeks leading up to the big day. If your teacher can mark your work for you then so much the better, but even if that is not possible the practice is still vitally important. This is because writing under examination conditions is so different from writing coursework in class. This chapter starts in the examination room but – this time – there is a guiding voice at your shoulder showing you how to think your way through the examination.

It's June. Although it is only nine o'clock it is already quite warm in the sports hall and the sun is beating through the windows behind the wall bars, making regular shadows on the rows of examination desks set out all around you. The examination paper is face down in front of you. This is it. Your day of reckoning. You've prepared as well as you can for this paper by practising on sample papers. Your coursework was all right as well. Now, it is down to this...

An examination paper

ENGLISH
PAPER ONE: NON-FICTION AND MEDIA TEXTS
2 hours

Candidates will be required to answer **all** the questions in Section A and **one** question from Section B.

SECTION A

Save our youth clubs!

Below are a number of news items and extracts relating to the closing of the city's youth service. Read them carefully and use your reading to help you answer all the questions below.

***Radio WRMB News Bulletin* – January 12th**
Walton City Council today recommended the shutting down of the City's Youth Service with the loss of over 200 jobs. Twelve youth centres will close from April 1st and some part-time workers will be made redundant before then. The cuts – part of a package involving educational administration and school meals – will save almost £2 million of the £8 million savings which the council has been told to make in the coming financial year.

Walton Observer – 18th January

ACTION TO SAVE YOUTH SERVICE

YOUTH workers have launched a massive protest campaign to fight plans to scrap the City's Youth Service. The plan, part of the City Council's attempt to keep within government spending limits, is intended to save £1.7 million.

The workers and their supporters packed into one of the City's teacher centres on Saturday to draw up battle plans. At the meeting, the Council's principal youth worker, Alison Hubbard, described the situation as unthinkable. "The service has been going on for over half a century. Families, teachers, the police and social services all rely on us to keep almost a thousand youngsters off the streets on any weekday night. I want us to make as firm a stand as possible," she said.

And she warned that once the service had gone, it would be impossible to get it back.

Lobbying

Youth workers will now be lobbying local councillors, MPs, the Prime Minister and even the Royal family in a bid to save their already heavily cut service.

In a highly organised campaign which will culminate in a massive rally in Market Street, the workers plan to bring the message home both nationally and locally.

Kevin Grimley, one of the organisers, said: "The youth service provides an essential safety net for some youngsters who might otherwise be involved in all sorts of trouble. It gives them a regular meeting place apart from parks and bus shelters and keeps them away from pubs and alcohol. What's more, it provides excellent returns when you see what it does and realise that schools are spending over £100 million a year".

The Observer speaks...

The cuts that kill

IT IS HARD not to feel a degree of sympathy for those who have campaigned so tirelessly on behalf of the city's youth service over the past few weeks. They have made clear to all that the Youth Service is popular, well-used and excellent value for money.

At the same time, one has to recognise that, when savings must be made, the non-essential services are likely to be the first to go. Our city is obliged by law to provide access to education, to clear refuse from the streets and to help fund the police force. It is not compelled to open halls and community centres for young people in the evenings, to provide coffee bars, table tennis tables and programmes of social events and entertainment.

It is necessary, therefore, to judge the Youth Service provision alongside the provision of bus passes and home helps for pensioners or of 'meals on wheels' for the housebound. Then, the issue becomes one of financial priorities for the community as a whole.

When such priorities are determined, one must appreciate that young people have the spark and energy to fight their own battles. The young people of Walton have shown in the past few weeks that, even without financial assistance, their effort and determination can bring an issue to the forefront of debate.

Perhaps that same dynamism can be focused on the continued voluntary youth provision which now offers the best hope for the future.

Walton Observer – 10th February

30,000 strong protest fails to stop the unkindest cut of all

WALTON City Youth Service will be killed off despite bitter protests from thousands of people. The City Council pushed ahead with the cuts at its meeting yesterday after receiving a 33,756-signature petition on the steps of City Hall, the Council's headquarters in Market Street.

CHARLES WATTS, Chairman of the Education Committee, told the meeting: "It is not our proposal to abandon the youth of Walton or abandon our responsibility for youth provision, but we cannot conjure up resources out of thin air.

"We had to make a hard choice and we had to protect our schools and the children in them from further financial cuts. The Youth Service is well used and popular, but it is the icing on the cake of our educational provision. We have asked schools to take over the running of the Youth Service and we are prepared to keep one officer on to co-ordinate the new arrangements."

But other members of the council claimed young people would be forced on to the streets where they could be enticed into taking drugs and alcohol or rioting. Councillor Ronald Wood said: "There will be fewer leisure opportunities for teenagers and no support, advice or guidance for these young people when things go wrong. Then sparks will fly and somebody will have to pick up the pieces. The police, social services or Alcoholics Anonymous?"

Councillor Mary Faithful argued: "The impact on the Youth Service will be disastrous. The professional workers are the core of the Youth Service and hold it together."

Other council members defended the cuts, saying tough choices had to be made to try and protect schools, but opponents claimed that schools would be indirectly affected, especially those community schools which currently offered youth services on site. Councillor Jack Bruce said: "These proposals are indirectly impoverishing the whole of the quality of life for thousands of families – not just the teenagers – in this community".

The recommendation that the cuts be made still has to be finally approved by the City Council's Policy and Resources Committee but that is usually just a formality.

Youth workers face redundancy

Unions representing youth workers have been told to expect large-scale redundancies, the City Council announced yesterday. Redundancy notices will be issued almost immediately in order to give the required three months' notice for permanent staff. Keith Relf, Branch Secretarial for the Community and Youth Workers Union, said: "It looks like large-scale redundancies but it is still not clear what the new proposed Youth Service will look like, or whether it will need any staff at all".

There are currently 25 full-time and 183 part-time youth workers in the city and, with unemployment figures already high, their prospects of finding other work are considered slim.

Walton Observer – 25th January

Dear Editor,
Of course no one wants to see the City Youth Service disbanded for the sake of it but people must recognise that money does not grow on trees and that local government has to make choices.

At the end of the day, someone has to pay the bill and, as a regular contributor to the City Council funds, I think that this saving is a sensible one.

It is the school's job to educate these young children and they should be at home doing their homework on weekday evenings not wandering the streets and hanging round at these clubs or getting into trouble with the police.

Maybe, if things improve, the Youth Service could start up again or perhaps it could be included in what the schools provide and they could stay open in the evenings?

Yours faithfully,
Katie Warren (Mrs)
12 Elizabeth Street, Strawton.

1 What are the main reasons put forward for keeping the Youth Service? Summarise them in a series of short paragraphs.

2 Set out and write a leaflet which can be printed and handed out on the day of the proposed demonstration. It should have three sections with these headings:

What's happening to our youth clubs?
Why we are fighting
How you can help

Make each section about 100 words in length and give your leaflet an eye-catching slogan. Make your writing both informative and persuasive.

3 Look closely at the newspaper editorial and the letter from Mrs Warren. Write a fully argued reply to be published in the newspaper. Refer to the points they make, as well as giving your own opinion.

Set your letter out formally, including your address and that of the newspaper. The newspaper's address is:

City Centre House,
36 Avignon Boulevard,
Walton,
WA31 8PQ

SECTION B

4 Imagine that the *Walton Observer* has asked you to write a feature article presenting the views of young people about the proposal to cut the Youth Service. Write the article, including some background information about the plans and the opposition to them and the views of some of your friends, teachers and adults. Give the article a headline.

5 Imagine that you became closely involved with the campaign to save Walton's youth service. Write some diary entries describing two or three significant days of events in the campaign, including the day of the demonstration. Write about your feelings and reactions, as well as describing what happened.

'Turn over your papers and begin. You have two hours.'

All this writing. All these questions. Oh no, not youth clubs. Never been to one.

Now wait, take a deep breath and relax. Look carefully at what you have to do. What have you been given?

Right, I'll try to calm down. There's a page of questions – tasks, I mean. There are five. No, wait a minute. I only have to answer one from Section B, so that makes four in all. That's about half an hour each. No, wait. There's the same number of marks available for each section, so I need to spend an hour on each section – well, maybe 50 minutes' writing time.

What else is there?

Um. A sheet with all the details on. There's some newspaper stories and a letter.

Good. What are you going to do now?

Get stuck into question one? Start scribbling down reasons as I read these newspaper stories? No, I remember. First look at the tasks, then the material. So, what have I got to do? Write a list of reasons, then a leaflet and then a letter. That's not so bad. Right. Let's read the material.

Read it slowly and carefully. Think about what you are reading. Notice that you have got two newspaper articles and one editorial. That will give somebody's opinion. Then, there is a news story from a radio bulletin and a letter – that will be opinion as well. As you read, underline the reasons you notice and highlight things that ought to be in your leaflet. Take your time.

Right. I've done that. But that's a quarter of an hour gone, and I haven't written anything. Ben is scribbling fast, Amy is staring into space holding her pen and Louise has already got the correcting fluid out.

Don't worry. There is plenty of time. Now look at Question 1. What have you got to do?

Write the main reasons... well, here goes. I'll just write 1–10 down the page and fill them in as I find them.

Hold on. Look at the task again. What sort of writing does it want from you? It doesn't ask for a list but a summary in a number of short paragraphs.

Oh, yes.

So what should you do?

Read through, make notes, then write them into a summary. Put the most important reasons first?

Exactly.

But there isn't time for that! Oh, well. Here goes. What's this? 200 jobs lost. Is that a reason? Yes, it could be. Think REASONS WHY. Think that 'because' is going to be the start of every reason. 'The Youth Service should be kept because 200 valuable jobs and the skills of the youth workers will be lost forever.' Yes, that's a reason but not a very important one. Make a note, '200 jobs'.

Here's another. It has gone on for half a century – that's 50 years. Make a note, 'well established'.

Everyone relies on the service... so what? Ah, here's the reason why. The youth service keeps youngsters off the street. Make a note, 'many clients'. Once it's gone it can't come back. That's a reason which links with the 200 jobs note. Link them together!

Keeps kids out of trouble... away from pubs... these reasons link to the 'many clients' point and keeping youngsters off the street. What's this? There could be trouble ahead. Tie that in as well. Let's start writing these down into an answer.

Hold on. Try to structure them more.

What do you mean? I see. Group them in some way?

Yes. How many groups of reasons are there?

Er..., three. Reasons to do with the youth workers losing their jobs, to do with the effects on the young people, the effect on society as a whole. Wait, there's another one. The amount of money involved is relatively small.

Anything else to think about?

9:55 No. Wait, yes. Putting them in order. Young people, effects on society, consequences for youth workers and then a last point about money. Let's get writing.

And remember, short, separate paragraphs.

Thanks.

10:05 Right, that's done. All the information down neat and tidy. Single line through the notes and then Question 2, here I come. I feel better already!

Question 2..., a leaflet. That's like a poster. Big headline, STUFF THE COUNCIL. That'll be good. Big picture of a riot going on as well. Border it in red – to show blood will be spilled if they go ahead!

Hold on. Look again. Put your pen down and think. It is a leaflet, not a poster. It has to have three sections, each about 100 words long. It needs a slogan and has to be both persuasive and informative. Imagine who it is for. Mrs Bhamra is out shopping and she sees these young people outside City Hall. Someone gives her a sheet of paper. What does she need to know?

10:06 What's happening? Why is there a demo? What she can do to help the young people if she wants to?

Precisely. Now you can see why the leaflet is structured like it is. The first bit is information, the second explanation, and the third persuasion. Remember that you have to show the examiner what you can do well and here is a chance to show you can cope with three different sorts of writing. Get on with those in note form. Leave the slogan until you have finished, rather than spend a long time now.

10:15 Done that. And I've thought of a slogan, 'The young are the adults of tomorrow – look after them well.'

Good, now write your final version. Check you are being informative – using facts and numbers and avoiding comment in the first part. Check that you are explaining in the second part – could the word 'because' go in front of what you say? Check that you are being persuasive in the third part – using phrases like, 'you should help', 'we need your help' and 'support us now!'

10:25 That's done. I've shortened the slogan, as well – 'Youth today, voters tomorrow' and I've underlined the word 'because' three times in the middle section to make it more eye-catching. The last section was a bit long – about 120 words – so I neatly crossed out one sentence. I think I'm a bit behind time, though.

Don't worry. Now you know the material, things won't take as long.

Question 3. Write a letter. Can I just bang this off and say what a daft old trout she is?

No. Look at what you have to show here. That you can argue against her points as well as giving your opinion and the letter must be formally set out – that means writing both your address and the newspaper's address at the top. Start with a rough draft of the points she makes and your responses to them.

10:30 That's done. She only really makes three points – about the money, about it being the school's job and about how the service could be restarted and I can answer all of them with arguments of my own.

Carry on. Remember to be polite in what you say and remember that you are writing to the Editor, not Mrs Warren. Start the letter, 'Dear Sir,' and end with 'Yours faithfully,' because you have not written to a named person. Write in separate paragraphs as you deal with Mrs Warren's points.

10:40 Thanks. I almost forgot the paragraphs! Now, Section B. I like writing imaginatively, so I think I'll do Question 5. Do you think that's a fair choice?

Certainly. Where you are given a choice, choose the task you will do best. But, again, think hard about what you are being asked for: not just to write a story but to weave in the events of the campaign and your feelings. AND you have to write in a diary format, with entries covering a couple of days.

10:45 Right, and I'll make my feelings change from hope to disappointment as it goes on. That'll be good. First I'll jot down some of the things I want to put in, from the material.

★★★

11:15 *Sorry to interrupt, but it's 11.15. You ought to be winding it up by now.*

Yes, I was getting carried away. It's fine as it is. So what next?

Read through all your answers. This is a check that you have covered all the relevant points and that you have not made mistakes in spelling and punctuation. In particular, check words which have been given to you in the passage and always expect to add some punctuation!

11:25 That's done. On the leaflet I'd left out about the Youth Service cut only saving £1.7 million, but I was able to slot it in neatly. I'd also called Mrs Warren, Miss Waren in one place in the letter! I spelled demonstration wrong as well and had to add quite a bit of punctuation towards the end of Question 5 where I got involved in the writing. It's fine now.

Well done!

'Please put your pens down. Don't speak until the papers have been collected...'

Of course, in reality you will not have a chance to talk over the questions with anyone else once you are in the examination room. But this is the kind of conversation you need to practise having with yourself.

The next paper is a slightly different one, based on reading. It uses a **pre-released extract** (sent to schools in advance) and an **unseen passage** (printed with the examination paper) to test your ability to read in detail and to respond to what you have read. With some examining groups all the material is unseen and with others the pre-released material comes in a larger anthology on which more of the examination is based.

ENGLISH
PAPER TWO: RESPONSE TO LITERATURE

2 hours

Candidates will be required to answer **all** the questions in Section A and **one** question from Section B.

SECTION A

Refer to this extract and answer Questions 1–3.

This passage is taken from *A Breath of French Air* by H. E. Bates. It describes how the Larkin family go on holiday to France. In the extract, Pop Larkin, Ma, their seven children and Charley (otherwise known as Mr Charlton and their daughter Mariette's husband) have their first meal at the Hotel Beau Rivage, somewhere in Northern France.

"Nearly an hour later, when Ma brought the children downstairs for dinner, closely followed by Charley and Mariette, Pop was already sitting moodily in a corner of the *salle à manger*, a room of varnished, ginger-coloured matchboard and glass built like a greenhouse shrouded with yellowing lace curtains against the westward side of the hotel. Some squares of glass were coloured blue or ruby. A few, broken altogether, had been patched up with squares of treacle-brown paper and it seemed generally that the whole ramshackle structure, battered by the Atlantic storm, might at any moment fall down, disintegrate, and blow away.

Driven by ravenous hunger and thirst to the bar, Pop had found it furnished with a solitary stool, a yard of dusty counter, a dozing grey cat, and a vase of last year's heather. The stool had two legs instead of three and all about the place was that curious pungent odour that Ma had been so quick to notice earlier in the day: as if a drain had been left open or a gas-tap on.

In the *salle à manger*, in contrast to the silent half-darkness of the bar, a noisy, eager battle was being waged by seven or eight French families against the howl of wind and rain, the tossing lace curtains, and more particularly against what appeared to be dishes of large unpleasant pink spiders, in reality *langoustines*. A mad cracking of claws filled the air and one plump Frenchman sat eating, wearing his cap, a large white one: as if for protection against something, perhaps flying claws or bread or rain.

Three feet from Pop's table a harassed French waitress with a marked limp and loose peroxide hair came to operate, every desperate two minutes or so, a large patent wooden-handled bread-slicer about the size of an old-fashioned sewing machine; a cross somewhere between a guillotine and a chaff-cutter.

This instrument made crude groaning noises, like an old tram trying to start. Slices of bread, savagely chopped from yard-long loaves, flew about in all directions, dropping all over the place until harassed waiters and waitresses bore them hurriedly off to eager, waiting guests. These, Pop noticed, at once crammed them ravenously into their mouths and even gluttonously mopped their plates with them.

Presently the rest of the family arrived: Mariette immaculate and perfumed in a beautiful sleeveless low-cut dress of emerald green that made her shoulders and upper breast glow a warm olive colour, Ma in a mauve woollen dress and a royal blue jumper on top to keep out the cold. Ma had plenty of Chanel No. 5 on, still convinced that the hotel smelled not only of mice but a lot of other things besides.

As the family walked in all the French families suddenly stopped eating. The French, Charley had once told Pop, were the élite of Europe. Now they stopped ramming bread into their mouths like famished prisoners and gaped at the bare, astral shoulders of Mariette, Ma's great mauve and blue balloon of a body, and the retinue of children behind it.

Most of the older French women, Pop thought, seemed to be wearing discoloured woollen sacks. The younger ones, who were nearly all tallow-coloured, bruise-eyed, and flat-chested, wore jeans. It was hard to tell any of them from boys and in consequence Pop felt more than usually proud of Mariette, who looked so fleshily, elegantly, and provocatively a girl.

“ Presently the waitress with the limp brought the menu and then with not a moment to spare hopped off to work the bread machine.

'Well, what's to eat, Charley-boy?' Pop said, rubbing his hands. 'Somethink good I hope, old man, I'm starving.'

Mr Charlton consulted the menu with a certain musing, studious air of English calm.

'By the way, Charley,' Pop said, 'what's "eat" in French? Haven't learned any words today.'

It was Pop's honest resolve to learn, if possible, a few new French words every day.

'*Manger*,' Charley said. 'Same word as the thing in the stable – manger.'

Pop sat mute and astounded. Manger – a simple thing like that. Perfickly wonderful.

Unbelievable. Manger. He sat back and prepared to listen to Charley reading out the menu with the awe he deserved.

'Well, to begin with there are *langoustines*. They're a kind of small lobster. Speciality of the Atlantic coast. Then there's *saucisson à la mode d'ici* – that's a sort of sausage they do here. *Spécialité de la maison*, I shouldn't wonder. Hot, I expect. Probably awfully good. Then *pigeons à la Gautier* – I expect that's pigeons in some sort of wine sauce. And afterwards fruit and cheese.'

'Sounds jolly *bon*,' Pop said.

Charley said he thought it ought to satisfy and Ma at once started remonstrating with Montgomery, Primrose, Victoria, and the twins about eating so much bread. She said they'd never want their dinners if they went on stuffing bread down.

'What shall we drink?' Charley said.

'Port,' Pop said. He too was stuffing down large quantities of bread, trying to stave off increasing stabs and rumbles of hunger. Ma agreed about the port. It would warm them all up, she said.

'I doubt if they'll have port.'

'Good God,' Pop said. '*What*? I thought you said the Froggies lived on wine?'

'Well, they do. But it's their own. Port isn't. I suggest we drink *vin rosé*. That'll go well with the fish and the pigeon.'

The harassed waitress with the limp, freed momentarily of bread-cutting, arrived a moment later to tell Charley, in French, that there were, after all, no *langoustines*.

'Sorry, no more *langoustines*,' Mr Charlton said. 'They've got *friture* instead.'

'What's *friture*?'

'Fried sardines.'

Ma choked; she felt she wanted to be suddenly and violently sick.

'Oh! Fresh ones of course,' Charley said. 'Probably caught this afternoon.'

'In that lot?' Pop said and waved a disbelieving hand in the general direction of the howling, blackening gale that threatened increasingly to blow away the *salle à manger*.

A second later a vast flash of lightning seemed to sizzle down the entire length of roof glass like a celestial diamond-cutter. A Frenchwoman rose hysterically and rushed from the room.

The chaff-cutter guillotine attacked yet another loaf with louder and louder groans and a long black burst of thunder struck the hotel to the depth of its foundations.

Alarmed too, the children ate more bread. Pop ate more bread and was in fact still eating bread when the *friture* arrived.

'They're only tiddlers!' the twins said. 'They're only tiddlers!'

'Sardines never grow any bigger,' Charley said, 'otherwise they wouldn't be sardines.'

'About time they did then,' Ma said, peering dubiously at piled scraps of fish, 'that's all.'

'*Bon appétit*!' Mr Charlton said, and proceeded enthusiastically to attack the *friture*.

Pop, turning to the attack too, found himself facing a large plateful of shrivelled dark brown objects which immediately fell to pieces at the touch of a fork. Scorched fragments of fish flew flakily about in all directions. The few crumbs that he was able to capture, impale on his fork and at last transfer to his mouth tasted, he thought, exactly like the unwanted scraps left over at the bottom of a bag of fish-and-chips.

'Shan't get very fat on these,' Ma said.

In a low depressed voice Pop agreed. Ma's great bulk, which filled half the side of one length of the table, now and then quivered in irritation and presently she was eating the *friture* with her fingers, urging the children to do likewise.

The children, in silent despair, ate more bread. Savagely the guillotine bread-cutter worked overtime, drowning conversation. And presently the limping waitress brought the *vin rosé*, which Charley tasted.

'Delicious,' he said with mounting enthusiasm. 'Quite delicious.'

At last the multitudinous remains of the *friture* were taken away, plates piled high with brown wreckage, and Ma said it looked like the feeding of the five thousand. Pop drank deep of *vin rosé*, raised his glass to everybody, and unable to think of very much to say remarked mournfully:

'Well, cheers, everybody. Well, here we are.'

'We certainly are,' Ma said. 'You never spoke a truer word.'

After a short interval the *saucisson à la mode d'ici* arrived. This consisted of a strange object looking like a large pregnant sausage-roll, rather scorched on top. Slight puffs of steam seemed to be issuing from the exhausts at either end.

Ma remarked that at least it was hot and Pop, appetite now whetted to the full by another sharp draught or two of *vin rosé*, prepared to attack the object on his plate by cutting it directly through the middle.

To his complete dismay the force of the cut, meeting hard resistance from the surface of scorched crust, sent the two pieces hurtling in the air. Both fell with a low thud to the floor.

'Don't touch it! Don't touch it!' Ma said. 'Mice everywhere.'

I'll order another,' Charley said. '*Ma'moiselle*!'

In silent patience Pop waited, but by the time a waitress could be spared from the bondage of bread-cutting the rest of the family had finished the battle with the *saucisson à la mode d'ici*.

With gloom, drinking more *vin rosé* to fortify himself, Pop waited while Charley explained to the waitress the situation about the unfortunate disappearance of his second course.

The waitress seemed dubious, even unimpressed. She simply stared coldly at Pop's empty plate as if knowing perfectly well he had eaten what had been on there and crushingly uttered the single word '*Supplément*'.

'She says if you have another you'll have to pay extra,' Charley said.

'Better order another bottle of vin rosy instead, Charley,' Pop said.

Weakly he started to eat more bread. He had, he thought, never eaten so much bread in his life. He no longer wondered why the guillotine worked overtime.

Suddenly thunder roared again, faintly echoed by the rumblings of his own belly, and presently the little man in pince-nez appeared, making his furtive mole-like way from table to table.

When he saw the Larkins, however, he stood some distance off, in partly obsequious retreat, an uneasy grimace on his face, his hands held together.

Once he bowed. Mr Charlton bowed too and Ma grinned faintly in reply.

'Nice to see that,' Mr Charlton said. 'Typical French. He's come to see if everything's all right.'

'Why don't we tell him?' Ma said.

'What do we have next?' the twins said. 'What do we have next?'

'Pigeons,' Pop said. The thought of stewed pigeons made his mouth water. In wine sauce too. 'Pigeons.'

'We want baked beans on toast!' the twins said. 'And cocoa.'

'Quiet!' Pop thundered. 'I'll have order.'

A moment later a waitress, arriving with a fourth plate of bread, proceeded to announce to Mr Charlton a fresh and disturbing piece of news. There were, after all, no pigeons.

Pop felt too weak to utter any kind of exclamation about this second, deeper disappointment.

'There's rabbit,' Charley told him, 'instead.'

Instantly Pop recoiled in pale, fastidious horror.

'Not after myxo!' he said. 'No! Charley, I couldn't. I can't touch 'em after myxo!'

“ Myxomatosis, the scourge of the rabbit tribe, had affected Pop very deeply. No one else in the family had been so moved by the plague and its results. But to Pop the thought of eating rabbits was now as great a nausea as the thought of eating nightingales.

'It started here in France too,' he said. 'The Froggies were the ones who first started it.'

'Have an omelette,' Charley said cheerfully.

'They don't suit him,' Ma said. 'They always give him heartburn.'

Pop could only murmur in a low, dispassionate voice that he had to have something, somehow, soon. Heartburn or no heartburn. Even an omelette.

'A steak then,' Charley said. 'With chips.'

At this Pop cheered up a little, saying that a steak would suit him.

'*Alors, un filet bifteck pour monsieur*,' Charley said, '*avec pommes frites*.'

'Biff-teck! Biff-teck!' the twins started shouting, punching each other, laughing loudly. 'Biff-teck! Biff-you! Biff-you! Biff-teck!'

Pop was too weak to cry 'Quiet!' this time and from a distance the man in pince-nez stared in disapproval at the scene, so that Ma said:

'Ssh! Mr Dupont's looking.'

'That isn't Mr Dupont,' Charley said. 'He's only the manager. Mr Dupont's dead.'

'Die of over-eating?' Ma said.

Pop laughed faintly.

'The hotel is run by a Miss Dupont—Mademoiselle Dupont,' Charley explained. 'But it seems she's away in Brest for the day.'

'When the cat's away,' Ma said.

'Well,' Charley said, 'I wouldn't be at all surprised if that didn't explain a slight lack of liaison.'

Pop, too low in spirits even to admire Charley's turn of phrase, drank deeply of *vin rosé*.

'Better order some more of the juice, Charley old man,' he said. 'Got to keep going somehow.'

'Biff-teck! Biff-teck! Biff-you! Biff-teck!'

'Quiet!' Pop said sharply and from across the *salle à manger* several French mammas looked quickly round at him with full sudden glances, clearly electrified.

Half an hour later he had masticated his way through a bloody piece of beef roughly the shape of a boot's sole, the same thickness, and about as interesting. He ate the chips that accompanied it down to the last frizzled crumb and even dipped his bread in the half-cold blood.

Ma said she hoped he felt better for it but Pop could hardly do more than nod, drinking again of *vin rosé*.

'Don't even have ketchup,' he said, as if this serious gastronomic omission were the final straw. ”

1 What impression does the passage give of the hotel and the French guests who are also eating there?

2 (a) In a few words, how would you describe Pop's reaction to the holiday so far? How does this reaction contrast with Charley's and Ma's?

(b) What impression do you get of Pop's character and personality? How is this brought out strongly in the way in which he speaks, contrasted with the language Charley uses?

3 Did you enjoy reading this extract? Discuss in some detail your reasons for answering yes or no.

Now read the following extract which is taken from another book about the Larkin family. Two neighbours, the Brigadier and Angela Snow, stay for dinner.

“ Soon the delicious unbearable fragrance of roasting pheasant was filling the house. Every few minutes the Brigadier sniffed openly at it like a dog. It seemed as if a long night, a grey mixture of solitude, sandwich lunches, bone-hard apple pies and cold bacon, was at last breaking and passing him by. He hardly noticed the arrival of a fourth and then a fifth whisky and it was from the remotest ends of a waking dream that he heard Pop calling with ebullient cheerfulness to Mr Charlton:

'Shall we have pink tonight, Charley boy? Why not? Get three or four bottles on the ice quick. Ought to go well with the pheasants, I think, don't you?'

'Darling, if that was champagne you were referring to I shall remain faithful to you for ever,' Angela Snow said. 'I adore the pink. It's absolutely me. Quite my favourite tipple.'

The Brigadier might well have wept again except that now, by some miracle, there was nothing to weep for. Had there ever been? He simply couldn't believe there ever had. He was beginning to feel alive again, terrifically alive. Pink champagne? By God, that took him back a thousand aching years. He was again a crazy subaltern on Indian hill-stations, lean and active as a panther: dances and parties everywhere, polo and pig-sticking, affairs with two married women running at the same time, servants everywhere as plentiful as beetles. He was the gay dog having champagne for breakfast, with a certain madness in the air, and nobody giving a damn.

'Glad to see you're perking up, General,' Ma said as she passed him with two deep glass dishes of strawberries, each containing half a dozen pounds. 'Got your glass topped up?' 'Splendid,' the Brigadier said. 'Splendid. Absolutely splendid.'

'Don't spoil your appetite, though, will you?' she said. 'Supper'll only be ten minutes or so.'

The Brigadier found it suddenly impossible to believe how swiftly the evening had gone. The time had whipped along like prairie fire. He took his watch out of his breast pocket and discovered it to be already eight o'clock. Spoil his appetite? He could have eaten horses.

Ma had cooked two brace of pheasants, together with chipolata sausages, thin game chips, potatoes creamed with fresh cream and the first Brussels sprouts with chestnuts. Brimming boats of gravy and bread sauce came to table as Pop started to carve the birds, the breasts of which crumbled under the knife as softly as fresh-baked bread.

'Tot the champagne out, Charley boy,' Pop said. 'And what about you, General? Which part of the bird for you? Leg or bosom?'

The Brigadier immediately confessed to a preference for bosom and a moment later found, his eye roving warmly across the table, in the direction of Angela Snow, who met the gaze full-faced and unflushed, though with not quite the elegant composure she always wore. This started his juices flowing again and with a brief peremptory bark he found himself suddenly on his feet, champagne glass waving.

'To our hostess. I give you a blessing, madam. And honour. And glory. And long, long health –'

The unaccustomed extravagance of the Brigadier's words trailed off, unfinished. Everybody rose and drank to Ma. The Brigadier then declared that the pink champagne was terrific and immediately crouched with eager reverence over his plate, the edges of which were only barely visible, a thin embroidered line of white enclosing a whole rich field of game, vegetables, sauce, and gravy.

Later, strawberries lay on the Brigadier's plate like fat fresh red rose-buds, dewed white with sugar. The visionary sherry-coloured figure of Angela Snow came to pour the thickest yellow cream on them, her voluptuous bare forearm brushing his hand. Then as she went away to take her place at the table a sudden spasm of double vision made him see two of her: a pair of tall golden twins of disturbing elegance who actually waved hands at him and said:

'You're doing fine, Brigadier, my Sweet. Does my heart good to see you. This afternoon I thought you were for the coal-hole.'

What on earth she meant by the coal-hole he didn't know and cared even less. He only knew he was doing fine. The strawberries were simply magnificent; they came straight from the lap of the gods. Only the gods could send strawberries like that, in October, to be washed down by champagne, and soon he was eating a second dishful, then a third.

'The General's away,' Ma kept saying with cheerful peals of laughter, 'the General's away.'

4 Compare and contrast this meal with the previous one. As you plan your answer, think about:
the meal and the way it is described;
the moods of the Larkins and their guests;
how the writer uses language.

SECTION B

5 On the days after their disastrous meal the Larkins visit other restaurants. One specialises in seafood, while another claims to offer 'traditional' English food. Write your account of what happens on either occasion.

6 Imagine that you are a member of one of the French families eating in the hotel. Write your account of the evening.

Assessing your progress

As you practise for the examination, you may often find it useful to compare what you do with the marking criteria for Reading and Writing (see pp.7–8). Asking your teacher to look over your work will also be valuable. This chapter looks at how to use self-assessment to improve your grade.

Making the grade

What makes someone buy and read a book like this? Well, the fact that you are reading it at all shows a number of positive things about you and your attitude to your work. You must be a committed student with a strong desire to succeed. You also recognise that by following advice you will be able to improve your chances of doing well.

You may have very particular reasons for reading this book. Many of you will need a particular grade in English in order to secure a place in further or higher education, or to be considered for a job you have set your sights on.

Some people in this group will need a better grade in English than in any other subject: if that Grade A or B in English materialises, they will be happy with Grade C for the other subjects.

There will also be some people who are very much better at other subjects than at English (often maths and science subjects) but who have frustrating problems with English: they know they are heading for Grade A in every other subject, but just cannot get on with the kind of work English requires, even though they know they will need a Grade B or C for a place in higher education.

Another group of readers will always have been 'good at' English, and love reading and writing. This group wants to continue their study of the subject after GCSE. They will do everything they can to ensure the best possible result.

If you recognise yourself as belonging to one of these groups you will want to know the same thing: is there anything more you can do, besides working hard, to get the grade you have set your sights on?

That is what this chapter of the book is about. While there is certainly no simple 'trick' which guarantees examination success every time, there are things you can do to find out more about how grades are awarded. One very easy thing to start with is to look closely at your examination syllabus. The other place to look is at the marking criteria which show you what qualities teachers will be looking for in your work when they award particular grades.

One conclusion you might reach is that different types of work allow you to demonstrate different skills. You will also notice that the skills are cumulative. This means that each grade builds something else on what you were expected to do for the grade below.

If you are to make much practical use of this knowledge to improve your grading, it is obvious that you will have to become skilled in the art of assessing your own work.

The skills you have to show

One place to start is with the grade descriptions for English: these form the 'mark scheme' against which the examiner will measure your progress.

For many GCSE candidates the most important step is from grade B to grade A and for others the step from grade D to grade C. The grade descriptions for grades A and C are printed below along with advice as to the kind of work you will have to produce, and the standard that you will have to reach, to make those grades.

Grade A

- Candidates articulate and sustain their responses to texts, developing their ideas and referring in detail to aspects of language, structure and presentation.

  As well as doing all that is required at Grade C, you need to aim to produce a rounded, polished response where the development of what you want to say as the thread of an argument is clear to the reader. That means showing plenty of insight and making clear points in each paragraph. You also need to make close references to the material that you read in both examination and coursework assignments either by quoting accurately or by paraphrasing arguments. In commenting on an advertisement, you might note how the elements — the images and the text — challenge the reader's expectations, relate to other texts or are aimed at a particular audience.

- They identify and analyse argument, opinion and alternative interpretations, making cross-references where appropriate. They make apt and careful comparisons within and between texts.

  You need to be able to see a text as more than just a book you have to read — perhaps in relation to an understanding of other texts written against the same historical and cultural background or in relation to the background of its writer. In talking about 'Animal Farm', you would be using the word 'allegory' with confidence and explaining the strengths and weaknesses of the novel as an allegory. You might be comparing it with an extract from 'Gulliver's Travels' or a similar story where animals are given human voices and emotions.

- Candidates' writing has shape and assured control of a range of styles. Narratives use structure as well as vocabulary for a range of effects and non-fiction is coherent, logical and persuasive.

  Your report on child abuse would have to be almost of professional quality in terms of its structure and layout and you might well use a word-processor to complete it. In a story you might be using flashbacks to help your narrative unfold, or the historic present to add excitement to a suspense thriller. You would have a clear understanding of the effects you wanted to achieve and the sort of stylistic devices you wanted to use. You would be able to change your writing in specific ways to match your intentions. You could write a sustained and persuasive argument about a subject you cared about.

- Punctuation and spelling are correct; paragraphs are well constructed and linked to clarify the organisation of the writing as a whole.

  You would be expected to make very few errors and to ensure that your spelling and punctuation showed complete control. That does not mean 100% accuracy in all circumstances but being able to identify where you are making errors and knowing how to use punctuation within sentences or to mark direct speech. Your paragraphing would have to be intentional, showing how you had thought hard about the final layout and shape of your writing.

Grade C

- Candidates show understanding of the ways in which meaning and information are conveyed in a range of literary and non-literary texts.

  For example, you have to be able to write about how an advertisement uses graphic illustrations, different sizes of print, slogans and emotive language to make its point. You could analyse the way a newspaper front page covered an important story, showing how the headline, the sub-headings, the page layout and the language of the story worked together to create an effect. See how this is a more advanced skill than explaining what you like about the advertisement.

- They give personal and critical responses to literary texts, referring to aspects of language, structure and themes in justifying their views.

  You need to be able to stand back from your subject. If you read 'Animal Farm', to achieve this statement you would have to write about what George Orwell was trying to tell his readers about people by writing a story in which animals took charge of their farm. You would have to write about why 'Lord of the Flies' is more than just an adventure story about a stranded group of boys on a desert island. Whatever you have read, pick a coursework task for yourself which focuses on what the writer is trying to achieve. Watch out for an examination question that targets this kind of understanding as well.

- They select and summarise a range of information from different sources.

  Retrieving and combining information are what is rewarded here. In coursework, make sure you have a task which draws on two or three sources of information. For example, you could write an essay on global warming, based on a newspaper report, some statistics and some scientific information. You could write a report on child abuse, based on eye-witness stories, social workers' views and government statements. Again, watch out in the examination for tasks which involve more than one piece of stimulus material, and make sure you draw your information from all the material you are given.

- Candidates' writing engages and sustains the reader's interest. It shows adaptation of style and register to different forms, including using an impersonal style where appropriate.

  This is asking for variety – especially in your coursework. Show that you can write an exciting story, a clear leaflet, and a persuasive speech in standard English. In the examination, watch out for places where you are challenged to go beyond your usual style by certain questions.

- Candidates use a range of sentence structures and varied vocabulary to create effects. Paragraphing and correct punctuation are used to make the sequence of events or ideas coherent and clear to the reader.

  Here, you are being asked to go beyond a simple story structure. A report on child abuse with sub-headings would show that you were thinking about the structure of your writing. If you wrote about a poem by dealing with different aspects of it in turn, that would have the same result. The punctuation would not have to be absolutely accurate but every sentence would need to have a capital letter and full stop.

- Spelling is accurate and handwriting is neat and legible.

  Spelling needs to be largely accurate and there should not be any repetitive mistakes. So check coursework carefully and revise work done in the examination. In at least one piece of coursework, consciously focus on the presentation of a leaflet or a poster or produce your report neatly using a word processor.

The importance of choosing the right task

One thing you will have noticed is that moving up a grade often involves doing a different sort of task, rather than doing the same thing better. This applies at all grades and it is also important in making sure that your coursework covers the criteria needed for the higher grades. Whenever you are set or choose a coursework task, think hard about:

- **Your purpose for writing**: Why are you doing this writing – apart from the fact that the teacher has told you to! Is it to inform, to persuade, to explain, or for another purpose?
- **Your audience**: Who is the writing for? Anyone, your peers, your teacher, old people, young people? Giving a writing task an audience can often make it easier than working in a vacuum.
- **The form of the writing**: Are you writing a story, a letter, a report, a commentary? If it is a poster or a leaflet, the form affects how you write, as well as what you have to say.

In examinations, you will often be told what form to use, or who your audience is. Think about what this tells you about the kind of writing you should be producing.

There is an enormous range of writing choice when you mix purpose, audience and form together. In general, when you have a prescribed purpose, audience and form, you are likely to be targeting the higher grades for reading and writing.

Putting this into practice

Purposes for writing

Study these alternative titles for some work on the character of Lady Macbeth in Shakespeare's play. What is the purpose and audience for each one? What form would you write in? Also, consider how different titles might meet the criteria for a high grade.

- Write Lady Macbeth's last letter to her husband.
- Imagine that Macbeth's plot succeeds and Lady Macbeth lives on. Write about how Banquo's heirs plot to seize the throne.
- Analyse the character of Lady Macbeth and the way it changes and develops throughout the play.
- Is there anything you like about Lady Macbeth?
- Use a series of private diary entries to trace the downfall of Lady Macbeth.
- Imagine that you are a courtier to Lady Macbeth. Write your account of the events of the play from the arrival of Macbeth's letter.
- Write Lady Macbeth's obituary as it might appear in two newspapers – one which supports Macbeth and one which is opposed to his rule.
- Pick two contemporary film actresses and say how you think they could portray Lady Macbeth in exciting new ways. If you were given the chance to play the part, what emotions and feelings would you try to convey? How would you want to dress and move around the stage?
- Imagine that Lady Macbeth lives and is put on trial for treason. Write two speeches, one defending her and the other on behalf of the prosecution.
- Analyse and compare three speeches by Lady Macbeth, identifying their key features.

The unwritten basics of good English

While it is possible to target and work towards grades in the ways outlined above, there are also some basic rules of good writing which can make a big difference to your eventual result. So in all of your writing, be prepared to:

- Change your style to suit your **task** (what you are asked to do) and your **audience** (the intended reader or listener).

  This means: you will need to demonstrate that you can write in a **formal** style for writing to, or for, people you don't know, and a **literary** style for writing about books, plays and poetry you have read. Of course, this is in addition to handling with confidence more everyday styles of writing, like stories or letters.
- Vary your vocabulary (the words you choose to use) enough to reflect the style you have chosen to use.

  This means: make yourself think about the words you use to **label** and **describe**. It is hard to describe what using a wider range of words means in practice but basically it is a matter of finding the best word for the job. Referring to a thesaurus as you write and reading widely are ways of increasing your word power. Other ways are using extra **adjectives** and **adverbs** (the describing words which go with nouns and verbs), or by putting **comparisons** (sometimes called **similes**, they use the words 'like' or 'as') into your work.

- Spell most common words correctly and also words which appear in the stimulus material, like the names of characters in a story or play or technical terms.
  This means: that you should not be confusing 'there' and 'their', that you should know the difference between words like 'practise' and 'practice' and that the letter 'i' normally comes before the letter 'e', except where they follow the letter 'c' in words like 'receive'. If you are writing about a character like Lennie in *Of Mice and Men,* don't write 'Lenny', or say that the book is by 'Jon Stienbock'!
- Punctuate your work appropriately.
  This means: that you should clearly show where sentences begin and end, using capital letters and full stops or question marks, and you should punctuate direct speech so that even if it is not perfect, it is clear who is talking when.
- Structure complex sentences in a variety of ways.
  This means: that you should write in longer sentences, which are made up of sections joined by words called **connectors**. The most common connector is 'and' and a good tip is to look at where you use 'and' to see if another connector might be better.
- Write work which demonstrates all these qualities at length.
  This means: that some of your pieces must be more than 400 words long – that is not always stated, but it is what most experts think of as extended writing. A few should be up to 600 words or so in length. Anything longer will not earn you extra credit, because to write even 400 words you have to be able to think ahead, plan, and organise your writing.
- Organise ideas into a logical sequence of well-formed paragraphs.
  This means: that you should always write in paragraphs. A paragraph is a group of sentences (more than one) which have something in common. Not paragraphing makes writing hard to read, follow or understand – no wonder examiners think it is important!
- Be sensitive to tone and atmosphere when you write about books.
  This means: that you have to be able to do more than re-tell the story. You have to make comments about what happens in the book, and consider what events show about characters, not just say what characters do.
- Recognise an author's purposes in using language and to write about these in detail with examples.
  This means: that you have to comment on a writer's use of language: not only recognise that he or she uses it in a particular way, but be able to say *why* and for *what effect.*

Going for grade A or A*

If you have ambitions in this direction, remember that grades are cumulative and that each higher grade requires something more than the one beneath.

Remember, as well, that you will have to demonstrate a uniformly high standard of achievement in all your work, no matter what it is. Your use of language will need to be consistently fluent and flexible enough to tackle almost any written task you are given. It should be obvious that you will have to achieve an extremely high standard of accuracy in technical skills like spelling and punctuation. If you have difficulty in either area, then you must do everything in your power to remedy your weaker points.

Your English Literature grade may survive a particular weakness in spelling or punctuation, because literature work is assessed primarily on the content of what you have to say. But your English grade will undoubtedly be lowered by such a problem.

There are also certain reading and writing tasks which will offer you the greatest possibilities to show off those skills which top-level candidates have, and which other candidates lack. The grade criteria help you to identify what these are. It is important that you make sure that the work you submit for assessment at the end of the course does reflect

that you have these particular skills. You will probably find that some pieces of work, by the nature of the task set, limit the number of skills you are able to demonstrate. For example, the script of a play set in a youth club would probably only allow you to demonstrate your ability to write in a very colloquial (chatty) manner.

Some creative assignments based on the literature you are reading will tend to focus your attention on the content of the book, rather than more complex matters like the language it is expressed in, or the issues which the book investigates. For example, newspaper articles based on a text you have read may do this, unless you are aware enough to show that you see more in what you have read than just a good story.

Also, if you base a comparative wider reading assignment on a 'best seller', or something specifically aimed at the teenage market, you would have to look much harder to find grade A insight into the reading than if you tackled a recognised work of literary merit. If all of your coursework was like this, it would be hard to judge whether or not you had shown evidence of grade A performance. You need to be careful that you do not limit your own level by falling into a trap like this. On the other hand, there are some tasks which encourage you to display grade A qualities. These are the ones where you pull out all the stops!

One way to think of reading and writing at grade A is that it not only reports, or even comments, but it also analyses an issue, a piece of writing or something you have read. **Analysis** means taking something apart into the elements which make it up, describing each one of them and its purpose. Good analytical writing does exactly that. It is the kind of writing you might need if you were discussing how a play is structured by the author to hold your attention. You would need to consider what was going on in each scene in order to keep the tension of the drama going.

Sometimes the analysis is accompanied by your comments, to sum up what you have discovered. Then the writing can be described as evaluation, especially where you put two possible views or solutions to a problem alongside one another. The opposite of analysis is **synthesis**, which basically means putting the bits you have analysed back together again or comparing two things to see, as you analyse them, what they have in common. It is another kind of writing where you can really show a wide range of writing skills. You might do this when you look at another play by the same author and see whether the same kind of structure is found there.

Comparing and contrasting is a form of writing which requires both analysis and synthesis. It is not too difficult to say how the heroes of two plays do similar things but it is much harder to analyse features about each of them and compare their use by the author – with detailed examples, of course.

So, firstly, if you want to go for grade A then you need to think about the material you are reading and the kinds of writing task you are being set. Both have to be sufficiently demanding for you to show what you can do. Then, in producing writing you will have to show that you are prepared to:

- Select an appropriate formal or literary style, knowing how your choice of style will affect your reader's response to your writing. You will be able to construct plots which are not just based on a simple chronology of events (saying what happened in the order in which it took place).

  This means: that you will be choosing the right style for writing, as well as showing that you can use it. If you write stories, for example, they must be structured in unexpected ways – using flashbacks, or writing as if you are a character in the story, or coming to an unexpected climax, etc.

- Use description as part of a narrative, for purposes like creating an atmosphere, or to reflect the mood of a character. You will also have to be able to use techniques like imagery and use the sound of words in a sophisticated manner.
  This means: that you will be using description self-consciously, knowing what effect you want to achieve. If you are writing about Dracula you may want to create the effect of a storm in the background: the crash of thunder should come through in the words you choose and the way you write.
- Write fluent formal prose where its use is appropriate.
  This means: that you will know when it is important to write formally and be able to do it accurately. In general, this is when you haven't met the person or people you are writing for, when you are writing objectively, rather than giving your own views, and when you are writing something like a report, a public letter, a set of instructions or explanations.
- Construct writing which argues a case or persuades your reader to agree with your point of view.
  This means: that you will be equally at home in tackling a controversial social issue as in arguing about the literature texts you have studied. You will be able to make a series of points, in a sensible order, and to back up each one by reference to examples and/or quotations.
- Discuss and illustrate, with evidence, the features of style and language use belonging to something you have read.
  This means: that you will be doing the analysing and evaluating referred to earlier in this section. You will write about the particular characteristics of a piece of writing and say what their importance is.
- Understand implicit meanings in your reading.
  This means: that you will notice things which are hinted at, or referred to indirectly, or suggested in your reading which are significant to the author. 'Implicit' means concealed or hidden within. It is the opposite of 'explicit', which means obvious or on the surface.

Beating your problems

Examiner's tip

re are ways to overcome
n the biggest problems
ore the examination.

Essentially, all the skills covered in this chapter are the ones which separate the different grades. But remember, being able to do these things is no good at all if the work you submit for coursework assessment or your writing in the examination does not actually show evidence of your ability. You may have one problem that carries right through your work and seems to reduce all of your assessments. Problems with English can be very hard to overcome, but there are some useful strategies you can learn.

Are you a poor speller?

The problem

Spelling mistakes can make any piece of work look worse than it really is! The spelling of English is tricky because it does not follow straightforward rules. If your general command of English is good and this is one area that really lowers your standards, then it is something you will have to cope with, not only for GCSE, but for the rest of your life.

The solutions

1. There are some rules to learn which will solve a number of common spelling errors. There are plenty of books which you can buy to help you learn these and your teacher may be able to supply one. Otherwise, buy one and read it. Make lists of words of the type you know you have problems with, and learn them.

2. Always use a dictionary when you are producing a final draft of a piece of work. If you are not sure of the correct spelling of a word, look it up. You can buy special spelling dictionaries which contain only words, not definitions.

❸ As you do this, compile a vocabulary book for yourself where you can keep lists of words you habitually misspell. Put into it any words your teacher marks or corrects in your writing, words you learn in school or while you are reading, and words you have checked in the dictionary. One word of warning. Do make sure they are spelled correctly. Find someone who will read through and check them from time to time. Get a friend to test you on the spellings. A good way to save this list is on a word processor because it can organise the words into alphabetical order for you and keeps printing out updated lists.

❹ In the case of really problematic (the ones you can never get right!) words, there is no substitute for looking at the correct spelling to fix it in your head, then writing it out from memory so many times that you will never forget it.

Is your punctuation terrible?

The problem

This is another difficult area. True, there are rules about where punctuation marks should be used, but knowing the rules is not quite the same as being able to apply them in your own writing. The more complex your sentences become, the more difficult they are to punctuate. Commas and apostrophes can be very slippery creatures when you are pushing your language abilities to full stretch! The first thing to decide is whether your problem is not knowing the rules or whether you just forget them when you are working through a piece of writing.

The solutions

❶ If your basic problem is that you do not know the rules, then, again, a self-help book will be useful. Going through a piece of writing in detail with your teacher should help you to see what you do wrong. After that, it is simply a matter of practice.

❷ Concentrate on your punctuation at the re-drafting stage. Reading your own writing through and correcting (which usually means adding) punctuation is the best way to make accurate punctuation a habit. If you find sentence breaks (where a sentence starts or stops) difficult, and are not sure about using commas, try reading your writing aloud with exaggerated expression, as if you are on a stage or talking to an eight-year-old! The pauses should then be obvious if your writing makes sense.

❸ Take an interest in the way punctuation is used in the things you read. Compare the way different publishers punctuate direct speech (the words actually spoken) in teenage reading books. Look out for mistakes in your local newspaper.

Is your vocabulary limited?

The problem

This is a common weakness which lowers the grade of otherwise fluent writers. The issue of choosing words appropriate to the task is bound up with the style you choose for different types of writing. If you tend to use the same basic, everyday words for every piece of writing you undertake, you are unlikely to reach a high grade. You will also run into problems when you read anything which is in any way complex. You are unlikely to be able to discuss a writer's choice of words if you don't even know what the words mean. Using a dictionary to look up the meaning of a word will be of only limited help if you are not familiar with that word in other contexts.

The solutions

❶ The only real remedy for this is a lifetime of reading. The greater your exposure to a wide variety of written language, the wider will be your understanding and use of vocabulary. Read widely from a range of books and magazines – not just those intended for a teenage audience.

❷ Take an interest in unusual words. If you hear a word you are not familiar with in conversation or whilst watching television, look it up to find out how it is spelled, as well as its meaning. While you are doing that, why not have a browse through the dictionary? You may be surprised at how much this sort of interest in words can increase your vocabulary.

❸ Use a thesaurus and a co-build dictionary. The thesaurus will introduce you to a whole world of words which you never knew existed and the co-build dictionary will show you how to use them.

❹ When you re-draft a narrative, consciously do the following:

(a) Look at each noun (the names or labels for objects, ideas and feelings). Try to change each of these for a more precise or interesting alternative. Don't use the same noun more than once in the piece of writing.

(b) See if you can change pronouns (words like 'she' and 'they') back into nouns with adjectives (the 'exotic model', the 'stumbling, exhausted animals').

(c) Make sure that each noun has at least one adjective to describe it. Add an interesting and descriptive adverb to each verb (the words which describe actions).

(d) Add a comparison to every paragraph.

Your writing will look a bit strange at first, but at the final draft stage you should edit it by cutting words to achieve the best effect. Use your thesaurus to give you ideas.

Only practice will teach you to use your new-found word power better, though. As with any new skill, you will not always get it right first time. Your teacher will always be the best person to advise about appropriate uses of new words which you are learning how to use in your writing.

Make a list here of any other areas of your English work which you think need more attention.

Your questions answered

Q Is it all right for me to use a word-processor to do my coursework on? Can I use the spell-check as I work?

A Different examining groups have different regulations about the use of word-processors and they keep updating them – generally to allow more use rather than less. It is best to check with the small print of your syllabus and to tell your teacher exactly what you want to do, but here is the essence of what is permitted.

Basically, it is fine to use a word-processor for all of the coursework pieces but one. This is because you have to show in your coursework that you can write legibly and spell correctly, and a word processor could conceal this. For some examining groups this evidence will be supplied by your examination papers as well.

Two words of warning. First, remember that a word-processor will show any weaknesses in punctuation and spelling, and don't get the spacing confused so that your paragraphing is lost. Second, it is the quality of your writing that counts, not its attractiveness, so don't waste time messing about with a computer when you could be writing.

One last thing: computer spell-checks are pretty good at spotting words that don't really exist, except through your poor spelling, but they can't tell you if you have written 'their' instead of 'there', or 'wear' instead of 'where' – because those words aren't actually misspellings – they're used in the wrong context. So you still need to proof- read your work for that kind of error.

Q I'm certain that my teacher does not like me and he always gives me lower marks than my friends. I'm afraid that this will lower my grade at the end of the course. What can I do?

A Firstly, stop worrying. Every student feels like this at some time during a two-year course. It is the teacher's job to criticise your work and there is never enough time to talk it through. Secondly, if there is a real problem, remember that your teacher is not going to be the only person to assess your coursework. The rest of the English department has to agree on the grades for the school as a whole and then the external assessor has to see a sample of folders as well. If you still feel anxious, it would be best to talk to the Head of the English Department and if he or she is the teacher in question then speak to the school Examinations Secretary, or your class tutor. Also remember that, whatever happens elsewhere, the examination is down to you!

Q I have a pronounced regional accent. Will this lead to me being awarded a lower grade for Speaking and Listening?

A No. The important thing about using standard English is that you are able to speak it when necessary. And you can speak standard English with a local accent. For example, if some foreigners asked you for directions, could you tell them so that they would understand you? There is some argument about whether you need to be able to speak standard English in formal situations, such as giving a speech. Doing this, you would have to avoid dialect constructions (changing the words themselves, or the word order), but it would be perfectly acceptable to speak with an accent (changing the sound of words).

Q If I am unhappy about my grade, can I appeal and have my work re-marked?

A This is quite a grey area because, yes, you are entitled to appeal if you think your work has been severely marked. This has always been allowed with examinations and, if you pay a fee, you can have your papers re-marked. But with coursework, the whole centre has to be re-marked because your grade relates to all the other grades awarded. So, if you really feel hard done by over coursework, then your best strategy is to find other students who feel the same and try to persuade the school to have all the folders checked. If everyone else is happy with their grades it is unlikely, because of how the assessment is done, that yours will be the odd one out.

Q When my older brother did GCSE English, he did an assignment on horror novels and he studied Stephen King and got a grade A for English. All we seem to read is Thomas Hardy and Wordsworth and the Brontë sisters. I don't mind reading older books, but why isn't our teacher giving us a choice?

A The rules and regulations about what GCSE students have to read for English and English Literature are very specific now. You have to read more books in total, and the authors of books written before 1900 have to be selected carefully if you wish coursework to be entered for English as well as for English Literature. You can still read your favourite novels at home for relaxation, and maybe you could make use of some of these influences when you produce pieces of writing to entertain? Any kind of reading may be turned to advantage on an English course.

Q I'm not very brilliant at writing, because I can't spell and I forget about paragraphs, but I'm a good reader and I love drama and acting. In Year 9, I regularly did Speaking and Listening activities that my teacher said were level 7 standard. Will this help me with my GCSE?

A Two comments to make about this. First, you will be pleased to know that your Speaking and Listening grade will be shown separately on your GCSE certificate, so if you perform to grade A standard, it will be there for all to see; also, a good mark for Speaking and Listening will boost your overall mark for English if you are able to use one oral assignment towards your coursework marks. Second, don't give up on the writing: you still have two years to make big improvements there. The fact that you know what your weaknesses are ought to help you to remedy these problems.

Q Who decides which work is chosen for assessment: me or my teacher?

A Both of you. This is a negotiated decision and it should not be left until the last moment. By Christmas in Year 11 you should have talked about this with your teacher and you should be starting to agree about what pieces to include and what still needs to be done. If you have not done that by then, you should make it a priority. And remember that your teacher probably has a lot more experience of what the assessor will be looking for than you have, so listen hard to her advice. You may be surprised by how much your teacher wants to leave out, but remember that it is not necessary to show the same skills over and over and it is important to show the range of your reading and writing in coursework. Because coursework has to show you at your best, you may find that most of the work has been completed in Year 11.

Q I'm proud of my coursework and I want it back. When can I have it?

A Once the results have been published in mid-August there is normally a period when appeals can be submitted, which runs until the end of September. After that, your school should be willing to return your work and, if it has been sent to the examining group for assessment, they should ask for its return on your behalf. One or two of the groups, however, do reserve the right to retain work for various purposes.

Q What are my parents allowed to do to help me with my coursework?

A Just as much as your teachers are. If they nag you into turning off the television at home and being a bit neater as well, it might be no bad thing. Some people have suggested that, because parents give varying amounts of help to their children, coursework is unfair, but really that has always been the case with homework.

Q If I get a lower grade than I had hoped for, can I re-take a Key Stage 4 examination in the autumn or in the following year?

A Yes and no! Your assessment in Year 11, when you are sixteen, is a compulsory national assessment and you cannot change that. But you can take any GCSE again and get a better grade for yourself. That involves some changes to your coursework and sitting a new set of examination papers. Different groups have different regulations about exactly how much or how little of your coursework you will have to change, and there may be special forms to fill in.

Q I know that someone in my group is cheating by copying work from someone in another group. What should I do?

A Tell your parents, your English teacher or your form tutor. If this person is found out, and the chances are that they will be, then all the school's grades could be delayed or questioned and the assessor might be told to be especially strict with all of them. This is a situation which could really affect your chances and you must do something about it.

Index

M

N

O

P

Q

R

Acknowledgements

The authors and publishers gratefully acknowledge the following:

'A Cream Cracker Under the Settee', reproduced from *Talking Heads* by Alan Bennett with the permission of BBC Enterprises Limited (pp.32–4); *Song of the Battery Hen* by Heathhead Winthrop, published by William Heinemann Ltd (p.36); extract from *Brave New World* by Aldous Huxley, published by Chatto & Windus and reproduced by permission of Mrs Laura Huxley (pp.65–6); extract from *Second from Last in the Sack Race* by David Nobbs, published by Methuen London (pp.67–9); extract from *The Fifth Child* by Doris Lessing, published by Jonathan Cape (pp.69–70); 'Girl' from *At the Bottom of the River* by Jamaica Kincaid, published by First Aventura Edition (p.71); extract from *Lark Rise to Candleford* by Flora Thompson, published by Oxford University Press (pp.72–4); extract from *A Ragged Schooling* by Robert Roberts, published by Manchester University Press (pp.75–77); extract from *I Know Why the Caged Bird Sings* by Maya Angelou, published by Virago Press (pp.77–8); extract from *A Traveller on Horseback* by Christina Dodwell, published by Hodder & Stoughton Limited (pp.79–80); extract from *Arabia Through the Looking Glass* by Jonathan Raban, published by Collins, an imprint of HarperCollins Publishers Ltd (pp.80–1); 'My Sister Betty' from *Song of the City* by Gareth Owen, published by HarperCollins Publishers Ltd (p.89); 'Incendiary' from *New and Collected Poems* by Vernon Scannell, published by Robson Books Ltd and reprinted by permission of Vernon Scannell (p.90); 'The Choosing' from *Dreaming Frankenstein and Other Poems* by Liz Lockhead, published by Polygon (p.94); extract from *Education Guardian*, reproduced by permission of *The Guardian* (p.105); extract from *Runaway Nurse*, published by Mills and Boon (pp.107–110); extract from 'Tea in the Wendy House' from *The Green Behind the Glass* © Adèle Geras 1982, published by Hamish Hamilton, permission granted by the Author (pp.110–12); 'At Castle Boterel' and 'Afterwards' from *The Complete Poems* by Thomas Hardy, published by Papermac (pp.116–7); World Wildlife Fund Marine Fact Sheet, reproduced by permission of WWF-UK (p.123); 'Mother Nature fights back', extract from *Daily Mail*, reproduced by permission of *Daily Mail*/Solo (p.124); 'A-plant "puts children at risk" – report', 'Safe in our hands' and 'A-plant fails test', extracts reproduced by permission of *Lancashire Evening Post* (pp.126–7); extract from pamphlet 'Nuclear Waste: What's to be done about it?', reproduced by permission of British Nuclear Fuels plc (p.129); extract from poster 'Radiation Protection At-a-Glance', reproduced by permission of National Radiation Protection Board (pp.130–2); extract from *Physics Matters* by Nick England, published by Hodder & Stoughton Limited (pp.133–4).

The authors gratefully acknowledge the Midland Examining Group, the Northern Examinations and Assessment Board, London Examinations, A division of Edexcel Foundation, the Welsh Joint Education Committee and the Southern Examining Group for permission to use copyright material.

Any approaches suggested for answering questions are solely the responsibility of the authors and have not been provided or approved by the examination boards.